IN THE SEVENTIES

adventures in the counter-culture

BARRY MILES

to Rosemary – met in the seventies

A complete catalogue record for this book can be obtained from the British Library on request

The right of Barry Miles to be identified as the author of this work has been asserted by him in accordance with the Copyright, Designs and Patents Act 1988

First published in 2011 by Serpent's Tail,
an imprint of Profile Books Ltd
3A Exmouth House
Pine Street
London EC1R 0JH
website: www.serpentstail.com

ISBN 978 1 84668 690 0
eISBN 978 1 84765 494 6

Designed and typeset by sue@lambledesign.demon.co.uk

Printed by Clays, Bungay, Suffolk

10 9 8 7 6 5 4 3 2 1

contents

introduction

The seventies are now more than thirty years ago – you need to be middle aged to properly remember them – and as they recede in time, just as the sixties did and the decades before that, the decade is taking on its own stereotype: a weird mixture of flares, Abba, punk, pornography and super-heavy drug use. All those elements were there, but I saw most of the seventies as an extension of the sixties; in fact for me, the sixties as a definable period of cultural history ran from 1963 until 1977: from the Beatles until the end of punk. It's not as convenient as a nice, easy, even-numbered decade but it encompasses the growth and collapse of a movement.

Journalist Peter Braunstein described the seventies as 'the last sexually free decade of the twentieth century' and he is right; in fact most of the excess attributed to the sixties occurred during the seventies: if there was ever a golden age of sex and drugs and rock 'n' roll this was it. Beginning with David Bowie in drag, and ending with Grace Jones naked at Studio 54, it was the era of massive cocaine use, of legal pornographic films, and fashions that even now no one has seriously attempted to revive.

This book is a continuation of my previous volume, *In the Sixties*, where I concentrated on underground, counter-cultural activities, mostly in London. That book described the 1965 Albert Hall Reading, the UFO Club, Indica Books and Gallery, the founding of *International Times* and the Beatles' spoken-word label Zapple.

Indica Books closed in February 1970 (the gallery closed in 1967), but *International Times* continued until 1974 – and flourished again later – and I continued to write for it, mostly reporting from New York.

My interest in the Beat Generation continued and this volume covers the time I spent on Allen Ginsberg's hippy commune in upstate New York, working with him in Berkeley, and cataloguing William Burroughs' archives in London. I also continued my rock 'n' roll journalism, this time at *New Musical Express*, where for several years I covered everyone from the Pink Floyd to the Clash, Brian Eno to Talking Heads. I spent much of this time in New York, reporting from CBGBs on the Bowery then, in 1978, I edited *Time Out*, the weekly London arts and entertainment listing magazine for a spell. It was a busy decade, I was privileged to work with some of the people I admired most in life, and at the end of it I finally figured out what I wanted to do with my life, which was to become a writer. The book opens in New York, where Sue, my first wife, and I had gone to recover from sixties London.

1 1970

off with a bang

The south side of tree-lined West 11th Street at Fifth Avenue in Greenwich Village is lined with elegant Greek Revival brownstones built in 1845, served by the sombre First Presbyterian church, across the street, built a year later, and set well back from Fifth Avenue. The house at number 18 was part hidden by a tall wooden fence until five minutes before midday on 6 March 1970, when a powerful explosion ripped open the whole front of the building. Flames were already billowing from the windows when two more blasts followed in quick succession. Clouds of dust billowed across the street, slabs of wall and flooring crushed the roofs of parked cars and filled the front yard and street, blocking the road and sidewalk.

Two dazed girls covered in soot staggered from the flames; one was completely naked, her clothes blown off by the blast, the other wore blue jeans. They were trembling and in shock. Part of the front wall crashed to the street, narrowly missing them, engulfing them in dust and smoke. By this time neighbours had begun to arrive and one of them, Susan Wager, the former wife of film actor Henry Fonda, quickly pulled them down the street to her house at number 50 and into her living room. The girls were shaking and unable to speak but they seemed physically uninjured so she took them upstairs to the bathroom and found fresh clothes for them to wear.

Soon the street was blocked off by police lines of blue and white wooden trestles and bundles of throbbing fire hoses that snaked along the gutters

She asked her housekeeper to make coffee for them, then returned to the burning building in case there were further casualties.

A crowd was gathering and the first of the emergency vehicles arrived, red lights revolving, radios crackling with static. Sirens and klaxons could be heard, converging on the block from all directions. Soon the street was blocked off by police lines of blue and white wooden trestles and bundles of throbbing fire hoses that snaked along the gutters. As the roof caved in, neighbours began to evacuate the nearby houses, among them Dustin Hoffman, who lived next door and left carrying a valuable Tiffany lamp. Mrs Wager returned to her house to check on the girls but they were gone, having told the housekeeper they were going to the drugstore to get some medicine.

The fire department quickly brought the fire under control and began damping down to make the structure safe to enter. Early in the evening the body of a man was found in the basement in pieces, and not long afterwards, the horribly mangled torso of a woman was discovered on the remnants of the ground floor. Police also found a number of handbags containing college IDs stolen from students in recent months. By now they were less convinced that the explosion was the result of a ruptured gas main. Floodlights were set up and late that same night police found more than sixty sticks of dynamite, a live military anti-tank shell, blasting caps and a number of large metal pipes packed tight with explosives. The neighbouring houses were evacuated. The police had discovered a Weathermen bomb factory.

The search continued. Using his fingerprints, police identified the dead man as Theodore Gold, one of the leaders of the 1968 student strike at Columbia University. He was twenty-three years old and a member of the Weathermen. The remains of the dead woman were identified only by the print on a severed finger. She was Diana Oughton, the granddaughter of the founder of the Boy Scouts of America and daughter of an Illinois state politician. After seven days of painstaking searching through the rubble the police located the body of another male, impossible to identify as only the torso remained. The Weathermen later gave him a name; it was Terry Robbins, one of their members. He had been blown to pieces when he accidentally ignited the six sticks of dynamite he was wiring up.

The house at 18 West 11th Street belonged to James P. Wilkerson, the owner of a Midwest radio station. His daughter, twenty-five-year-old Cathlyn Wilkerson, was home on $20,000 bail for her part in the Days of Rage protest the previous autumn when a group of Students for a Democratic Society (SDS) members armed with baseball bats and wearing helmets to protect themselves from police batons vandalised shopfronts along Chicago's Gold Coast. One of her best friends, Kathy Boudin, had been released on $40,000 bail after hitting a police officer with her club during the same action. Kathy was staying with Cathlyn at West 11th Street at the time of the blast.

They were both known members of the Weathermen, the

breakaway radical arm of the SDS. These were the two women who escaped, unharmed, from the blast. The bombs were intended to 'bring the war home' by blowing up a non-commissioned officers' dance at Fort Dix, an action that would undoubtedly have resulted in many deaths. Two weeks earlier, on 19 February, the Weathermen had caused explosions in three New York office buildings and at buildings in California, Washington State, Maryland and Michigan. After the debacle of the town house explosion, the Weathermen never again attempted an action that would harm human life. Cathlyn Wilkerson remained underground for ten years before turning herself in. She served eleven months of a three-year sentence for negligent homicide in connection with the explosion. Kathy Boudin stayed on the loose until 1981 when she was captured as a participant in the hold-up of a Brinks armoured truck in which two cops and a security officer were killed. She received a prison term of twenty years to life and was released on parole in September 2003.

At the time of the explosion I was staying with my then wife, Sue, at a friend's apartment on the eighth floor of 51 Fifth Avenue, on the corner of 11th Street, just ten doors from number eighteen. I remember the piles of rubble, the police lines blocking the street and the shockingly exposed interior of the house, visible through the gaping hole of what was once its front. The odd thing is that I cannot remember whether I was there when the explosion happened or not; it is possible that I only flew in from London the next day.

I was writing about the New York counter-cultural scene for *International Times*, the London underground paper that I had helped to found back in 1966, and my fact-gathering and reporting of events, and my actual memories, have become entangled as one. It poses an interesting question about authenticity; was I there or did I just hear about it? I certainly remember the aftermath, the closed street and the emergency vehicles. It is rather like the childhood memories of events that you only remember because parents have described them so often; are they real memories or received information? There is an element of this in this book; sometimes I have added factual details to give an event context, but it is all a first-person memoir.

I arrived in New York exhausted after years of close involvement with the London underground scene: running Indica Bookshop, on the editorial board of *International Times*, writing regular book reviews and record review columns as well as articles for *IT*, *Oz* and many US and European underground newspapers, working as label manager of the Beatles experimental Zapple label, and producing a dozen spoken-word albums. It was with a sense of relief that I had taken up Allen Ginsberg's kind offer for me to come over and catalogue his tape archive, an open-ended job that could easily take a year. Indica, the bookshop I started back in 1965 with John Dunbar and Peter Asher, had finally closed on 29 February; I resigned from the various companies that had been set up to manufacture and sell psychedelic posters, sublet the flat, and Sue and I set off for Manhattan.

The grim reality of the political situation in America was brought forcefully home to us by the explosion on East 11th. At the beginning of the seventies America was a society divided; opposition to the Vietnam War was at its height and the right-wing establishment was using all its powers to crush the anti-war, pro-youth counter-culture; in fact it sometimes seemed that America regarded all college students or any young person with long hair as the enemy. The hippies were becoming radicalised. It was a time of huge demonstrations, and of violent political activism.

Many of the central figures of the counter-culture were in jail or being harassed by the police. John Sinclair, the leader of the Detroit White Panther Party, was jailed for ten years for possession of one joint, having been set up by narcs posing as hippies. On 19 February, Timothy Leary was convicted for possession of two roaches (probably belonging to his daughter) and also held in custody. For some time the police had been looking for a way to contain Leary, who was seen as something of a loose cannon; an establishment figure gone bad. Allen Ginsberg sent the judge at Leary's trial in Santa Ana, California, a telegram: 'Pray release the pioneer psychologist Dr Timothy

Leary on normal bond till sentencing. He is considered by many good people to hold honourable if controversial opinions and it is not useful to deny bond and abruptly jail so famous a theorist for his unpopular views – such an imprisonment is proper neither to science nor jurisprudence. Allen Ginsberg – Guggenheim fellow poet / National Arts Letter grantee.' He was ignored, of course, and like Sinclair, Tim was given a ten-year sentence. On 11 March Leary was denied appeal bail as 'an insidious influence' and sent to Vacaville State Penitentiary for processing.

Meanwhile, the great Chicago Conspiracy trial was still playing itself out. The Youth International Party (Yippies), in collaboration with the National Mobilization Committee (MOBE), had organised a series of demonstrations to take place during the Democratic Party National Congress in Chicago in August 1968. The Yippie role was to sponsor a 'Festival of Life' during the convention and in March that year they applied to the Chicago Parks department for an appli-cation to hold demonstrations as was their democratic right. Then on 5 August, only three weeks before the convention and with thousands of young people planning to attend the Yippie festival, Deputy Mayor Stahl decided not to grant permits to allow sleeping in the parks.

Despite the efforts of the Civil Liberties Union, the city refused to budge, and on 22 August, MOBE organisers warned them it would be 'suicide' not to allow demonstrators to sleep in the parks; it was just asking for a confrontation. The next day, as cops tacked up '11 p.m. curfew' signs on the park trees, MOBE and the Yippies began training demonstrators in karate, snake dancing and other forms of self-defence. They needed it because on the 25th there was a police charge. People attending a concert in Lincoln Park were clubbed to the ground by their nightsticks and the next night police, with their nametags removed to avoid prosecution, attacked about three thousand people in the park with clubs and tear gas. The violence culminated on the 28th when the police ran riot, beating up everyone: demonstrators, spectators, the press, innocent bystanders, and CBS cameramen, all live on national television. The plate-glass window of the Hilton Hotel was pushed in and cops ran inside and began beating up people in the lobby, including members of the international press. The thin veneer of the American police state had finally cracked and middle-class Americans were shocked.

Then the long legal proceedings began: a federal grand jury indicted the 'Chicago Eight' in March 1968 and in September the trial began under Judge Julius Hoffman. The trial was a travesty of justice. Black Panther Bobby Seale, who had arrived in Chicago only two days before the convention and who had no part at all in the planning of the demonstrations, was ordered to be bound in chains and gagged because of his courtroom outbursts demanding to represent himself. Eventually, on 5 November, his trial was severed from that of the others but not until the American public had seen the sorry spectacle of a black man, bound and gagged, sitting before the all-white court.

On 18 February, the jury found five of the seven defendants guilty of violating the Anti-Riot Act of 1968 and Hoffman gave them all jail sentences as well as additional time for contempt of court. Even their lawyers were given several years in prison for contempt. (The contempt convictions, including those of their lawyers, were reversed by the Seventh Circuit Criminal Court of Appeals on 11 May 1972, and the convictions themselves were reversed on 21 November 1972.) The sentences provoked fury across the nation, with many college campuses erupting with spontaneous demonstrations. There was a riot at Isla Vista, California, followed up on 25 February by a violent demonstration during which the Isla Vista branch of the Bank of America was burned to the ground by college students from UC Santa Barbara. This prompted California governor Ronald Reagan to comment on the subject of student unrest: 'If it takes a bloodbath, let's get it over with.'

This was a prescient remark as a month later, on 4 May, on the campus of Kent State University, Ohio, National Guardsmen opened fire on unarmed students, killing four of them. Two of them were only walking to their classes; naturally no one was prosecuted. Ten days later, police killed two more students, this time at Jackson State College during violent student demonstrations against Nixon and Kissinger sending American troops into Cambodia. Astonishingly, the killings at Kent State met with wide approval from patriotic right-wing Americans, and two days later New York construction workers, their hard hats adorned with American flags, attacked an anti-war demonstration on Wall Street, screaming and yelling obscenities. Even the Spanish waiters at the El Coyote restaurant attached to the Hotel Chelsea showed their patriotism by putting little American flags on the tables; something that provoked several bad-tempered rows when Chelsea residents drew swastikas on them or set them on fire.

It was against this increasingly polarised background that Allen Ginsberg, Sue and I, attended the Holding Together benefit for Leary held at the Village Gate in mid-May, where Allen was to perform. Self-appointed youth leaders Abbie Hoffman and Jerry Rubin, both high on acid, seized the microphone and denounced Allen as 'a CIA agent' and the organisers of the benefit as 'half CIA', which seemed a bit feeble.

'They'll never let Leary out,' screamed the flushed, wild-eyed Hoffman, a dirty bandana tied round his head. 'You're looking for a religious martyr but this is a political revolution and he is a prisoner of war – a political prisoner!' Allen stood to the side of the stage, also sweating, looking worried and confused as the Hoffman–Rubin circus roared out of control. With us were a number of Allen's friends, including Claude Pelieu and Mary Beach, his French translators, who were clearly confused; they regarded both Leary and Hoffman–Rubin as counter-cultural spokesmen, and now they didn't know which side to support.

It seemed pretty obvious to me that the already massive egos of Hoffman and Rubin had been so inflated by all the media attention that the trial and sentencing received that they really did think they were revolutionary leaders. But they represented no one, they were not in any organised political party, they had no constituency. They were leaders only in their own eyes and that of the media, who loved their pranks. As their two enormous egos buffeted around the room like weather balloons, squeezed into the remaining space, present to support Leary, were Fernanda Pivano, the Italian translator of Allen Ginsberg, Kerouac and the Beats, and her husband, the celebrated designer Ettore Sottsass. Ettore happily took photographs; his English wasn't up to following the arguments and he very sensibly saw it all as a media spectacle. Having spent much of the Second World War in a concentration camp in Yugoslavia, he was not overly impressed by these wild antics; to him they were merely playing at politics. Jimi Hendrix played a fine set backed by Johnny Winter, whom I knew from the Hotel Chelsea where he lived. Jim Morrison was supposed to be there, presumably to read poetry, but if he was I missed him.

Although I was already organising Allen Ginsberg's tape archive, in preparation for listing and cataloguing it all, I did not want to stop writing for the underground press. I filed regular stories with *International Times* back in London and began working for *Crawdaddy* magazine, one of the first underground music mags, then edited by Peter Stafford. Peter saw the mag as being about rock culture, rather than directly tied to rock itself. He thought music would fill only about half of its pages. His guiding principle was to make the reader wonder: 'What the fuck is *Crawdaddy* up to?'

The editorial offices were in the sub-basement of a cast-iron office block at 510 Sixth Avenue on the corner of 13th Street. The ground floor housed a huge store selling scented candles, joss sticks, tie-dye clothing and hippy paraphernalia on a vast scale. The patchouli oil caught in your throat as you walked in the door. The basement was used for storage and offices and below that was one vast room, the ceiling supported by dozens of metal columns. On one wall was a huge metal door with a complicated metal lock, like in a submarine, that led through to the subway on the other side; we were on a level with the tracks and could hear the trains thunder by. Most of the room was empty, but huddled in one corner, in a pool of fluorescent light, was the group of desks that constituted *Crawdaddy*.

In another corner, far away across the gloom, were more desks in another pool of light; this was where the *New York Review of Sex* was produced, one of the sex papers that started around the same time as Al Goldstein's *Screw*. There was something wrong about the whole set-up, and the way the paper was printed gave a few clues.

When the boards were ready, some large Italian men would come and collect them. A few days later, the magazine was on the stands. We did not know who printed it, or where, or how many. Our job was to fill the paper, and in this we had complete freedom. I wrote regularly for *Crawdaddy* for six months, then one day Peter called the staff together for a meeting. 'I am not sure that the wage cheques are going to be paid this week,' he told us. 'I understand that an IBM Selectric goes for pretty good money these days. I am going to take a walk around the block and I do hope no one steals any of our typewriters while I'm gone.' I took a nice fire-engine red one back to the Chelsea, along with a couple of different golf-balls, and eventually shipped it to London. I later got to know Bob Salpeter, who helped design the first IBM ad campaign for the Selectric. His ad read: 'Our typewriters are different. They've got balls!' They fired him of course.

2   1970

allen ginsberg's hippy commune

Cherry Valley in upstate New York was first settled in 1740. It remained a village of just two streets, slowly acquiring a hotel, a feed store, bank and, of course, several churches as well as a scattering of traditional white clapboard houses with porches. The most memorable event in its history was the Cherry Valley Massacre of 9 November 1778, when the Tory, Walter N. Butler, led a force of Rangers and Six Nations Indians behind American lines to attack the village. They left behind forty-six corpses: sixteen soldiers from the Cherry Valley garrison and thirty-two settlers, mostly women and children, tomahawked and scalped by the Seneca Indians, who were looking to avenge the destruction of three of their villages by the Americans. White settlers subsequently seized the land from the Indians, who are now restricted to a few small reservations, but their invisible presence is still felt in the place names: Oneida, Oneonta, Mohawk, Sauquoit, Canajoharie and nearby Otsego Lake, headwater of the Susquehanna river, a name I'd known from American folk songs and ballads but had never identified as a real place. It leaves Otsego Lake at Cooperstown, home of the Baseball Hall of Fame.

Allen Ginsberg showed me around the Hall of Fame. We saw Babe Ruth's shirt and baseball bat; baseballs autographed by long-ago batsmen and pitchers, and a huge collection of colourful pennants.

Allen explained the rules and history of baseball in a loud voice until several visitors, after forcefully frowning and glaring at him to no effect, acted in unison and asked him to be quiet. They informed him, somewhat bluntly, that his understanding of the game was faulty on numerous counts. These they then elucidated in rather more detail than Allen and I would have ideally liked. Despite such erudition, it still seemed like rounders to me, a game that in England is played only by schoolgirls, along with hockey, lacrosse and other violent sports.

Allen was suitably subdued; however, he soon perked up at the Cooperstown Farmers' Museum, an extraordinary collection of a dozen houses, brought together from a 100-mile radius, and ranging in age from 1795 to 1829: a country store, a printing office, a school-house, farm and so on, all moved from their original locations to be reassembled to make a new 'historic' village. At the Farmers' Museum Allen was on firmer ground, explaining the story of James Fennimore Cooper, author of the Leatherstocking Tales, whose father founded the town. I had read *The Last of the Mohicans* when I was a child and it was wonderful to see the Glimmerglass Lake itself; you could almost see the Indians in their canoes, moving silently among the reeds at the bank. This of course would have been very unlikely as the lake is now completely dead so there are no fish to catch. The poisoned water is crystal clear, bereft even of algae.

Many of the people in Cooperstown had pointed Allen out in loud whispers. This was the period of his most intense political activity and consequently of his greatest public fame: he was frequently on television and in the newspapers and, with his balding pate, long black hair curling over his collar, and large Whitmanesque beard, thick black-rimmed glasses, dark work clothes and baggy jeans, he was easily recognisable. His move to upstate New York had been the subject of much gossip in Cherry Valley and the surrounding villages.

The Poetry Farm was five miles from Cherry Valley on East Hill, and stood in 99 acres of pasture, which sloped down to a river, beyond which was state forest. The Seneca name for Cherry Valley was Karightongegh, meaning 'Oak Woods', but the ancient forest had been logged many years before and now consisted entirely of characterless second- or third-growth pine. At the top of the meadow the land was bordered by trees, which sheltered the tarpaper shack where Ed the Hermit lived; you could sometimes see the flash of sun on his field glasses as he spied on the girls bathing in the fishpond below the barn. The land was first settled by a family called Millson and their gravestones stood next to the house, in a grove of saplings behind the propane tank. The white-painted wooden farmhouse had a crude stone-lined storm cellar, and consisted of a large kitchen-dining room and a living room, the two divided by a staircase. Above that were four bedrooms and a large high-ceilinged attic. There was another ground-floor room off the porch. Next to the house stood a traditional red and white painted barn and various lean-tos for the goats and chickens.

When Sue and I arrived in late May 1970, the occupants were Allen Ginsberg, then aged forty-three; his lover Peter Orlovsky; Peter's twenty-year-old girlfriend Denise Mercedes, who was sixteen years younger than him; Peter's catatonic elder brother Julius Orlovsky, rescued from the mental hospital; farm manager Gordon Ball; Beat poet Ray Bremser; his wife Bonnie and their three-year-old daughter Georgia; Lash the horse; Bessie Smith and Jennifer the cows, plus one unnamed calf; three goats: Shiva, Junior and Rama; three dogs: Godley, Radah and Mirabelle; one nameless white rabbit; two cocks and thirty hens; ten ducks; three cats: George, Tiger and Blackie, and one gerbil called Geoffrey. The previous year the farm had been home to a pair of African geese, male and female, but they were so aggressive that they had to be sent away before they really hurt someone; their speciality was pecking the buttocks of rapidly retreating guests. They could deliver a painful nip.

The winter of 1969/70 was the first time that Allen had tried to live there year round. Gordon Ball and Peter Orlovsky had panelled the walls with insulation behind tongue-and-groove pine boards to 'winterise' the building, as they put it, but it was still bitterly cold when the freezing winds and snow came. It must have been a harsh existence for the original farmers. I was surprised by the building's flimsy, unsubstantial construction; in Europe it would have been built of stone throughout.

Early in February a bathroom was built off the kitchen to replace the outhouse, which had become a major point of contention. Each week someone was elected to empty the bucket beneath the smooth wooden seat but many people refused and it was usually Allen himself who did it. The only source of water had been a clanking green-painted hand pump in the kitchen sink, but now a deep well had been dug below the house down to the spring to install a complicated gravity pump which used the weight of many cups of water to force one cup of water up the hill to a storage reservoir above the house. Seventy times an hour there was a reassuring click in the pipes, which confirmed that the system was working and that the Poetry Farm was equipped with running water. Cooking was done with the aid of a large propane gas tank to the side of the house, and there was a telephone; Ma Bell was compelled by law to provide a service no matter how remote.

Unfortunately it was a party line, and Allen used it so often that his neighbours sometimes became exasperated at not being able to get through. Most days Allen spent an hour or two, sitting uncomfortably on a little child's chair, just inside the kitchen door, his knees in the air, fingers dialling, his voluminous address book open on his lap; calling the *New York Times* to complain about something in that day's Op-Ed page, raising support for this group or that, arranging readings, translations, visitors and finances. I never understood why he didn't replace it with a normal-size chair.

One major convenience lacking on the farm was electricity. I knew the farm was too remote to be connected to mains electricity but I'd assumed they used a generator for refrigeration and to power Peter's television, but this was not the case. A generator was considered polluting and unecological; I was told it would disturb

Life on the Poetry Farm: from left to right top row: Peter Orlovsky, Denise Mercedes, Don't Bite Me (the pig), Julius Orlovsky, Gordon Ball. In front: Allen Ginsberg, Georgia Bremser, Bonnie Bremser, Ray Bremser, Gregory Corso

the peaceful atmosphere and produce fumes, but surely no more than the clapped-out 1959 Ford Galaxy and '56 Oldsmobile 88 that chugged up and down the driveway emitting clouds of blue smoke. Allen's cousin, who worked in Mayor Lindsay's office, offered to get him a generator at a discount through the city, but Allen was adamant.

Peter and Denise used car batteries to power a specially converted television in their bedroom off the porch and Allen would sometimes join them there to watch the news. Denise was not too keen on the other guests visiting; she wanted to have her own space. She had been with Peter only since October and it was hardly a conventional relationship; for a start Peter and Allen were still on-off lovers. Since my reason for being there was to catalogue and edit Allen's huge collection of tape-recorded readings it was immediately clear that I would have to start by devising an electricity supply.

In 1969 I had produced an album of him singing William Blake's *Songs of Innocence and Experience* to tunes that he had composed himself; we know that Blake sang them, but the music was not preserved, if it was ever written down at all. Allen had become very interested in audio recording and, in a wonderful act of kindness, he had recognised that I was exhausted from my life in London so he had invited me to spend a season on the farm, editing his tapes into shape, with a view to releasing them as a ten-album boxed set through Fantasy Records in Berkeley.

We knew there were undoubtedly some gems hidden in the tape boxes as he had material going right back to the forties, including some reels on paper tape, which Allen was sure contained a recording of a sex orgy with Jack Kerouac. These I carefully restored, repairing all the tears with splicing tape, but when we played them through, to Allen's chagrin, there was no orgy, just poorly recorded table talk.

We did, however, find a 1952 recording of Allen reading his poems in a T. S. Eliot voice at Neal Cassady's house in San Jose, as well as the famous 1960 *Big Table* reading in Chicago with Gregory Corso, and the notorious Los Angeles reading where he took his clothes off in front of Anaïs Nin, described by Lawrence Lipton in his book *The Holy Barbarians*. Our intention was to find the best reading of each of Allen's published poems, but as the quality of recording was often terrible, we also had to take fidelity into account. It was a long job, but first of all I had to listen to all of the tapes – 300 of them – and catalogue which poems were on each. If they were recorded on 'one side' only, I would insert leader tape between each poem so that we could find it again easily.

A system was rigged up to power my tape machines from car batteries but this was obviously inefficient as they needed to be charged up twice a week, and that meant carrying them out to the car and driving over to Myron's place where the friendly local farmer would charge them overnight ready for collection the next day. Peter had the big powerful physique of a Russian peasant and the heavy batteries were no problem for him to carry around, but it was a waste of his time. If I was to spend the summer editing Allen's tapes we had to get a proper power supply.

At the end of the sixties, young people began leaving the cities to set up communes, to grow organic vegetables, and attempt a self-sufficient life outside the consumer society. Stewart Brand's *Whole Earth Catalog* was an immensely popular counter-cultural alternative to the *Sears-Roebuck Catalog*; it provided everything eco-warriors could possibly need to live the alternate lifestyle. It was here we found a suitable windmill to generate our own electricity. Allen could not afford to buy a full-size windmill, capable of providing enough power for lights and a fridge, so we settled for a small unit that we hoped would power my tape machines with a bit left over for the hi-fi. The rickety barn was not strong enough to withstand the stress of a vibrating windmill so it was decided to build one above the wellhead where the gravity pump was installed. A DC cable could then lead down the well to an AC converter and car batteries which would be stored down next to the pump, below the frost line.

I had produced Allen's William Blake album at Apostolic Studios in New York and one of their engineers, Paul Berkowitz, now came up to help out. Paul and I built a six-foot wooden frame as a foundation for the windmill's metal tower. We creosoted it into the ground, ruining a good blue shirt of mine, and bolted together the tower, like building with a Meccano set as a child. I had not done any physical labour like this – apart from humping boxes of books around – for many years and it felt very good. The generator was attached directly to the propeller at the top of the tower. To prevent power simply feeding back from the batteries on the circuit and driving the windmill on calm days instead of storing its energy, Paul inserted a diode into the loop. He also assembled the AC/DC converter, which, like the windmill, arrived in kit form from an address in the *Whole Earth Catalog.*

Paul and I were both too weedy for heavy digging so Gordon and Peter cut a trench a couple hundred feet up to the house to bury the AC cable and a separate cable for the on-off switch for the converter. Drainage channels were dug to secure the foundations of the windmill. Finally an electric power point appeared on the wall in the living room. This gave me an absurd sense of achievement. Now all we needed was wind. There was really not enough and we were always checking the battery levels with a hydrometer and having to carry them up and down from their dungeon home on a ladder. Sometimes we would wait for days for enough energy to store up for me to spend a few hours editing, then Maretta Greer, who had recently arrived from India, would blow it all by thoughtlessly playing Dylan records so we had to wait even longer.

> The little dakini playing her bells
> > & listening to late baritone Dylan
> dancing in the living room's forgot almost
> > th' electric supply's vanishing
> from the batteries in the pasture   [AG: 'Ecologue']

There were four bedrooms off the small upstairs hallway. Sue and I were given a room at the front that had a connecting door through to Allen's big room at the rear. Gordon had the other front room, over the living room, and the remaining back room was occupied by Julius. A ladder continued up to the attic where Ray Bremser and his family lived. Gregory Corso and his girlfriend Belle Gardener previously occupied this and it still contained a moth-eaten lion skin originally bagged in Africa by Belle's father. It lay mouldering in the dusty attic, spreadeagled on the floor, a terrible snarl on its face, its fangs yellowing, glass eyes smeared from three-year-old Georgia's tiny fingers. The eaves sloped down to the floor and the inaccessible space was filled with piles of old *New Yorker* magazines that Ray was methodically reading his way through. There was plenty of room. At the end, a large window, covered in fly spots, looked out at the rickety barn, which was painted in traditional reddish-brown and white panels.

Peter and Denise's room was accessible only from the porch, which gave them privacy. Peter's relationship with Allen was a complicated one. They had been lovers since they first met in San Francisco in 1954 and had spent time living in Tangier, Paris and India as well as years in New York. Despite Allen's frequent pronouncements about their gay marriage, Peter's sexual orientation was heterosexual, and even when having sex with Allen he fantasised that he was a woman. He came from a very dysfunctional family and several of his siblings were in a mental hospital. He was enormously generous and good willed, but the pressures on him from family and friends sometimes made him resort to drugs or alcohol in prodigious amounts.

When Sue and I first arrived at the farm at the end of May, Peter was on speed. It made him terribly paranoid. He thought that the rednecks were going to come up from Oneonta and kill us all. He became convinced that his portable Sony television was watching him and attacked it with an iron bar. He smashed its car batteries too, for good measure. Denise was understandably annoyed about the TV and so he had to buy another one, but three days later he smashed that up as well, throwing the tangle of electronics and coloured wires out into the front yard where Allen then stood, bending forward, tugging at his beard, contemplating it with horror. Peter began pondering Allen's rather unorthodox views on sex and decided that there was a grave danger that he might attempt to fuck Lash the horse. Accordingly Peter took to sleeping in the barn in order to protect her from Allen's amorous advances.

His withdrawal from speed was anguished and very painful to watch. His voice sounded like gravel – his 'leper's voice', as he called it (in 1961, he and Allen had lived in Benares, near Dasad-sumad Ghat, where the lepers gathered, and he had got to know some of them). Peter had a boisterous speedy humour when he was up, which counterbalanced the torment as he tried to kick it. One evening we all sat around the dinner table eating while Peter lay outside on the path, banging his head on the stone flags, crying and issuing terrible groans, cursing himself: 'Why do I do it? It's poison, it's fucking poison!'

Allen hovered around him, wringing his hands, helpless, offering advice, suggesting that they chant together the Hindu prayers they learned in India to ease the pain. Peter angrily retorted: 'That stuff doesn't work! You don't really believe in all that chanting, do you?'

Allen, sorrowful, sat with him, worrying, wiping away the sweat as Peter burned up and writhed on the damp evening grass. Eventually Allen came in to eat.

'Go get your camera and film Peter,' he told Gordon.

'No, I couldn't,' said Gordon. 'Peter's a friend.'

'He'll thank you for it later, if he gets over it. And maybe it'll show someone else what speed'll do to you! You *should* film it. It's real. It's much more real than all those sunsets and trees you film...' Allen was quite insistent.

Gordon slowly shook his head and crouched low over the table, not looking up. Allen raised his voice, almost shouting. 'That's what being a film-maker is about. Showing things as they are. Well, that's Peter out there groaning. That's how he is!'

Allen was suffering almost as much as Peter.

'Yeah. Go-wan. Why not?' demanded Denise. She sounded desperate. She had done everything possible. Their biggest worry was that Peter had still more amphetamine hidden round the farm and that he would have to go through his withdrawal all over again. He had sold letters from Jack Kerouac, Neal Cassady and Allen and spent all $12,000 on speed in a matter of months, making false entries in his bank-book so that Allen would not know. Trips to Manhattan were a constant danger because he had friends who would give him more. Allen was determined that he kick it; it was one of the reasons he bought the farm. He saw it as a refuge from the city, somewhere that Peter could kick speed, Gregory Corso could kick junk and, in his fantasies, that Jack Kerouac could come and dry out. The

Committee On Poetry, Allen's charitable foundation which owned the farm, was dedicated to helping poets, particularly the vulnerable survivors of the Beat Generation.

Peter gradually calmed down; his voice eventually returned to normal. He stopped ordering his brother Julius about so much; he became less distant and more warm and friendly. It had been a terrible period and Julius had taken the brunt of it. Catatonic Julius simply did whatever Peter told him to do, without speaking or dissenting. Peter made him carry heavy rocks all day, or spend hours digging the soybean patch in the hot summer sun. Sometimes they forgot him and would have to return to the fields in the evening to find him, still standing where they last left him, head lowered, large stomach protruding over his pants, hair sticking up in clumps.

Once off speed, Peter began to work compulsively. In his manic phase he had already planted out asparagus beds, strawberry beds and peas. Now he decided that soybeans were good for you. He would plant more, maybe an acre. He and Gordon fenced off land with posts and wire and planted frantically. He built a larger chicken run to give the hens more space to run around but we never were able to hatch out any eggs because Julius would always disturb the sitting hens in the mornings before we got up, searching for eggs to scramble. During the day the hens flapped happily in dust baths near the house wall. Peter began to fence the land, all 99 acres of it. Each day he would disappear with Julius and not return until the evening meal, still filled with energy, his body muscular and burned brown in the sun. Allen was relieved. The farm had worked. It had broken Peter's addiction. Every dollar spent was worth it.

Julius clearly benefited from life in the open air but it did little to improve his mental state. Every night he had to be told to go to bed or else he would sit on the settee all night, staring straight ahead. Once upstairs he had to be told to take his boots off, or else he would sleep in them, but he knew how to undress. In the morning he would wait in the upstairs hallway until someone told him to have breakfast: 'Go and have breakfast, Julie,' and down he would go and make himself some eggs. Sometimes three different people would tell him to eat breakfast and he would eat three breakfasts. He liked to hang around outside my room in the mornings because he knew where I kept my cigarettes and that I'd give him one if he gave me his imploring look.

One time Peter told him to lay a crazy paving round the side of the house to the barn to stop mud being walked into the kitchen. He gave him a big pile of flat stones and showed him how to do it. Julius put on his big yellow work gloves and set to work. Hours later we were amazed to see the pathway. It started out as it should be, with the stones carefully arranged to fit together, but it became narrower and narrower until, as it turned the corner of the house, it was just a line of tiny pebbles, not even an inch across. Allen summoned everyone to come and look. Julie seemed quite pleased with his work and stood next to it, smiling contentedly. Unfortunately, shortly afterwards an empty hay truck drove out of the barn and ran over it, cracking and burying all the stones.

Julie rarely spoke, once saying nothing for a whole year. His rare pronouncements were therefore of great interest. One time, out of the blue, he told Gordon Ball that he felt as if he were encased in a suit of copper, and when asked by Gregory Corso, 'What is the best way to live?' Julie told him, 'Repose.' Another time, when he became suddenly voluble, he was asked why he hadn't spoken in so long. 'I didn't have nuthin' to say,' he said.

We didn't see much of Ray Bremser. He knew that if he left the attic he might be asked to help out. Ray was an old-time Beatnik poet. He read *Howl* shortly after it was published when he was in the Bordentown Reformatory in New Jersey, doing six years on two counts of armed robbery. Somehow he got Allen's address and wrote to him at the Beat Hotel in Paris, sending him his poems. Allen put him in touch with LeRoi Jones, who published them in *Yugen*, one of the best Beat Generation magazines of the time.

When Ray got out in November 1958 he was feted by Ginsberg, Gregory Corso and Jack Kerouac, who recognised genuine raw talent when they saw it and appreciated the jazz rhythms in his work. Many years later, Bob Dylan was attracted to his work, but Ray always remained a minor character in the Beat pantheon. Ray was skinny with a hooked nose and a miserable downturned mouth. He reminded me of Magwitch, the criminal in Dickens' *Great Expectations*. He looked tough but he was soft and hypersensitive, often tearful. Prison and drugs had broken him. He was born in Jersey City and had a strong Jersey accent. He liked to recite the words on the huge sign outside the condom factory where his mother Gertrude had worked: 'What Jersey City Makes, the World Uses'. His mother used to bring home pockets full of prophylactics, which she put to good use about the house. They were ideal, for instance, for covering the tops of glass milk bottles once they were opened.

Ray was a hopeless case, always in trouble, often in jail. He found life easier, cheaper and safer in Mexico and Central America, where he could lay around all day and send his adoring wife, Bonnie, out to prostitute herself in order to pay for his heroin habit. She wrote about it in her harrowing memoir *Trioa*. Ray's behaviour towards Bonnie did not endear him to most of the people living on the farm who thought his patriarchal attitude was despicable. Ray had written to Allen on 29 October 1969, from the St Lucie county jail in Fort Pierce, Florida, to say that Bonnie had left him, his mother had died and that the State Department had flown him to Miami when he applied for repatriation from Guatemala. 'I'm destitute & in shit of trouble,' he told Allen. 'You are my only friend; so forgive me for imposing again – I need some money to pay fines for drunk/disorderly & breaking the peace. $150 would cover it.' He explained that he had had an accident in Guatemala, leaving him with a broken shoulder, four broken ribs, a broken elbow and little finger, and sprains. He didn't think he was in good enough condition to hitchhike up through Georgia and the Carolinas. 'Please help me return to New York' he begged. Naturally Allen sent the money. Ray reunited his family – if they were ever split up – and Ray, Bonnie and little Georgia arrived on the farm in mid-December 1969.

We would all retire to our rooms shortly after it got dark. The oil lamps gave plenty of light, but they also gave off a lot of heat and it was already very hot. Though people retired early, Allen was usually up late, reading, writing and dealing with his voluminous correspondence.

I had produced a spoken-word record with the poet Charles Olson the previous year at his home in Gloucester, Massachusetts, and Allen knew that he was an old friend of mine. One evening Sue and I were already in bed when Allen came into our room and began talking about him. Olson had died a few months earlier on 10 January 1970 and Allen had been a pallbearer along with Ed Sanders, Ed Dorn, John Wieners, Harvey Brown and others at the funeral in Boston. Allen told me that Charles's last word was 'Beautiful!', describing his death visions. Allen said that one of Charles's friends, who was in the insurance business in Gloucester, had stood before the coffin wearing a dapper hat and crying aloud for a minute, 'You're glorious, Charlie, now you're glorious!', shaking his head back and forth. Allen had been standing next to the bed and now, with a flourish worthy of a stage conjuror, he produced a deathbed photograph of Charles and thrust it in front of my face: 'Ha! That'll get rid of your hard-on!'

One evening Allen could be heard fussing about in his room with his dusty papers and Gordon could be heard loudly fucking some girl from Cherry Valley High School he had persuaded to come home with him. Silence reigned in Julius's room. Suddenly, lights! Action! Gordon ran into Allen's room and there was an earnest discussion. Then came a knock on my door. 'Come in.' Gordon stood there, shining a flashlight on his face to show that it was him, creating a strange interplay of shadows on his shining sunburned features, making him look like a bronze statue. He looked very concerned. Then he beamed the light down on to his cock. At first I didn't understand. Then he explained that this was the cause of the trouble. It was bleeding. I hadn't been able to see anything wrong in the poor light. His naked girlfriend stood anxiously behind him. I leaned forward to see, wondering what was the correct viewing distance to adopt while examining a friend's injured member. He held it out in the palm of his hand, relieving me of the need to handle it myself. Eighteen inches seemed to be about the right distance for an examination, indicating solicitude, as it required almost falling out of bed, but not inviting any suspicion of prurient interest. Gordon adjusted the flashlight so that Sue could also assess the situation. We ascertained that his still-naked girlfriend was not the owner of the blood; at this point Gordon formally introduced us and we shook hands. She must have arrived after dark. We discussed whether or not the penis had a bone that could be broken. I was sure that there was no bone, the penis relying entirely upon blood for tumescence. We concluded it must have been a broken blood vessel caused by too vigorous lovemaking. (It turned out to be a urinary tract infection, nothing to do with the girl at all.)

After the excitement, with oil lamps lit and much discussion, including Allen's lengthy reminiscences about breaking a blood vessel in his cock while fucking Dusty Moreland back in 1952, something that left him with a permanent crick in it, we were just settling down again when Allen, taking advantage of everyone being awake and all in one place, appeared carrying his Aladdin lamp and two petitions to sign. One was about stopping sonic booms over the forest, the other to Save Blue Whales. Gordon's teenage girlfriend from the village read them through carefully before signing, obviously wary of this extraordinary household. Even something as straightforward as signing a petition could be turned into a surrealist event at the Poetry Farm: in the kitchen, a few days before, a previous petition had been signed by Allen and passed to Julius for his signature. Julius had carefully and neatly added his name in his best copperplate, but unfortunately he had written it right on top of Allen's signature instead of on the line below. Allen held his head in his hands and moaned quietly. This time Allen had Julie sign first.

The Trailways bus from New York to Cherry Valley left from the Port Authority Terminal on 10th Avenue and I always used the occasion to visit Carl Solomon, who at that time worked at the Port Authority bookstall. I liked his quick humour and strange asides. The full title of Allen Ginsberg's famous poem is 'Howl for Carl Solomon'; he was one of the best minds of Allen's generation, which had been destroyed, in this case by insulin shock treatment in the mental hospital where Allen, also an inmate, met him.

In June the summer visitors began to arrive and Carl was among the first. Carl called his mother from Crain's Drugstore in Cherry Valley as soon as he got there. This was where the Trailways bus deposited its daily load from the big city 250 miles away. Allen then talked for a long time with Carl's mother, assuring her that Carl would be OK, while Carl and I sat at the fifties drugstore counter and had egg-creams, that wonderful New York concoction that contains neither eggs nor cream, in tall glasses. It was like being in a fifties teenage movie.

That evening Carl and Allen lounged in the living room, Carl reclining on the settee looking like the famous photograph of the rotund Apollinaire with his head bandaged. Carl's head had the same pear shape.

'We're not young and pretty any more,' said Allen.

'No, but we can be old and bestial,' replied Carl, and they looked at each other and laughed.

At one point the conversation took a political turn and Carl froze. He quickly said that he couldn't discuss these things because his uncle wouldn't approve of it and it made him nervous. This was the same uncle, A. A. Wynn, owner of Avon Books, that Carl worked for in 1953 and whom Carl persuaded to publish William Burroughs' *Junkie* as a mass-market paperback.

The English poet Nathaniel Tarn was visiting for a night and he and Carl talked at length about French poetry, a subject dear to Nathaniel, who was half French and who worked as an editor and translator of French poetry for the London publishers Jonathan Cape. Carl seemed to enjoy an intellectual discussion; he was obviously extremely well read and highly intelligent; he just found everyday life very difficult to deal with. He said that when he came out of the mental hospital his mother bought him *How to Dress for Success*. 'She thinks the answer to my problems is to get a better wardrobe,' he cackled.

In the morning Nathaniel bounced down to breakfast, dressed in what would have been appropriate clothes had he been staying the weekend in an English country house: white trousers and tennis shoes. As he stood at the foot of the stairs and looked out of the window his face took on an air of disbelief. There in the backyard stood Peter, naked, facing away from the house, legs astride, bent over, washing his ass with great care while yodelling 'The Raspberry Song'.

'I see,' said Nathaniel. Then realised everyone at the kitchen table was smiling at him and saw the joke.

Sue and I had been having problems before we went to the farm. We had been together since the early sixties and had essentially grown up together but we had become very different people. Though we had had relationships with a few other people, the move to the farm was in some ways a last attempt to mend the marriage; we had been through so much together that neither of us could face the idea of a clean break, though that is what, in the end, we did.

Being on the farm, without the distractions of London and our friends, brought problems to a head and she left for the city to stay with friends in the Lower East Side. I went down to see her every few weeks and we talked on the phone at least twice a week, but it seemed as if the break was a permanent one. 'I wondered why I never heard you fucking,' commented Allen.

The final break-up came in New York at Jane Fuller's apartment at 11th Street and Fifth Avenue where we first stayed when we arrived in New York in March. Sue left to walk to the Lower East Side where she had a room in another friend's flat; I stayed up all night, sustained by Alison Steele's all-night progressive rock show on WNEW-FM. From then on, every time I heard the introduction to her show, I remembered that square room high over Fifth Avenue, and the swirling, uncoordinated thoughts, the painful constriction of the chest, literally 'heartache', that came with the final decision to part: 'The flutter of wings, the shadow across the moon, the sounds of the night, as the Nightbird spreads her wings and soars, above the earth, into another level of comprehension, where we exist only to feel. Come, fly with me, Alison Steele, the Nightbird, at WNEW-FM, until dawn.' Pretentious as it might sound today, then it was fantastic, helping to ground me in some kind of reality. From then on I have never doubted the power of the radio DJ in people's lives.

Back on the farm I reorganised my room, arranging my typewriter, papers and oil lamp on the desk by the window. The sound of my Olivetti portable countered that of Allen's bigger, heavier machine in the next room. At night you could hear the wind through the trees and the propeller on the wind charger whirring. Allen lent me a small portable radio and I sometimes lay in the dark, listening to advertisements for restaurants and car tyre companies in faraway Buffalo, on one of the few stations I could receive. The living-room radio could pick up WRPI-FM, a student underground rock station from Troy, NY, with no advertising, that played Zappa, Hendrix and the Dead. I had never felt so alone.

I devoted as much of my time as I could to editing and sorting Allen's tapes, but this was determined by how much electricity we had and I could rarely work for more than three hours at a stretch unless the wind was blowing. I set myself up in the living room, clearing shelves for the tapes and connecting the tape machines to each other, arranging my editing block, leader tapes, single-edge razor blades and empty spools. As soon as we had electricity installed I ordered a professional tape machine: a Revox A77 with built in speakers so that we didn't have to all wear headphones for playback. I also bought a pair of Electrovoice microphones and microphone stands and a remote control so that we could make professional recordings of Allen when he did readings. He was very pleased to find that I could adjust the EQ to increase the bass end of his voice, making him sound like an ancient bard, and insisted that all our recordings utilise this feature.

There were a number of discoveries made during the project. We found recorded versions of poems Allen thought were lost for ever because he no longer had manuscript copies. These included 'Credo'; 'Green Valentine'; 'Saints Marching In' and one of his 'Psalm' series of poems. I recognised that I was privileged to spend so much uninterrupted time with Allen, talking in his room and walking with him in the meadows and forest, and knew that once the project was over I might never have such an opportunity again.

There was a beaver dam in the state woods near the far corner of Allen's property where a large area of forest was flooded or swampy. Allen and I went to see it, Allen wearing oversize wellingtons and the same green parka that he wore when he and Gary Snyder climbed Glacier Peak in Washington State in 1965. After considerable difficulty we were able to reach the dam itself. It must have been an old dam because the central area of destruction was enormous and a scene of incredible desolation with many of the trees now rotted and covered in huge fungi. Only about one in eight of the trees felled by the beavers had been of any use to them; many had caught in other trees or fallen across other felled trees remaining many feet above the waterline. A visitor to the farm, however, specialising in ecology, explained that what looked like desolation to me was in fact a very rich ecosystem and that dozens of species depend on the beavers to create these very conditions. The dam was very wide, creating a deep pond. The beavers plopped in by the dozen as we approached. In the same section of woodland was an old hemlock tree that Allen liked to visit, the only remaining tree from the original forest, too gnarled and twisted to be of use to the loggers.

Allen's room was the most peaceful and pleasant in the house. There were a lot of books in the living room, but they were an odd collection either left behind by departing guests or review copies, sent by the publishers in the hope that Allen would comment on them. The books in Allen's room, however, were a selection from his personal library, brought up from New York City. There were works by William Blake, Whitman's *Leaves of Grass*, several volumes by Tim Leary, a number of dog-eared paperbacks by Kerouac, Wyeth's volumes of haikus, books by Ed Sanders, Robert Creeley, Gary Snyder and his other poet friends. A row of mystical books included the Zohar, the Upanishads, the Kabbalah, the *Tibetan Book of the Dead*, Goddard's *Buddhist Bible*, Suzuki on Zen Buddhism. There were Gnostic fragments, the Gita and Soma Veda, the Mahanirvana and Hevajra tantras, books on comparative religion and magic mushrooms. Recent titles included Leslie Fiedler's *Being Busted* and books by Abbie Hoffman and Jerry Rubin. There were piles of poetry magazines, mostly mimeographed, including *Adventures in Poetry*; I always thought that was a good title for a magazine. Allen had underground comics, *Class War Comix*, *Zap*, *Yellow Dog*, and the one about the trial of the Chicago Eight, *Conspiracy Capers*.

Strings of Yoruba beads hung in front of the window and there was a coiled rope fixed to the floor beneath – as in all the bedrooms – to escape in case of fire. There was an old Tibetan tanka on the wall, the sole survivor of the many Allen brought back from his long sojourn in India. Lower East Side speed freaks stole all the others. The image was faded and darkened by butter smoke but still beautiful. The panel of Chinese silk – the door to the tanka – was fresh and bright but the stitching around the edge was frayed and worn. There was also a *dorje* – a Tibetan thunderbolt used in tantric ceremonies – brought from India, and a Tibetan *mani* seal and a tablet of red wax that Allen sometimes used on letters.

The panelled walls were hung with pictures: a photograph of bathers at a Ganges ghat, standing in the water in their white robes with Brahmins on the bank sitting under raised umbrellas; a photograph of Walt Whitman in his old age with a long white beard; the famous oval photograph of the young Arthur Rimbaud that Allen always had on his wall wherever he lived – there was another in his kitchen in the Lower East Side – and a full-colour poster of the view of Earth from outer space: intense blue oceans, brilliant green Amazon jungle and brown eroded Andes. There was a calendar from the Cherry Valley Bank on the back of the door, a round wall mirror, and a battered top hat hanging from a nail.

Allen had a hard single bed covered with a heavy thick prickly diamond-patterned Mexican blanket brought back from his travels. There was an old office desk, piled high with boxes of letters to answer, notebooks, bound journals, manuscripts and typescripts of his poetry. A huge floppy Xerox copy of Kerouac's *Visions of Cody* was marked by inserted slips of paper; Allen was writing a scholarly introduction to it. 'It really is his great masterwork,' he told me. 'His Ulysses.' We agreed that *Finnegans Wake* might be a better analogy, but I reminded Allen that when he first read it in the fifties he was horrified by its unedited transcriptions from tape recordings, its written equivalent of scat singing and its apparently random structure. He had been expecting a straight narrative. 'I recognised that it could never be published in that form,' Allen said. 'And I was right. It's only now he's dead that it'll come out.'

Allen was working on an investigation of CIA involvement in the narcotics trade in South-East Asia, and he had scores of folders of clippings and Xerox copies of papers and articles on the subject. Next to his bed there was a bronze ashtray, even though Allen was always trying to give up smoking – 'It's more addictive than heroin' – and a brass hash water pipe, though drugs were officially banned on the farm. He had a rocking chair and, leaning against the wall, an acoustic guitar left by one of his boys.

Denise liked to collect patchwork quilts, and there were many to be found in the barn sales on sleepy country roads. They were usually all unravelling and would have taken months to repair, but she recognised the work and creativity that went into them. One day, in mid-July, Peter, Denise and I were driving somewhere north of Cherry Valley in the '56 Chevy looking for a barn sale, when we passed a scrapyard piled high with auto wrecks. We wandered round inspecting the cars, each one a frozen moment in time, evidence of a violent event in the universe, theorising on the nature and type of impact that could have caused each one. Some of the cars didn't look damaged at all and we marvelled over what appeared to be a very cheap 1958 Chrysler with huge tailfins.

The owner also ran a farm and the two things were inextricably mixed up. Chickens pecked around the wrecks and the big barn was filled with pigs as well as small auto parts, rows of headlamps, silencers, fenders and strange chrome shapes that fitted together like a jigsaw to make up the grilles of huge fifties cars. Peter decided to buy a pig for Denise's birthday. 'Oh God,' I thought, 'Allen will go nuts.' He was always worrying about the animals as it was. No one ever rode or groomed Lash the horse and her hair hung off her in great black tufts like shadows. She waited hopefully by the fence, licking her salt block, desperate for company. Peter sometimes washed her down with the hose in the backyard, singing and chortling to himself, usually completing the work by lifting her tail and giving her a big smacking kiss. The billy goat served no useful function except cropping the front yard in a circle from his long chain; he butted anyone who came near and made such a smell that most people stayed well clear of his shed. Bessie provided the milk and the chickens delivered eggs but a pig would just eat a lot of food and I knew Peter and Denise would obviously never kill it.

I tried to remonstrate but Peter was determined. The farmer was given $15 and the pink, squealing, wriggling creature was put in a sack and Denise sat holding it in her lap as we drove back. Though I sympathised with him, Allen's face was priceless to see when the sack was opened and the pig exploded from it and ran round and round in confused circles in the yard. The pig was named 'Don't Bite Me' and soon began to root up the garden, the patch of grass and everything not fenced with chicken wire, but it always came when they whistled. It slept in Peter and Denise's room and used to lie on their bed at night, grunting contentedly. It quickly grew to an enormous size so that it had to be moved to the floor to sleep or else there was no room for them. It was a fine sight to see them in the evening sitting out on the porch making music together, Peter playing his banjo, his long ponytail bobbing, and Denise on an acoustic guitar, Don't Bite Me lying relaxed at their feet grunting and snorting.

Towards the end of June poets Bill Berkson and Jim Carroll arrived on their way to California. Jim Carroll later became well known for *The Basketball Diaries*, his 1978 memoir of his days as a 'teenage Catholic junkie' that was made into a film in 1995 by Scott Kalvert where Carroll is played by Leonardo DiCaprio. He also had a burst of rock stardom in the Jim Carroll Band in 1980 with his *Catholic Boy* album. He had Irish good looks with high cheekbones, straight lank blond hair and a skinny wiry body. He had a slightly tremulous, strangled voice, as if every word had to be fought for. I could see that Allen was very attracted to him. Carroll is very funny about Allen in his later memoir *Forced Entries*. When he and Berkson arrived Allen was recovering from a bout of dysentery and had been sleeping and idling in his room all day but, cheered by his visitors, he produced a big map of America and together they studied the mountains and deserts they would cross.

I played them Bob Dylan's new album. I was on Columbia Records' press list and they had sent me an advance copy of *Self Portrait*. Allen and I had been arguing about it for several weeks and, knowing that Carroll appreciated Dylan's work, Allen decided to sacrifice some electricity and get his opinion. The result was predictable: I still thought the album was pedestrian and not a patch on his earlier work and said so but Allen and Carroll, both Dylan fanatics, defended it vehemently. Allen described it in his journal as 'all differing emotions and moods from corny blue moon nostalgia hokum to hysteric-voiced Wight-Isle honk'. I liked the Isle of Wight honk, which was a live recording of 'The Mighty Quinn'; in fact I had been privileged to have fifth-row seats at the festival when it was recorded, but Dylan's Nashville recordings of 'Let It Be Me' and 'Blue Moon' were hard to take. I also objected to the fact that Leadbelly's 'Alberta', which appeared on the album twice, was credited as a Dylan original.

Allen's father, Louis, and his wife Edith, Allen's stepmother, drove up for a week at the end of June. Allen gave them his room, the most comfortable in the house, and moved in with Julius. Louis was seventy-four years old but still taught English composition at Rutgers State College. He should have retired from teaching when he was seventy but as he was such an active member of staff, and as he had been there for twenty-four years, they retained him on a year-by-year basis. 'I'm like a ghost haunting the corridors,' he said. He was alert and had a fierce intelligence masked by a protective shell of truly terrible puns. These were so much a part of who he was that he ran a weekly column of puns in the Paterson weekly paper. 'Not every beard is a bard, but with Allen it grows on you.' I accompanied Allen and his parents on some excursions round the countryside in their big new Ford. Edith allowed me to drive some of the way on the dirt roads amid untended woods, as I was learning to drive. The woods in upstate New York seemed strangely dull, lacking in energy compared with Vermont or New Hampshire or Maine. Maybe they have been logged too often and the pines do not allow enough of a mixed growth of bushes and plants.

I explained what we were doing with the tape archive and we decided to record some of Louis's reminiscences. Louis told the story of the family laundry in Newark and the saga of Allen's grand-father's horse. His memories were as evocative as the fading brown photographs of Jewish life in turn-of-the century America in the family album: images of the overcrowded tenements, the shouts in the streets, the struggles to make good. Edith, Louis, Allen and I would sit around the kitchen table at night, everyone else in their rooms, the oil lamp turned low because it gave off so much heat, moths fluttering around its tall glass shade, Louis's voice cracking a little as he described once more Allen's mother's madness and eventual death. Louis did not really like the tape recorder running and it was only after I had turned it off that he could relax.

It was fascinating to see the interaction between Allen and his father. Both men had strong opinions and were not afraid to express them, and the peaceful air was shattered several times by raised voices as they returned to their ongoing argument over the Black Panthers, whom Louis regarded as anti-Semitic and Allen did not. Allen believed that their anti-Jewish remarks stemmed from the fact that most of the merchants in the black ghetto and many of the slum landlords were Jews and that the black intolerance stemmed largely from dissatisfaction at the high prices they charged rather than a blanket hatred of all Jews. The argument usually came down to statements made by LeRoi Jones, whom Louis had met on many occasions in the late fifties when Jones published *Yugen* and later *Floating Bear*, two of the most exciting Beat Generation-era magazines. Now Jones was known as Amiri Baraka and had become a strident voice in the separatist Black Panther movement. It was an argument that could not be won, but they each tried, vociferously, until Edith would finally interject and smooth the ruffled feathers. Aside from political disagreements, it was obvious that Louis was immensely proud of his son's achievement as a poet and was prepared to tolerate those aspects of Allen's life he found distasteful; for instance, he was clearly very fond of Peter even though Allen's homosexuality had initially been repugnant to him.

3 1970

the summer people

As summer filled the meadows waist deep with wild flowers and dancing butterflies we saw a lot more of little Georgia. A hammock was strung between the trees in the front yard and she played on the grass in front of the house where she could come to no harm. Bonnie sat reading, watching over her, and seemed content with her life on the farm, though arguments and sobbing often came from upstairs in the early evenings.

> Man and wife, they weep in the attic
>> After bitter voices.
>>> Low voices threatening. [AG: 'Ecologue']

Bonnie clearly loved Ray even though he was a pathological liar and completely idle. He did have a certain charm and a strange innocence and childlike vulnerability. He spent his days sitting in the attic, rolling up his Bugler tobacco, surrounded by dust and dead flies that it did not occur to him to clean up. He ordered Bonnie around in a way that most women would have found intolerable, particularly in those days when women's liberation was a subject of hot debate. But this was a subject that Bonnie just didn't want to hear about. Ray's refusal to do his share of the cooking was irksome and Bonnie saying that she would do his share for him didn't help. They embodied a different era, living in a time warp of old-fashioned fifties male chauvinism. They kept themselves to themselves.

Cooking was something that I had also had to deal with. Sue had run the café at the Arts Lab in London in the sixties; she was trained as a cook and later became a professional chef; she had always prepared the food. I never even boiled an egg during the time I was with her. Now I had to learn to cook fast. On a visit to New York I picked up a copy of Julia Child's *Mastering the Art of French Cooking*, which explains every detail of preparing and cooking each dish as if she was talking to an eight-year-old. The farm was technically vegetarian, which was fine by me; I was quite prepared to leave out meat for a bit, so I cooked my way through all the vegetarian dishes in the book, learning all the time. Within weeks I had them eating *Céleri-rave rémoulade* (celery in a mustard sauce) and *gratin dauphinois* from freshly dug potatoes.

There were often many mouths to feed as Allen's friends began to take summer breaks and visit. Herbert Huncke arrived with R'lene Dahlberg and Elise Dorfman. 'Man, we have such boss wheels outside,' said Huncke, entering the farm door as if it were a midtown bar. His face was ravaged and twisted into an extraordinary grimace of greeting, the pickling effects of decades of hard drugs. This was the man who showed William Burroughs how to use morphine back in 1944. 'Dig these threads!' he shouted as he grabbed Allen's hand in order that he might feel for himself the quality of the cloth. 'We've brought pink gin. Where shall we put it?' he said happily. Allen was immediately in a state of panic, stepping from leg to leg. It was obvious that Ray would get completely smashed and maybe Peter would get drunk too and, with his guard down, try some more speed. Peter had burned most of the plastic bags of speed in a dustbin, but as he had spent all his savings on it Allen was convinced that more was hidden all over the farm. Gordon had already found some in the gutter pipe beneath the eaves. Allen was in a quandary; he could not stop Huncke, R'lene and Ellie from drinking – he had invited them up for a vacation, not to dry out. He begged them to keep it as secret as possible. A hopeless task, of course.

Huncke was a brilliant raconteur and the evenings were filled with enjoyable accounts of low-life behaviour. Huncke came from a wealthy Chicago Jewish family, but they became estranged when his father found the teenage Herbert dressed in drag, picking up men on the highway. I was familiar with his story from *Huncke's Journal* which Diane DiPrima published in 1965. Huncke seemed scared of the countryside and rarely left the immediate vicinity of the house unless accompanied by Allen or one of the women for a walk. His New York City sartorial elegance – clashing patterns in the worst possible taste and high collars to hide his scrawny neck – looked strangely out of place. The sunlight was too bright for his eyes, more conditioned to Times Square neon than to daylight. He had been a junkie since the early forties and was bony, sly, razor sharp, big-city slick and utterly untrustworthy; he was the man who got Allen arrested and put into a mental hospital by filling Allen's apartment with stolen goods. I found him in my room one day looking through my things. 'There's nothing here to steal,' I told him.

'I got lost, I went into the wrong room,' he lied. He knew the farm very well; he had spent time there the previous year with his boyfriend Louis Cartwright. Huncke was a man with no ethical or moral values whatsoever. He would steal from anyone, no matter how sick or destitute they were. Years before, when he worked as a male prostitute on Times Square, the cops, who had seen some pretty despicable behaviour in their time, nicknamed him 'The Creep' and sometimes banned him from the Square altogether. Huncke imposed on anyone who treated him with respect or kindness until they could take it no more. Burroughs grew to dread his whining voice on the telephone and, when he later moved from New York to Kansas, he refused to allow Huncke to visit, but Ginsberg, with his enormous tolerance for human foibles, continued to see him.

An example of his character came when Sue moved to New York. Huncke knew that she was working at the East Side Bookstore

Ettori Sottsass

Sue with M in New York, April 1970

on St Marks Place. Timing it so that she was the only other person in the store, he casually opened the cash register and took out a twenty. He knew that Sue did not have a work permit and that she would, anyway, not call the cops. He was quite happy to see her get into trouble when only weeks before he had been socialising with her and Allen. There was always a new generation of impressionable young kids who thought that Huncke was the *real thing*. Huncke knew exactly how to play up to the romantic notions they had of him as the angelic thief, telling them stories about Burroughs and Kerouac, Ginsberg and Corso in the forties and fifties. He told great stories and it didn't matter much whether they were true or not, he had recounted them so many times they were perfected, smoothed-out, shining vignettes, many of which he later used in his memoirs. Those who listened had to pay, often in ways that came as a surprise to them when they found that drugs, money, books or anything portable of any value had gone missing.

One day an old milk delivery truck appeared at the top of the drive and slowly trundled towards the house. It was the sort where the driver had to stand up to steer and had a top speed of ten miles per hour. A number of us sat on the grass outside the house while Allen wondered who it could be as no one had called. It was Ann Buchanan and Rick Fields who had been fruit picking over towards Buffalo and thought they would visit for a while. They had fitted the van out with a mattress and storage bins and had been living in it since the spring. Allen was very upset to see it in the car park; he was convinced that it would remain there always, up on blocks, and insisted that they drive it about every few weeks to make sure it still worked. He had a terror of the farm looking like many of the others in the area, littered with the hulks of rusting cars and pick-ups.

Ann was an old friend of Allen's from San Francisco where she and her then boyfriend Charley Plymell shared a house and often a bed with Allen, Neal Cassady and Neal's girlfriend Ann Murphy on Gough Street. Ann was petite, with long thick black hair and a steady, wide gaze. She was from the Midwest: Griggsville, Illinois, a small town with one wide shopping street dominated by a tall mast covered with nesting boxes. It dubbed itself 'The purple martin capitol of the world' – purple martins are like swallows or swifts and eat mosquitoes. It was the Bible Belt and her family were religious. Ann, however, was a Buddhist. She was a misfit in rural Illinois and left as soon as she could, moving to San Francisco and then New York. It was not until Gerard Malanga told me later that I found out she was one of the stars in Andy Warhol's *Ten Most Beautiful Women*. Ann never mentioned it. I had seen stills but it was not often screened and I did not get to see it until January 2002 when I was walking through the Andy Warhol Retrospective at the Tate Modern and entered a room given over to the screening of Warhol's films. I turned the corner and there was Ann, filling an entire wall of the room. It was an unexpected shock. It was made long before I met her, but she told me that all she did was stare at the camera and wait for a tear to roll down her cheek, and this is what happens. She had no interest in fame or celebrity and I was always being surprised by newly emerging facts about her: that she had spent time with Allen and Bob Dylan, for instance. She was honest and straightforward to the point, sometimes, of rudeness.

I began to explore the area with Ann, trundling along quiet country roads in the milk truck at a speed only slightly faster than walking so we could see every tree and creek, visiting sleepy little villages, occasionally attending a barn sale where great piles of unravelling hand-stitched quilts were for sale for a few dollars each. At one barn there was an old pump organ, originally from a village church. We told Allen about it and the next day we went with Allen, Peter and Denise to buy it. It was a beautiful old instrument, in need of minor repair, with filigree woodwork and even a pair of folding candleholders on the front. Soon it was squeaking and rattling in the living room as Allen furiously pumped the pedals and slowly coaxed the melody he had written to accompany William Blake's 'Night' from its dusty keys. It was a very hot night and Allen and I sat up talking until very late, listening to the house groaning and shifting with the temperature change when a breeze got up.

Ann seemed to be breaking up with Rick and slept in the attic of the barn. You could see the light of her candle through the cracks in the red-painted wood at night. After a while she began sleeping in my room. She was a Tibetan Buddhist and had taken Sonam Kazi as her teacher. Kazi had been the Dalai Lama's interpreter in India, and had studied with Dudjom Rinpoche, the head of the Nyingma sect, the oldest order of Tibetan Buddhism. (I was told that the sight of his hat alone was supposed to confer instant enlightenment. Years later I recorded a talk by him at Chelsea Town Hall and was therefore able to get a good look at it but I didn't feel any different. There may have been a misunderstanding here, because traditionally it is the Karma

Kagyu sect who particularly venerate their leader's black crown, not the Nyingma.) Part of her religious ritual entailed tantric sex, which we used to practise in the long grass: the man adopting the lotus position with legs crossed, and the woman locked into place on his lap, her legs wrapped around his body. It is a meditative exercise, with no movement or friction allowed but, after a bit of practice, I found I could keep it up for a half-hour or so sitting still, but I always cheated in the end.

Although the farm was officially vegetarian, on one occasion Peter developed such a craving for chicken that he and I drove all the way to Oneonta in the '56 Olds to buy some as nowhere in Cherry Valley would have been open at that time of day. He drove fast, like his friend Neal Cassady. I didn't mind the lack of meat but I would have enjoyed a bottle of wine with my meals. Once in the supermarket we succumbed to temptation and not only bought enough chicken for the evening meal, but also an enormous bargain pack of bacon. We had lunch at a diner that Peter liked on the main street and he reminisced about the several years that he and Allen lived in India in the early sixties and of his experiences in London on his way back to the States; Allen had gone on ahead, returning to the States via Japan. I had heard many stories of Peter's time in London and how he walked the cold autumn streets barefoot, wearing colourful Indian clothes, long hair and a woolly hat, the first bona fide member of the Beat Generation anyone had ever encountered.

Gregory Corso arrived on the farm in the first week of July to kick his heroin habit. I had first met Gregory in London in 1962 when he was living in a squat on Regent's Park Road along with a group of poetry magazine editors. I got to know him better in 1965 when Allen Ginsberg was staying with me at the time of the Royal Albert Hall reading as Gregory was a frequent visitor. When I first met him Gregory still had the classic Italian looks of Frank Sinatra, but by the time he arrived in Cherry Valley, the drugs had taken their toll: the loss of teeth, the pugnacious thrust of his jaw and low furrowed brow now gave him a distinct simian cast, a Neanderthal look that was to increase with age. He arrived angry and belligerent but focused most of his aggression on Allen.

He was enormously jealous of Allen's success as a poet. As far as Gregory was concerned they had started out together and it was the 1956 *Howl* obscenity trial which had propelled both Allen and Lawrence Ferlinghetti to fame, not the quality of their poetry. In fact Gregory had been an equal partner in the Beat Generation pantheon throughout the fifties. When he and Allen visited Chicago to read in support of *Big Table* magazine's obscenity trial, they were front-page news and both feted by society hostesses and the local intelligentsia. Gregory's poem 'Bomb' and his collection *Happy Birthday of Death* were commercial as well as critical successes. It was his escalating addiction to heroin which was his downfall; giving him a patchy output, as poems got lost or notebooks stolen or sold for money for drugs.

At first there were some good days on the farm with Gregory when he would even do his share of the cooking. Once I fixed the salad while Gregory made pasta: the linguini with clam sauce that Allen liked so much. Italian opera played loudly on the portable radio and Gregory hummed along with the aria, clearly relaxed and content. 'Miles, you've been to Italy,' he said. 'You realise how food should be. It's got to have *endente*. Not the way these fools cook it.' But then he began his paranoid ramblings about a plot against him formulated by Allen. Though it is pointless trying to reason with a junkie, I tried to convince Gregory that this was the product of his imagination. Gregory looked at me slyly and quoted William Burroughs back to me: 'Even paranoid people can have real enemies.' Sometimes, however, he came out with some really good lines. While walking in the yard with Claude Pelieu he suddenly asked, 'When did the first man smile?'

Claude Pelieu was a well-known avant-garde poet in his own right back in France, married to the translator Mary Beach. In the sixties they had published Ginsberg, Burroughs, Lawrence Ferlinghetti and others in their small press, Beach Books, Texts and Documents, and were

Allen and Burroughs's French translators. Mary was a Connecticut Yankee, very straight looking with full make-up, lipstick, powdered face, and permed hair. She was a niece of Sylvia Beach, the publisher of James Joyce's *Ulysses*. Claude and Mary were on the farm in order to work with Allen on the French translation of *Planet News* for Editions Christian Bourgeois. I first met them in 1969 when I spent several months living at the Hotel Chelsea. Claude and Mary had a two-room suite there, with their own television and phone line so they were spared the terrors of the Chelsea switchboard. Their living room had a gigantic collage all across one wall of pictures clipped from pornographic magazines and *Life* magazine. They worked all day at their typewriters, Mary at her desk, Claude standing up at the marble fireplace with his typewriter on the mantelpiece. One of Mary's own books from this period was called *Electric Banana* and was written using William Burroughs's cut-up collage technique.

For several days Allen sat outside, slumped in a chair beneath the maples by the propane tank, reading the bulky manuscript and making notes. The dogs lay in the shade near him, panting. Claude and Mary spent the mornings walking in the woods after working late with Allen on the translation. There were some wonderful exchanges.

'Do you have geeks in France?'

'A geek? What is that?'

'You know, in the country where they cut off the heads of chickens...'

'Oh, yeah, yeah,' Claude interrupting. 'We have a word, what is that, Mary? A man who is a poodle-fucker!'

In the evenings they would sit around the kitchen table with Allen, the two oil lamps heating the room to tropical temperatures. Allen's French seemed to be quite good though Mary sometimes had to correct the grammar that he suggested. They made numerous corrections to each poem. The French translation must be the most perfect of all Allen's translated works considering the lavish attention paid to each poem. Small errors such as Paul McCartney playing guitar instead of bass in 'Portland Coliseum' were rectified. Even the most minor points were argued through; there was one heated exchange between Allen and Mary over whether Martin Buber's name was spelled in Yiddish or Hebrew which only ended when they were drowned out by the noise of Peter and Denise having a shower together. I think Claude and Mary got great satisfaction in knowing that it was a superb translation. They were hardly doing it for the money.

Claude and Mary were used to decent food and cleanliness and the farm provided neither of these. The lifestyle of many of the people seemed alien to them and they made little effort to get to know most of them. They were old friends of mine so we spent a lot of time together. They found Ray's drunkenness amusing. One incident, in which Gregory directed some particularly unpleasant vulgarity at Mary, almost resulted in him being flattened by Claude, an ex-paratrooper who was about twice Gregory's size, but with great reserve Claude allowed Mary to defend herself, which she was quite capable of doing; her tongue being an even match to Gregory's. Unfortunately, Gregory's rudeness to Mary caused Ray, in a sudden spurt of drunken chivalry, to defend her honour, bringing Gregory's wrathful tongue down upon himself. Instead of immediately backing down Ray slapped Gregory's cigarette from his mouth, surprising both Gregory and himself. Ray unfortunately then spoiled everything by bursting into tears when Gregory taunted him for being a jailbird. The pain this always caused Ray suggested that something truly horrible had happened to him when he was in the Bordentown Reformatory all those years ago. You could taunt Gregory about being in jail and he would revel in it.

In his rambling monologues, Gregory had one particular line that he kept returning to, that the only reason he was on the farm was to kill Allen, that Allen was dead anyway, and that Peter was just a parasite on Allen. He, Gregory, was Allen's oldest friend and he had to kill Allen to save him from all this. He claimed he had friends or relatives who were 'made men' in the Mafia and they

Barry Miles

Allen Ginsberg in the kitchen at the Cherry Valley farm, spring 1970

were going to get him; he was really getting into his Italian ancestry (in fact Gregory later had a minor speaking role in *Godfather III*). In the end, after one such vituperative tirade filled with death threats, Allen flopped back in his chair and said, in an exhausted voice, 'You know, even though I've known you for so many years, I don't think I like you so much any more. It's been a long time since there was any friendship, it's all been unpleasantness...' This time Gregory seemed to register what Allen was saying; somewhere down inside his head something clicked and he fell silent.

A few days after Gregory arrived, I was walking down by the pond, planning to sit and watch the frogs and smoke a quiet Camel. Then I saw something that I knew would provoke the most fearful row, a collection of objects guaranteed to cause recriminations, several of them, floating about ten feet out from the bank. I hurried back up to the farm to tell Allen. Beer cans in the lake! Allen, the vocal spokesman for ecology and organic vegetables, has beer cans floating in his lake, recently built with a government matching grant for water conservation and only just stocked with fish. Beer was banned on the farm, as were speed and junk. Allen originally bought the Cherry Valley farm as a haven for poets to kick drugs: Ray Bremser was supposed to be drying out there and Gregory was on the farm to kick junk. I even encountered opposition to my smoking cigarettes, but Allen was not in a position to say much because he still secretly smoked when he thought no one was looking and even bummed them from me when he was desperate.

The discovery of the beer cans swiftly developed into a major incident. A full-scale investigation began with all eyes upon Ray and some on Gregory. Eventually it was revealed that they were both guilty, having walked the eight miles into town and finished up with a six-pack down by the lake. This exploded the idea that they didn't get along together, which was the impression that Gregory always tried to give, not wanting to be classed alongside a common ex-con, even though Gregory himself had served time for robbery. Gregory saw himself as a great poet, driven only by the muse, but when it came to their mutual need for alcohol he and Ray formed an alliance and became pals. The inquisition by Allen resulted in Ray breaking down and crying, saying he wouldn't do it again, and Gregory being abusive to Ray for implicating him in the guilt.

Allen recorded in his journal entry for 13 July: 'Beer cans found in the pond & their smiling faces turned snarling & screaming at each other at dusk – Peter drunk also screaming in garage – second day all calm & a wave of happiness passed thru tranquil grassy yard – yesterday more vodka's screaming & threats of death.' Allen had been very worried at first to find Peter incoherent, rolling on the stone pathway outside, and was enormously relieved to find that it was as a result of alcohol, not speed.

Allen: 'Why are you so unhappy? You got your youth, you got a
     girlfriend, you got all of nature, you got the whole earth to play
     with.'
Peter: 'I know, I know. (Grunts, animal sounds) It's not play.'
Allen: 'It's not play? Don't work so hard, then, play more.'
Peter: 'Gotta eat!'
Allen: 'Well, there'll be food. (Peter groaning) You wanna come in
     and eat?'
Peter: 'No, I don't, I don't.'
Allen: (finally broaching the subject) 'What did you take?'
Peter: 'Oh, oh, uh, wine.'
Allen: 'What kind?'
Peter: 'Port.'
Allen: 'You feel all right?'
Peter: (has attack of hiccoughs) 'I think I'll kill myself.'
Allen: 'Don't do that.'
Peter: 'If I do, it don't matter.'
Allen: 'Yes it does, it matters to me!'
Peter: 'No it don't.'
Allen: 'I'd cry, I'd cry.'
Peter: 'Oh, *big deal*!'
Allen: 'Well, that's the biggest deal there is, a broken heart.'
Peter: 'In order to break your heart, you gotta take it and go,
     Stummmbbah! (Sound of Peter banging head on ground) You
     gotta take a rock and Tummbah! it on your skull, and then you
     break your heart, that's all. You know if you ever break your
     skull you can always put it together again. (Strange laugh)'
Allen: 'Ha! Ha! Ha! You're drunk!'
Peter: 'That's all, that's about all!'

My friend Steve Abrams, the man who placed the full-page advertisement in the London *Times* in 1967 demanding that the laws against
marijuana should be changed, came to visit during this bad period

and found Allen stressed out from it all. They spent a day in Allen's room discussing pot laws and the effects of pot, and going through Allen's bulging files on the role of the CIA in opium trafficking in South-East Asia. In the evening, Steve got stoned and Allen, after a few tokes, took on a persona I had not previously seen; that of an Aleister Crowleyan guru. He produced one of Sir Arthur Avalon's immense books and incanted the whole of the Siva ritual, Siva being ganga or pot. Steve, and everyone else, was visibly bored as the lamp heated the kitchen like an oven but there was no stopping Allen. No one was quite sure whether Allen regarded Avalon's ramblings as serious or some kind of elaborate pothead joke, so it was somewhat difficult to join Allen in his obvious enthusiasm. Years later Allen would sometimes do the same thing in reciting the lineages of various Tibetan gurus to people who had not the slightest interest and who did not, in any case, believe in reincarnation. It was some sort of grounding exercise.

Gregory shouted a lot but it wasn't until he had been on the farm for two weeks that he turned violent. It was during Steve Abrams's visit. Paul Berkowitz was also visiting and we were preparing to take Steve into Cherry Valley to catch the bus back to New York. Gordon was going to drive us to the bus stop so Gregory demanded that he buy him some beer in the town, trying to assert his authority, hoping that mild-mannered Gordon could be cowed. But Gordon said no and as he turned to open the kitchen door and leave, Gregory leapt upon him from behind, flailing like a madman at Gordon's head, giving him a black eye. We all leapt upon Gregory and pinned him to the floor. He squealed even louder than Don't Bite Me. In the course of the struggle Gregory swung at me, knocking my glasses across the room but fortunately not breaking them. Everybody was in favour of putting Gregory on the bus with Steve but Allen overrode us, proving once and for all that it may have looked like a commune, but it was Allen's commune and not a democracy. He was the one who paid the bills and he chose who would live there.

While Gordon nursed his bruised eye, I went with Steve to Cherry

Valley, driven by Paul Berkowitz. Naturally we had missed the bus, so Paul drove Steve to Albany, about eighty miles to the east. Though Steve was originally from Beverly Hills, his years studying at Oxford had given him the accent and demeanour of an Oxbridge don along with a tendency to tell extremely long stories. Paul was astonished by Steve's encyclopedic knowledge of marijuana. Throughout the drive, drawing on his experience as a chemist, he opined on the merits of different isomers of the tetrahydrocannabinol molecule and their various uses.

When he was safely on the bus Paul took off his little granny glasses and rubbed them. 'I didn't know there was so much to know about pot!' he said. Allen faithfully recorded the events in his journal: 'July 21: 1970: Gordon Ball with a violet bruise under his left eye where Gregory attacked him from behind – screaming to the bottom, "assholes" drunk anguish with sour cream on unsuspecting finger tucking in the cigarette holed shirt.' I liked the sour cream observation.

Some of Allen's stress was caused by Maretta Greer, who had arrived on the farm two days before Gregory. She had been Allen's on-off girlfriend since the Human Be-In in San Francisco's Golden Gate Park when she sat on the stage with him chanting alongside the other self-proclaimed 'gurus' of the counter-culture. She was very thin, with long straight blonde hair, and saw herself as something of a religious teacher. She taught Allen lots of mantras, writing them in his notebook, but she had never actually studied with a guru of her own. She called Allen from New York, weeping on the telephone, to say she had been kicked out of Pakistan after being discharged from the Holy Family Hospital in Rawalpindi, West Pakistan. They thought that they had enough beggars of their own without having an American on the street.

On Maretta's previous visit she had spent weeks in solitary meditation in the attic, rarely making an appearance. On this second sojourn she was a little more in evidence, if only to play records and use up the electricity. Allen lost his temper with her when she burned copies of *Oz* magazine she found there because she thought they were 'obscene'. He remembered 'she ran up the ladder flashing eyed angry to the attic where she did prostrations smoked hemp and masturbated and insisted that she loved me as Lord Shiv'. Though Maretta was desperate for sex with him Allen rebelled: 'I was turned off, she was so thin, her cunt like a shark fin out to get me, and her skin was mottled, she didn't wash herself.' And so another casualty was added to the roll of inmates.

There were scores of visitors: poet Paul Blackburn arrived thin and wan, chain-smoking the French cigarettes that would eventually kill him and joking about dying of cancer; I wonder, did he already know he had it? He was very interested in the tape project and said that he had assembled a large collection of spoken-word recordings himself; he assiduously recorded all the local New York poets. It was Blackburn who moved the weekly readings at the Metro Café to St Mark's Church and established the Poetry Project there, where it remains to this day. The translator David Rattrey and his wife spent a week, reminiscing about the New York jazz scene in the fifties and the close relationship between heroin and jazz. John Chamberlain, who made life-size sculptures of people fucking out of scrap metal and old cars, arrived with poet John Giorno, inventor of Dial-a-Poem, who was to become a frequent visitor.

Lucien Carr, Allen's oldest friend, came with his family for a week. They first met in 1943 when Allen arrived at Columbia University, and it was Lucien who introduced him to William Burroughs and Jack Kerouac. Listening to their table talk was a delight. Lucien had no illusions about his famous friends. He was scathing about Kerouac's behaviour and dismissed his *Vanity of Duluoz*, which contains a highly romanticised version of Lucien's killing of David Kammerer, as 'silly shit'.

When Allen and Lucien were at Columbia University in the early forties, Lucien was shadowed everywhere by a predatory admirer, David Kammerer, his one-time scout troop leader, who followed him from school to school, and from University of Chicago to Columbia.

Lucien, Kammerer and Burroughs all knew each other from St Louis and Kammerer always managed to ingratiate himself into Lucien's circles, making it impossible to ignore him. When he finally made a lunge at Lucien, late one night when they were sitting talking on the banks of the Hudson, Lucien stabbed him with his boy-scout knife, then panicked, weighted the body down with rocks and pushed him into the river. He served two years on the grounds that it was an 'honor slaying'. Lucien wanted to keep that side of his early life as quiet as possible, and had not been pleased when, despite Lucien's objections, Kerouac decided to use it as subject matter for a book. Allen tried to defend Kerouac but was no match for Lucien's scorn.

Lucien had many hilarious stories to tell about William Burroughs in St Louis and in Chicago in the early forties: how William – whom he called 'Billy' – would drive his roadster across people's front lawns, and what a great womaniser he was: 'There's a fire in my chest!' William would cry, beating on it with his fist. Apparently it impressed the ladies. Lucien told a story of how a group of them had stripped off and had sex in the mud on the banks of the Missouri. To Lucien these were just his old friends from college days. He was uninterested in the cult of personality that had grown around them and was much amused that anyone would regard any of them as gurus or teachers.

Lucien had been to the farm on a number of occasions, usually to dry out. He told me, 'I'd say, Allen, I need to come up the farm for a week, because I'd gotten to a point where I could not stop drinking in New York. Could not stop drinking if liquor was available. So I went up there a couple of times with Peter, couple of times with Allen and Peter, couple of times with whatever girl I was living with, and they would take the car away and so if you were going to get a drink it meant an eight-mile walk to Cherry Valley and I was never up to the eight-mile walk so I got dried out for a week and after a week drying out I was able to come back to New York and not drink for a while.'

Ann Charters came to stay and, though Allen was busy, he was able to give her quite a bit of time to talk about Jack Kerouac for her groundbreaking biography of him. It is always hard writing the first biography and she was hampered by the fact that she was not permitted to quote directly from Kerouac's books and had to paraphrase. She sparked a deluge of books but hers remains one of the best introductions to the man and his work. She took a lot of photographs of the farm and its occupants which she published in her photo book, *Beats and Company*. I liked her very much and Ann and I had dinner together with her husband Sam at their house in Brooklyn Heights before they left to live in Sweden as a personal protest against the Vietnam War.

The farm was a convenient journey break for people en route to the University of Buffalo (SUNY), and so Robert Creeley stopped off several times. These evenings were very literary, and almost entirely devoted to poetry, though Creeley listened attentively to Allen's pet project: his investigation into the role of the CIA in the opium traffic of South-East Asia. Though Creeley was an old friend of Allen's from the mid-fifties, he seemed rather reserved in his company, as if Allen's lifestyle and values were too far out for him. It was hard to imagine him as the man famous for his bar fights and rabble-rousing.

Allen DeLoach, editor of *Intrepid* magazine and a professor at SUNY, always broke his trip at the farm and would give lifts to anyone heading back to the city in his VW camper, the vehicle of choice in those days. He was an ex-speed-freak and one time gave Allen and I a lift back to the city. Though he claimed to be no longer taking speed, DeLoach talked continuously from Cherry Valley to Manhattan and not even Allen could get a word in edgeways. It was through DeLoach that Allen managed to get Gregory some kind of teaching post at SUNY and, miraculously, within a few days of his attack on Gordon, Gregory was brooding his fate on the banks of Lake Ontario.

It was very pleasant to sit outside in the shade of a tree, watching the swallows swoop and dive around the barn and make the occasional foray to the pond to scoop up water on the wing. Sometimes Radah and Godley would discover garter snakes in the hay and run in circles, excitedly barking, but mostly the atmosphere was one of utmost tranquillity. With an average of a dozen people at the house at any given time, people soon established their own chosen spaces outdoors. Rick Fields liked to meditate in the sun at the edge of the pond, whereas Ann preferred the shade of a tree some distance from the pond. Bonnie and Georgia liked to sit on the bank, watching the fish. Sometimes Georgia discovered a frog and would run after it in excitement until it jumped into the water and disappeared. It seemed a pity that there were no other four-year-olds around for her to play with but she seemed content. If not in his room, Allen worked at a small table set up near the propane tank at the side of the house beneath the maples. Ray stayed in the attic and Gordon, Denise, Peter and Julius slaved in the soybean patch. If there was electricity I would be in the living room at my tape machines but at the height of the afternoon heat I preferred the cool gloom of my wood-panelled room with the smell of new-mown grass coming through the open window. Next door, Gordon would sometimes escape the heat outside and work on the farm receipts. Green light filtered into both our rooms through the whispering branches of the maples outside. Green was the predominant colour even at night, when the air was filled with the green neon flashes of the fireflies.

In the morning Gordon was the first up, calling to Bessie in the woods to come and be milked. Julius was usually standing outside his door at an early hour and would be sent to collect eggs for breakfast. Gordon was trying to get the thirty hens to produce chicks, but every time one got broody and began to sit on a clutch of eggs, Julius would shoo her away and take them. Allen was usually up at 6.30 or seven. I would hear the front door squeak as he went out to the field for a morning piss.

Ed the Hermit was usually standing outside to greet him, dressed in his regulation bib overalls, work boots and greasy peaked cap advertising Agway Foodstore. Ed, who had already heard the forecast on the radio, would hold his finger to the wind, study the clouds and the horizon and accurately predict the day's weather to

Allen's eternal astonishment. Ed kept a few black alpine goats up at his shack adjoining Allen's land. As he had never cleaned them out, they walked about on top of a pile of dung almost as high as a man. Ed had raised the sides of their enclosure to compensate. It seemed an odd way to farm to me – why not move the enclosure to one side? Ed was the most sociable hermit I'd ever met; he loved to talk and had some good stories. It was a pleasant walk across the meadow through the long grass and flowers, surrounded by clouds of butterflies and prancing cicadas, to the top road and to Ed's; the noise of the cicadas sometimes deafening.

After his long years in the Lower East Side, Allen was charmed by the bucolic environment and began some nature poems, including a long 'Eco-log' (later 'Ecologue') which balanced his appreciation of nature with a gloomy prognosis for its survival: 'In a thousand years, if there's History / America'll be remembered as a nasty little Country...' He first performed it at a poetry reading in Albany in the university gymnasium. We took a carload of equipment. This was the first time that we had used the Revox in a location setting. Recording was impossible at the farm because the AC/DC converter put a square-wave hum on the line that we could reduce in volume but not get rid of. Ray Bremser read, so did Gregory Corso, who was still on the farm at that time. There was a large audience, which softened the live acoustics, and the directional microphones provided a perfect stereo recording. Allen was delighted at having his own road crew to position his chair and microphone stands, just like a rock 'n' roll star. Our first live recording was a great success.

From then on, unless he was flying somewhere to do a gig, Ann and I usually accompanied Allen on readings to record them. One time we drove up from Manhattan to a Catholic school in Tarrytown, NY, where a Sister Elizabeth, who had recently married Daniel Berrigan, was on the staff. Allen, provocatively, read 'Please Master', about wanting to be fucked in the arse and beaten, but this was not what puzzled the nuns. Afterwards one came up and asked about the reference to the 'Sacred Heart of Jesus'. They said this was a very conservative Catholic cult and they were surprised to hear Allen mention it. It turned out that Allen didn't really know much about it; it was something he'd heard about from Kerouac and had used largely because he liked the way the words sounded. The nuns remained puzzled.

Another time, Allen, Ann and I flew up to Ithaca in upstate New York carrying the Revox and microphone stands. The town was deep in snow and we were all put up in an old campus building as college guests. It was a glimpse of old New York: polished wooden floors, a case clock that ticked so slowly that you waited anxiously for the next tick in case it had stopped, ancient creaking wooden bedsteads with hand-sewn quilts. Allen pottered around after all the guests had left, making last cups of coffee; the three of us like a family.

In September a phone call brought the news that Tim Leary had escaped from jail. He had been given a ten-year sentence in January for possession of marijuana and once he was transferred to jail they added another ten years from a previous offence in 1965. The two were to be served consecutively: twenty years in prison for less than half an ounce of marijuana. He was forty-nine. When Leary arrived at the San Luis Obispo penitentiary he was given the standard psychological tests that were used to determine appropriate prison work. As Leary actually wrote the tests himself – the 'Leary Interpersonal Behaviour Test' – he knew exactly how to answer them in such a way that the authorities would consider him to be a very conventional, conforming individual with a great interest in forestry and gardening. Because of this, he was assigned a job as a gardener in the low-security wing. Leary had seemed to be holding up well; in a letter to Allen he said: 'I watch the stars & the planets every nite… study basic science texts… botany… physics… electricity… entomology… it's all there in every science… all so obvious… positive-negative charges… double helix…' And so on. But when his appeal was rejected he knew that his subsequent appeal would not be heard again for at least another year. He knew then that the only way out was to escape.

His draconian sentence, imposed for a tiny amount of pot, was just a flimsy excuse for holding him as a political prisoner. By encouraging young people to 'tune in' – to question the lies and American values the schools and advertisers had fed them all their life – to 'turn on' – to experience hallucinogenic or mind-altering drugs that enabled them to see how shallow American consumer society is – and 'drop out' – to reject establishment values in favour of a more life-affirming and people-oriented, anti-war, peace-loving, more spiritual existence – he was seen as a serious threat to the very foundations of everything that the establishment held dear. They set out to destroy him and they ultimately did, but not until later.

It seemed so unreal, somehow, looking out of the kitchen window at the gently moving leaves as Allen gave us the news. Leary had risked his life to climb a twelve-foot link fence, patrolled by armed guards in two gun trucks, to be met by members of the Weather Underground who spirited him away southward down US-1, leaving his prison clothes two miles down the road. He was reunited with his wife Rosemary and together they were smuggled out of the country to Algeria, where they stayed with Eldridge Cleaver and the Black Panthers' 'Government in Exile'. Before leaving, however, Tim, Rosemary and Bernadette Dohrn, one of the leaders of the Weather Underground who had also been living underground since the March town-house explosion, all got very stoned and went to see *Woodstock*. Leary told Allen in a letter how very much he enjoyed the film.

Leary posted a statement he said was written before climbing the wall, but in which many people detected the heavy hand of the Weather Underground in the call for armed struggle. Most of it, however, was pure Leary: 'Listen. There is no compromise with a machine. You cannot talk peace and love to a humanoid robot whose every Federal Bureaucratic impulse is soulless, heartless, humour-less, lifeless, loveless... Love life... blow the mechanical mind with Holy acid... dose them... dose them... dose them. Resist physically; robot agents who threaten life must be disarmed, disabled, discon-nected by force. Arm yourselves and shoot to live... Listen, Nixon.

We were never that naïve. We knew that flowers in your gun-barrels were risky... We begged you to live and let live, to love and let love, but you have chosen to kill and get killed.' He ended with a warning that he was armed and should be considered dangerous to anyone who threatened his life or freedom. For the next two years American agents monitored his every move and in 1973 they caught up with him in Kabul, Afghanistan. Though Afghanistan had no extradition treaty with the USA, federal agents forcibly detained him on a plane at the airport and whisked him back to the USA.

Then Jimi Hendrix died in London on 18 September 1970. He was only twenty-seven. I could imagine the atmosphere back in town and could envisage the excited gossip and the conspiracy theories, but Jimi had been in bad shape and unfortunately it was not too unexpected. We sacrificed some electricity to play some of his albums in a gesture of respect. This was followed by the news that Janis Joplin died on 4 October of a heroin overdose. This was a real surprise because everyone made her for a lush. Once again a few hours' electricity were used to give her a good send-off. She was not just a singer; her looks, her clothes and no-holds-barred behaviour had made her the most iconic woman on the scene. She represented the freedom that the counter-culture was all about, particularly for the women, many of whom took her for a role model. I last saw her that spring at Steve Paul's Scene in New York where Dr John and Sha Na Na were playing a double bill. Janis sat at the next table to us surrounded by huge Texans with ponytails. She was wearing her signature feather boa in her hair and was covered in sequins and beads. She ordered whiskies thick and fast. At one point she summoned the waiter, counted her party, doubled it and added an extra one for herself, 'As I'm fucking paying!', which came to seventeen doubles.

Then came the dog days. Lash the horse standing at the gate amid swarms of flies. Denise practising acoustic guitar and Peter strumming his banjo in their room off the porch. Allen sitting reading next to the propane tank. The last visitors gone. The farm began to prepare for winter. The oil heaters were brought up from the cellar and cleaned. Julius filled them all with gasoline instead of kerosene but Peter noticed the smell and another disaster was averted. Hundreds of glass Ball jars were bought and sterilised in boiling water. I used my mother's recipe for bottling runner beans in salt (canning, the Americans call it). Gordon, Peter and Denise also canned squash, corn, cucumbers, lima beans, soybeans, carrots and over two hundred quarts of tomatoes that had been growing in long rows in the fenced-off vegetable garden, protected from deer. The smell of tomatoes bubbling on the stove lingered for days. Potatoes, beets, parsnips and other root vegetables were carefully stored and covered with old sacks.

Peter had an old juicing machine in the backyard and filled scores and scores of jars with apple juice and tomato juice, more than enough to last the winter and with a lot left over to sell. He and Denise took a carload down to New York to a health food shop. We made dill pickles. The recipe for the preserving liquid seemed absurdly complicated but we found all the ingredients and, even though we made gallons of it, it covered only a few inches of the bottom of the big stone jar next to the gerbil cage in the kitchen that Peter was determined to fill. They were good, though.

The shelves in the storm cellar were packed tightly with food. The leaves on the birch tree went bright orange, then apple red. The wind in the darkness at night now whistled through the stand of maples and the Milky Way was a thick band of light, surrounded by crystal-bright stars in the clear sky. By mid-October the temperature dropped below freezing every night and in the morning the grass sparkled with frost. Allen decided to stay at the newly insulated farm throughout the winter, but for us it was time to return to the city, where Ann and I were going to continue the tape editing at Allen's apartment in the Lower East Side.

4 1970

chelsea days

In mid-October, Peter drove Ann and I down to Manhattan in the Oldsmobile, demonstrating how Neal Cassady used to execute certain manoeuvres. Peter was a fine driver, having been a New York cabby at one point. All our possessions were in the car, along with all of Allen's tapes, three tape recorders and several boxes of papers that Allen wanted transported.

Allen's apartment was at 408 East 10 Street, between Avenues C and D; the heart of Alphabet City, a run-down apartment building, built to house immigrants around the turn of the century to absolute minimum legal standards and now encased in a lattice of metal fire escapes. Allen lived in a terrible neighbourhood, even by New York standards. All the shops had massive metal grilles across their windows and doors, any wall less than 20 feet high had razor wire looped along the top and every apartment had permanently closed metal grilles behind their windows. The north side of Allen's block had been demolished and huge pile drivers worked all day, driving enormous metal beams into the rock in order to build a high-rise housing project that you knew would become another instant slum. The sound of the steam hammers was inescapable, the hiss of escaping steam followed by the thump as the hammer hit the girder, pounding it deep into the earth. Four blocks away, the Con-Ed power station's chimney stacks belched a cloud of black smoke over the neighbourhood, depositing a layer of soot over the buildings, the washing lines strung across the back courts and in people's lungs. Despite the onset of winter, a fair number of locals still sat on their stoops, mostly Puerto Ricans. It was obvious that we didn't belong in the neighbourhood. One day one of them calmly felt the material of my raincoat and nodded, as if to say, 'That will do nicely.' Another time, we were standing on the front stoop, about to open the front door, when a Puerto Rican casually opened the brown paper supermarket sack and looked in to see what we had bought.

New York in the seventies was going through one of the most violent periods in its history. In 1972 there were 1,691 murders, more than ten times the number for the whole of Britain, and more than 20,000 reported assaults; most people didn't bother to report a crime unless an insurance claim was possible. Inevitably, given where we lived, it was not long before we were robbed. One day we came back from the A&P supermarket at 8.30 in the evening, walked up the stairs to apartment 4C and, just as I was fiddling with the key, someone tapped me on the shoulder. I looked round to stare down the stubby barrel of a handgun held by a large black man. His partner was holding Ann against the wall at knifepoint.

They had me put down my shopping bag, relieved me of my watch and wallet containing $60. Then, as no one seemed to be around, they made us let them into the apartment. It was a railroad apartment, opening first into the kitchen, then a short hall with the bathroom on the left, followed by a living room and bedroom. They pushed us roughly through the rooms, checking each one out. They cut the telephone wire and tied me up with string they had with them. They used two of Allen's neckties knotted together to tie up Ann while they ransacked the place. 'Where's the money?' they kept asking. 'Where's the money?'

I kept explaining that I was not from New York and was simply borrowing the apartment from a friend. 'Where's the money?' the guy repeated and rubbed his gun suggestively up and down his thigh.

'Look,' I told him, 'If I had any money, do you think I'd be staying in an apartment like this? I'd be in a hotel!'

'Shut up,' Ann whispered, but it seemed to do the trick. I was very scared, not so much that they would kill us, since they had bothered to tie us up, but that they might rape Ann; there had been a number of rapes in the area in the last few weeks. One of them stuck a cigarette in my mouth and lit it. I had given up smoking a few weeks before but sucked on it gladly even though my hands were tied behind my back. They carefully piled everything of value to them near the kitchen door: Allen's Uher tape recorder, unfortunately with a tape on it of auto poesy recorded at Big Sur that we had no copy of, a Sony television that Allen bought from Claude and Mary when they left the Hotel Chelsea to live in Britain, a cheap Sony tape recorder and an FM/AM radio, along with five microphones: two Sonys, one Uher and two expensive AKGs worth $125 each. They even took the stopwatch I used to time tracks and the leads for the tape recorders. Then they hauled us to our feet and shut us in the bathroom, saying that they would be back.

There was in fact some money; I had hidden it in a book. Allen's apartment had thousands of books, covering several walls from floor to ceiling. It would have taken a massive search to find it. After a lot of wriggling, Ann managed to pick up a pair of nail scissors from the sink and cut me free and I immediately rushed into the hall and locked the door in case they returned for the Revox, the most expensive item of all, but very heavy. It took me about twenty minutes to reconnect the telephone cable by Scotch-taping the severed wires to a sheet of card.

Allen had said that if we had any problems with the apartment, we should ask the advice of Mrs Parker, the old Puerto Rican lady in 4D next door. I wanted to call the police but Ann disagreed. I thought the social conditions in this area would never be rectified if the crime statistics were inaccurate. Mrs Parker agreed with Ann: 'I've been robbed seventeen times but there's no point in reporting it. How can they catch them? The boys probably only live round

Claude Pelieu and Mary
Beach had a two-room
suite at the Hotel Chelsea

the corner in the projects on Avenue D. They've probably sold your
things already for ten dollars and used it to buy drugs.' She opened
her hands despairingly and shrugged. She was used to it; being
mugged and robbed was normal life for her.

We didn't report it, but I was freaked out. I quickly packed
our things and we took a cab to the Hotel Chelsea and checked in.
There was no way I was going to stay in the area. I had spent several
months living at the Chelsea in 1969 and walking into the lobby and
seeing Big John behind the desk and Josie at the switchboard was
like coming home.

We took room 420 on a monthly lease, unpacked, and settled in.

There was a two-ring hotplate and they even brought us a new fridge for the room. Two days later we somehow moved 200 reels of tape, the two remaining tape recorders, the microphone stands, booms, amps, record deck and my books across town during the taxi strike using rogue cabs. I wired up the record deck through the Revox and was able to play the hundreds of review albums that had accumulated while I was up on the farm. I replaced all the essential items of equipment, such as leads, that had been stolen, and we resumed work.

Not long after we had moved in I was awoken at about 7 a.m. by a tremendous banging on the door. I got up and sleepily answered the door to the police; there was something in the way they knocked that made it obvious it was the cops. I had no drugs in the apartment and I had not overstayed my entry permit so I had nothing to fear. A young uniformed officer stood in the doorway; he was skinny and his uniform looked too big for him. Another stood back from him in the corridor. 'Whadda you know 'bout this?' he snapped.

I blinked sleepily. 'Sorry, officer, I don't understand what you are talking about.' I was looking at his face. He raised his hand between us and extended his forefinger upwards. As I watched, he twisted his wrist to make the finger point downwards to my feet. I looked down. There lay a body, completely blocking my door.

'Blimey,' I said. 'What's wrong with him?'

'He's dead,' said the cop. 'Someone shot him. Did you hear anything?' I shook my head, now fully awake. 'I didn't think you woulda, looks like he crawled here from the other end of the corridor. He was making for his room down there,' and he pointed to the opposite end of the corridor. 'OK, bud, you can get back to bed.'

It seems that the dead man had tried to rob a fellow junkie living at the other end of the corridor, who had reacted by shooting him. They were both SRO (single room occupancy) residents, imposed on the Chelsea by the city. So many SRO hotels had closed that the city had resorted to commandeering rooms for welfare cases in hotels such as the Chelsea. It was not an auspicious start to our stay.

I was first introduced to the Hotel Chelsea by Allen Ginsberg. It was the summer of 1969 and I was in New York to make a recording of Allen singing William Blake's *Songs of Innocence and Experience*, which he had written some music for, so I needed somewhere to stay for several months. Allen looked knowingly at me and said, 'I know just the place.'

I knew of the Chelsea, of course; Dylan Thomas was living there when he drank himself to death, Bob Dylan wrote 'Sad Eyed Lady Of The Lowlands' there; I had seen Andy Warhol's *Chelsea Girls* and the Chelsea was where Arthur Miller escaped to when he and Marilyn Monroe split up. In fact, as Allen and I crossed the lobby, the first person we ran into was Miller, whom Allen had known for many years.

Stanley Bard, the owner, was behind the desk that day, and together he and Ginsberg decided upon a rent as Allen was paying. The Chelsea is a residential hotel, with few facilities for transients. There was a desultory room service if Percy wasn't too drunk, but there were no televisions or air conditioning units or any of the things that normal hotels regard as standard, because most residents installed their own. You could rent them from the hotel, but I was later assured by residents that they were so old and beaten up that they never worked properly.

When the building was erected in 1894, it was designed as a cooperative apartment house and each of the members of the co-op designed their own apartment layouts. As a consequence no two rooms or floors of the Chelsea are the same, so the room size has some bearing on the rent. By no means all the rooms had their own bathrooms, so those with a bathroom down the hall were cheaper. Quite a few of the original apartments survived, with beautiful parquet flooring and mahogany panelling and tiled fireplaces. Most were on long leases, but I was once able to sublet one of them.

Stanley's criterion for setting the rent was based on creativity. If you were a painter or writer you were charged considerably less than if you were a stockbroker. Artists were effectively subsidised by the wealthy people who lived there for the artistic ambience. In fact at that time there was only one stockbroker living there, and the element of subsidy came from a number of Harlem pimps who wore long coats and gold chains around their hats and congregated in the lobby. Then the rent also depended on who introduced you. Most people were introduced by existing residents and Stanley never charged less than the person who introduced you was already paying, usually a little more. By having Allen Ginsberg introduce me I got an extremely favourable rent as Stanley respected him and Allen had never lived there, so there was no precedent. I received my key and after inspecting the room, Allen took me to meet some of the other residents.

The rule at the Chelsea was that people always rang on the house phone before visiting the rooms. Privacy was very much respected in the hotel. Generally speaking, people met in the lobby or the El Quijote, the Spanish restaurant next door, which still has its own entrance into the lobby and had originally been the Chelsea's communal dining room. One could usually find several of the hotel's residents ensconced at the long bar. The restaurant is decorated in the worst of taste with large paintings of El Quijote and Pancho and even the wallpaper has an El Quijote theme. When I first visited in the sixties there was a banner proclaiming the seventeenth anniversary of the restaurant draped across the top of the bar, which had already been there for some time because the restaurant opened in 1936. All through the seventies and early eighties the banner remained in place, thick with New York dust, until someone finally got on a stepladder and cleaned the upper reaches of the bar. The decor remains the same as it ever was. The menu has changed little but the jukebox no longer has 'The Dawning of Aquarius' in Spanish on it.

At the Chelsea you could close the door and work and no one would bother you, but if you felt sociable the hotel had 250 units and most evenings there was an event or a party on somewhere. There were many film-makers living there and they often held screenings in their rooms; there were performance artists who performed, and many painters had open studio days. If you wanted to know where the party was, you asked Josephine, the telephone operator. She knew everyone's business because she listened in to their phone calls. She knew who knew who and if you received a phone call from outside it would not take her long to trace you to someone else's room. To find the party, all you had to do was ask her, but she would only tell you about parties where she knew you would be welcome.

This was how I met Virgil Thomson, the composer. Virgil had been in the building since 1935 and had one of the original co-op apartments. He was a link to pre-war bohemia. When he was living in Paris he had written an opera with Gertrude Stein called *Four Saints in Three Acts* and his conversation was studded with references to Cocteau and Picasso and the Ballet Russe. His rooms were crammed with memorabilia, and as he moved around, fussing, arranging papers and books, he reminded me of the cartoon character Elmer Fudd. He was famous for his musical portraits of people and loved to play them for you. He gave wonderful parties.

There was also a connection to Paris in even earlier days. Alphaeus Cole in room 929 looked every inch the artist, with a long white beard, long sensitive fingers and an artist's smock. He was born in 1877 and had studied painting in Paris in the 1890s. He liked to talk about Daumier and Doré and Victor Hugo and the pranks the art students used to get up to at the Arts Ball, parading nude models through the streets. It was sometimes hard to understand what he was saying because his false teeth were very loose and rattled around his mouth as he talked. He painted in the academic manner of the time and in 1971 he had a show of recent oil paintings and water colours. He was then ninety-four. Alphaeus died at the hotel in November 1988, aged 112, after living there for thirty years. He disapproved strongly of all the art that was displayed on the walls of the lobby by previous Chelsea residents such as Larry Rivers and Christo.

Film-maker Sandy Daley lived in a suite on the tenth floor with a large pure-white living room, empty of everything except some silver pillow balloons by Andy Warhol that clustered around the corners of the ceiling. Light poured in from the windows overlooking 23rd Street. There were a few cushions on the floor and a large hi-fi. I loaned my Revox A77 to her for use in recording the soundtrack for her film *Robert Having His Nipple Pierced*, a documentary about Robert Mapplethorpe with voiceover sound by Robert's then girl-friend Patti Smith (she and Robert lived in the room next door to Sandy on the tenth floor). Robert and Patti had moved into the hotel in 1969 and immediately became friends with Harry Smith, Peggy Biderman and Peggy's musician friend Matthew Reich. It was easy to get to know your fellow residents even though Proust could have been describing the Chelsea when he remarked: 'This hotel is like a stage setting for the third act of a farce'; there were so many weird and eccentric people there, including two rival wizards who sometimes held magical battles in the lobby, frantically twisting their fingers into obscure mudras and snarling at each other.

The Chelsea quickly became home again. We entertained friends and visited other residents. Among the people we saw were Claudia Dreyfus and her boyfriend. Claudia had worked on the *East Village Other*, the first New York underground newspaper back in the sixties, and I knew her because I wrote a London column for them. She was now very involved with reporting on the women's movement, which was the subject of enormous public debate in New York. We spent endless evenings discussing gender roles and trying to isolate conditioned behaviour. So many things were automatically accepted which were in fact gender determined. Ann always made a point of opening doors for men, which certainly confused a lot of people, but there were other areas in which we tried to even out our behaviour – for instance, I would buy the contraceptive cream on every other occasion.

I must say it seemed to me that Claudia and her boyfriend had not so much evened out the roles as swapped them; Claudia was a forceful personality and dominated the conversations. She appeared to take a very male role in their relationship, but because of the times, this was also something we could discuss. It was a very productive period and I certainly learned a lot, if only about myself and my conditioned behaviour patterns. One thing on which Claudia and I disagreed was Germaine Greer's *Female Eunuch*, which Claudia thought was reactionary; she thought it actually set back the women's movement whereas I thought it was a very positive contribution to the debate. There were of course cultural differences between the British and American movements, with the American one being much more strident and hard-line. These differences could be seen in the way Ann and I interpreted gender equality, with Ann being totally inflexible, whereas I was more relaxed. It was a fascinating debate, and one which was engaging many of our friends in the hotel.

Allen and I were delighted by a review by Ellen Willis in the 12 December 1970 issue of *New Yorker* of the Blake album I produced which read: 'Allen Ginsberg has recorded an album of Blake poems set to Ginsberg music, "William Blake: Songs of Innocence and Experience" (Verve FTS 3083). It's a beautiful record, which makes me happy every time I hear it – but then most of what Ginsberg does has that effect on me. He should be persuaded to record a collection of mantras next.'

Not that Allen needed any encouragement; he was already planning to do a mantra album once we got the spoken-word albums sorted out. We had arranged a deal with Fantasy Records in Berkeley to release the best of the recordings I had been cataloguing and editing, but it was for five albums, not the sixteen we had originally planned, which would have included a recording of every poem Allen had ever published. Allen liked to think big. Fantasy now wanted to buy back the original Blake album from MGM and for us to record a second Blake album so they could release the complete Blake's *Songs of Innocence and Experience* as a double album.

They offered a reasonable advance and free studio time to master the tapes. All this was to be done before Allen flew to Australia in June 1971. After that he was talking of spending a year in India, so we had to get the spoken-word tapes finished. Though we had already edited more than a hundred recordings, Allen now systematically contacted the various colleges where he had read to request tapes and several dozen boxes arrived through the mail, and Ann and I flew with him to record his various readings at campuses across the country. The relaxed lazy days on the farm were now replaced with long work hours as each one had to be listened to in real time.

Allen even dropped some tape boxes off for me at the Chelsea reception desk on Christmas Day, prompting John, the night clerk, to call my room to say that Allen Ginsberg had left a Christmas present. That increased my status at the Chelsea no end. There were still quite a few poems that we had no recordings of, mostly long difficult ones that Allen had deemed unsuited to public performance. Now he slipped at least one into each of his readings for Ann and me to record.

5 1971

the golden west

In March 1971, Ann and I arrived in Streater, Illinois, Pop: 16,868, 'Glass container capital of the world', named after the early industrialist, Dr Streater. All these Midwest towns seem to be the capital of something: 'Griggsville, Illinois; Purple Martin Capital of the World', 'Quincy, Illinois; Hog Capital of the World'. There were two hotels; we chose the bigger of the two, the Plumb Hotel – a large peeling structure with a once elegant façade, red neon sign broken, greasy and flickering against Greek Revival columns, its wooden clapboards peeling and warped.

The previously fine proportions of the faded brown lobby had been destroyed to make room for a ground-floor bar, but even this upheaval had clearly occurred many decades before. A huge television, its colour hopelessly in need of adjustment, blared in the corner with no one watching. A sad old black porter sat hunched over in a wooden-backed chair that had stuffing bulging from a huge rip in the upholstery. The desk clerk seemed surprised to see us. No one ever stays in Streater. 'Yew the new go-go girl?' he asked Ann. He spoke in a long slow drawl, not relaxed, just tired and bored. She glared at him. We were given a big dusty room, with a faint smell of urine from generations of travelling salesmen pissing in the sink, and of sweat and dirty clothes from years ago.

Nothing for anyone to do in Streater except get drunk and hang

around the railroad yards, looking for trouble. In the local supermarket cafeteria everyone was very suspicious of the strangers but
we found a cheap Mexican restaurant with chilli in disposable paper
bowls and plastic cutlery. Next day the air hung heavy with silence,
bright sun bleaching everything as we walked to the RR station.
Old bells dinged and ancient equipment buzzed. The railroad men
wore greasy vests as in a cowboy movie. I half expected a 1920s
steam locomotive to chuff into view. Then the 'San Francisco Chief'
arrived. A long silver snake from another place, longer than the
town, bringing a glimpse of a different reality to the good ol' boys
lined up on the bench and the kids playing in the dusty marshalling yards. There was no platform in Streater so the porter hopped
down with a footstool. It was 11.35 a.m.; 2,467 miles to go to San
Francisco. The journey would take three days. We had already made
the New York City–Chicago leg of the journey and spent some time
with Ann's family in Illinois. Now it was time to get back to work.

'I got beer, whuskey, ev'rythaaang!' said the black bartender in
the beautiful polished wood club car, and the bottles gleamed behind
him as if we were in some downtown Chicago hotel. A ticker-tape
machine with a fishbowl top stood in the corner of the lounge car
and one could imagine fat old robber barons studying the emerging
tape. Now it was turned off. Upstairs in the bubble-domed observation car, we sat in swivel armchairs and watched the passing show.
It was just like being in a fifties *National Geographic* magazine, with
Negro waiters and everybody dressed up. I felt I should be wearing
a hat. The passengers were mostly older couples who were afraid
of flying or preferred the leisurely pace of the Santa Fe. But sadly
the train was being closed down. This was the last but one 'San
Francisco Chief'. The last was to leave Chicago the next day, but
no one talked about that; in fact the train was two-thirds empty,
probably the reason for closing it down. I hoped they would keep
the observation cars with their bubble domes for some future train,
or Nostalgia Express.

We passed through Marceline, Mo., named after the daughter of

The San Francisco Chief

the first resident. This was Walt Disney's boyhood home. No wonder he had such an imagination; there was nothing to see there except the vast sky. There were fewer than three thousand people there in 1971, spread out across the vast plain. The size of America never ceased to amaze me; there are vast, unimaginable distances between towns and dirt tracks wander off to the horizon, scores of miles away. We had a suite in order to accommodate all the tape recorders and tapes, as well as our own luggage, and it was slightly bizarre to be sitting in our massive armchairs, facing a picture window, viewing the passing countryside. Most trains ignore the view and the passenger faces the direction of travel, or the opposite wall. In the golden age of the train, the view was all important, thus the observation cars and picture windows.

There was a half-hour break in Kansas City. The station appeared to be crumbling to rust, dirty metal girders, oil dripping on iron, polluted air, crackling, incomprehensible messages over loud-speakers. Nothing but sex books at the station bookstand and bizarre 'souvenirs' of KC. Bent, twisted fire escapes on tall grime-caked office blocks faced the RR tracks. It was hard to imagine that so much beautiful music came from such a place. Decades later I was once again in KC and went in search of Charlie Parker's birthplace. The whole area had been levelled for a freeway, and where his house once stood is now a broad expanse of greensward. His high school and junior school still stand, however, though many people looked askance as I photographed them. There is a jazz museum at legendary 18th and Vine, but what remains standing in this area was largely reconstructed by Hollywood for a film about KC jazz, though the 1912 Gem Theatre looks original. In the museum the pride of place in a display of artefacts associated with Ella Fitzgerald is given to her American Express card; she was one of the first black Americans to get one. Boarded-up buildings nearby have an ominous notice stencilled on the doors and windows: 'Secured By Penitentiary Labor'.

Darkness had already fallen by the time we left Topeka, Kansas: Indian word meaning 'a grand place to dig potatoes'. By the time we woke up, we had passed through Oklahoma and the whole of Texas. We were just leaving Bovina, Texas, on the New Mexico border, and the flat farmland was long gone. At Clovis, Buddy Holly's birthplace, the porter knocked on the door to tell us to set our watches back one hour. At 11.35 a.m., we crossed the Rio Grande. Enormous desert with rocky outcrops on the distant horizon. Near the tracks were small Indian adobes with bread ovens made from mud bricks in the backyards, first adobe I'd seen. We passed run-down shacks, clapped-out autos lurched lopsidedly down bumpy dirt tracks followed by a plume of dust, old jalopies up on blocks, huge scrap-metal heaps, garbage everywhere on the desert, barbed wire and a tangle of twisted steel of wrecked cars. We hummed past adobe liquor stores and adobe motels with neon signs; the neon looked strangely out of place with a horizon 40 miles away. There were five uranium mines in this area, the biggest concentration anywhere in the US. An Indian sitting by the side of the tracks had no shoes. There were signs of poverty everywhere, not a new car in sight.

We passed the famous two-miles-wide meteor crater near Winslow, Arizona, but it was several miles from the RR tracks and couldn't be seen. That night we travelled through the Mojave Desert.

Next morning we woke up in California! Now we were surrounded by palm trees and orange groves, rich red earth, lush vegetation and golden sunlight. I felt a tingling excitement, to actually reach California. I believed in the legend of the golden west; the sunlight was so intense it hurt my eyes. I could understand how dust-bowl farmers must have thought they had reached paradise when they first saw it (before they realised the grim reality of their situation).

At 8 a.m. we stopped at Stockton, blocking the RR crossing next to the station. Cars and pick-up trucks backed up, Mexicans in the backs of trucks on their way to the fields. Thick palm fronds shaded the road. Roofs were of red tile in the Mediterranean style. Flowers bloomed everywhere in the gardens by the tracks and on the sides of the embankment and climbed the trees to make each branch a bouquet of colour. Palm trees, geraniums, hummingbirds and crickets: southern California. At 10 a.m. we reached Richmond. The end of the Santa Fe Railroad tracks. From here a trainside bus took us on a forty-five minute ride to San Francisco, where we were deposited at a dusty marshalling yard in the middle of nowhere. It seemed an ignominious end to such a trip. In Europe one would have arrived in a glorious cathedral-like station, filled with soaring arches and columns to the glory of travel and arrival. Here, even after a trip across the nation, we were left standing on an open-air wooden platform, with not even a station building to be seen.

Lawrence Ferlinghetti, with his slow smile and grey beard, was waiting in the bright sunlight to meet us with his VW van to help us unload the cases of tapes and recording equipment. He had stayed with me in London in 1965, just after the Albert Hall poetry reading and I had recorded a spoken-word album with him in 1969 in San Francisco for the Beatles' spoken-word label Zapple. It had not been released but the tapes came out on two subsequent Fantasy Records albums so the work was not wasted. I always regarded him as one of

Allen Ginsberg (glasses, beard); the author (glasses, half beard); Gordon Ball (tongue), Albany, NY, 1971

the most overlooked poets in America; neither true Beat Generation nor establishment.

We were anxious to find somewhere to live and work as Allen was due to arrive the next week and we had only four months to complete the project. At first Ann and I moved into the Sam Wong Hotel on Broadway, very cheap and mostly Chinese. Many people left their doors open, and walking down the corridor we could see glimpses of entire families crowded into a single room, with old women hunched over the stove or doling out noodles into ceramic bowls. From there we moved to the Swiss American, across the street. Allen Ginsberg recommended it on the phone because Kerouac stayed there and also Lenny Bruce, who apparently once fell from – or jumped from – his window there. It was a flop-house. The street door led directly on to a steep flight of stairs. The upstairs lobby had a big coffee urn with Styrofoam cups, a television and some ratty armchairs.

Our room had bright green patterned wallpaper which had not been improved by the fact that someone had thrown what appeared to be a frying pan full of fat over it. A wide arc of grease, longer than the bed, made a very dramatic addition to the room's decor. The window overlooked the street, and it was fun to lean on the sill and people-watch. The door was flimsy and anyone could have used a card to pop the lock, so I was worried about the tape recorders. I hid them under the bed, covered with blankets, and hoped that they would be safe.

There were lots of junkies in the hotel but they would have had to carry the tape machines past the desk and down the stairs so we asked the desk staff to make sure that no one except Ann and I walked out with a Revox A77 in their arms. There was one lost-looking junkie girl who roamed the corridors wearing a thin night-shirt and nothing else. She was always sitting in the lobby drinking coffee from the white polystyrene cups, her eyes wide, her long hair uncombed as if she had just that moment got out of bed. Maybe she didn't have a room; she was always around for the whole week we stayed there. Next we moved to the UC Hotel on University in Berkeley which was more secure.

When Allen arrived we looked for an apartment for the three of us to share, but the Bay area had become expensive. We looked at what appeared to be sheltered housing for old people, Allen asking all sorts of interested questions about the central vacuum pipes that ran around the walls so you could just plug in a hose instead of having to drag a vacuum cleaner from room to room. The puzzled realtor kept asking 'How old are your parents?', thinking it was for them. Allen brightly told him, 'Oh, my mother died in the madhouse fifteen years ago.'

Another place we looked at was tempting but dangerous. It was a large villa in Berkeley, with a swimming pool, lots of bedrooms and two large German shepherds patrolling the garden. The owner lived there but was happy for us to have two of the bedrooms for six months as there was plenty of room and he admired Allen and his work. The long-haired hippy owner did not want any rent. Smiling, he gestured to a large ceramic bowl on the sideboard and said, 'I don't need any bread from you, man. In fact, if you want any money just help yourselves! It wouldn't cost you a thing to live here.' The bowl had several thousand dollars in it in cash, loose rolls of tens and twenties. We went away to consider his kind offer. We had to decline; he was so obviously a drug dealer that it was too unsafe for Allen to live there.

Eventually we found shelter in a hippy commune at 1801 Woolsey Street in Berkeley, not far from where Allen had once lived on Milvia Street – 'A Strange New Cottage in Berkeley' was written there – where we were given two adjoining rooms. 1801 Woolsey was a large Victorian – or Victorian-in-style – house with turrets and a backyard with a tall palm. Ann and I had a large room overlooking the street with a bay window containing window seats. The bathroom was on the same floor, but for several reasons there was no privacy if you wished to take a bath or use the facilities. A young man called Wesley lived in a room that could only be reached by

walking through the bathroom and climbing a staircase, and consequently both he and his friends needed access, so there was no
lock on the door. Wesley was a fine printer, a specialist in hand-
printed editions, and most of his business meetings took place in
the bathroom. One day I was sitting in the tub, washing my hair,
when three people I had never seen before came in and conducted
a drug deal.

The house was owned by Dan Moore, a doctor, who lived with
his wife on the ground floor in a large room where the walls were
completely covered with psychedelic murals of the most violently
clashing colours and shapes. We saw very little of them but they
seemed kind, committed to the communal ideal and friendly. More
people lived on the top floor. Everyone seemed to have regular
jobs; one of the top-floor girls went out to work each day at 8 a.m.,
always dressed in a short green minidress with a scalloped hem
like Tinker Bell.

She was the one who most rigorously defended the house rules.
There were a number of rules in the commune that I found irksome:
coffee was not allowed, nor was sugar, though a strange organic
substitute from the local health-food store made from figs was
permitted. This caused several arguments between myself and my
fellow communards as it was quite a long way to walk to the nearest
coffee shop and I can barely function in the morning without a large
cup of coffee. Smoking was also not allowed and the cuisine was
vegetarian. A number of geese lived in the backyard and wandered
freely in the kitchen, as did several cats. There was no insistence
that anyone engage in communal activities, though advance warning
had to be given if you wanted to dine. There was a long refectory-
style table in the kitchen and half the people seated there were liable
to be completely naked.

In Berkeley there were three branches of the Co-op supermarket;
they used the same logo as the British Co-operative Society and
appeared to have the same principle of member ownership. They
had a large section devoted to generic goods, all in plain white boxes

with black lettering: soap powder, cornflakes, flour, rice; it was very refreshing to get away from the brand names, and they were also half the price of branded goods. Many of the items, a notice informed us, actually came from the same suppliers, as it is well known that half the brand names do not manufacture their own products. Being Berkeley – the counter-cultural capital of the world at that time – the stores also had enormous public noticeboards with sections for New Age activities, babysitting, car pools, political meetings and demonstrations. Such boards are now common, but I had never seen them before. More than any other city, Berkeley had become the centre of the free-speech and anti-war movements, of radical politics, of communal and other lifestyle experiments, and a centre of considerable sexual and drug-related experiment; the latter heavily influenced by the presence of Timothy Leary, who had lived there before his arrest and imprisonment.

We went over to Fantasy Records almost as soon as Allen arrived. It was a huge compound exactly filling the block, looking like a prison with pebbledash concrete walls and no windows, as if built to withstand a siege. There was a front door and a service entrance for groups to take in their gear. Fantasy had been a small independent until they achieved massive success with Creedence Clearwater Revival. The sales of 'Proud Mary' and 'Bad Moon Rising', the albums *Bayou Country* and *Green River*, had swamped Fantasy, posing such accounting and cash-flow problems that the group finished up owning half the company. Some of the money was used to construct this purpose-built studio complex with state-of-the-art equipment, a secure tape vault and the record company offices. It was built in a warehouse neighbourhood and a large railroad freight car was parked right outside on one of the many railroad tracks that wove in and out of the buildings. Inside it was luxurious.

We went to see Al Bendich, one of the owners of the company, whom Allen knew from way back when Bendich was one of the lawyers from the Council for Civil Liberties who defended *Howl* in the 1956 obscenity trial. I was very impressed by him; he clearly loved jazz, he knew and understood what was happening in progressive rock and his heart was definitely in the right place. The other owner was Ralph J. Gleason, a pipe-smoking, tweed-jacketed anglophile who had been a co-founder of *Rolling Stone* magazine. I had enjoyed his book *The Jefferson Airplane and the San Francisco Scene* and told him so. We established an immediate rapport and I would often drop by his office while we were working there just to hang out and chat.

There was no studio available for a block booking as Tom Fogerty, the main songwriter of Creedence, was recording a solo album, but we only needed a deck to master Allen's tapes so we took over the mastering room. They rarely needed to make acetates or cut masters so we had it pretty much to ourselves. The Neuman lathe was state-of-the-art; they had a similar one at Apple Records in London which most of the London independent studios hired, so I was familiar with what it could do, and in any case, there was an engineer to operate it. It had better EQ than the studio desk and we were able to tidy up a lot of Allen's tapes with it. We began work in April. I made a note of the sign attached to the lathe by the Fantasy engineers:

ACHTUNG! ALLES LOOKENSPEEPERS

DAS SWITCHING MACHINE IST NICHT FUR GE
FINGERPOKEN UND MITTENGRABBEN. IST EASY FUR
SCHNAPPEN DER SPRINGENWERK, BLOWEN FISEN, UND
POPPENCORKEN MIT SPITZENSPARKEN. IST NICHT FUR
GE WORKEN BY DAS DUMMENKOPFEN, DAS RUBBER-
NECKEN SIGHTSEEREN. KEEPEN HANDS IN DAS POCKETS
– RELAXEN UND WATCH DAS BLINKEN LIGHTS!

Shortly after we arrived, Lawrence Ferlinghetti gave Allen a royalty cheque from City Lights. It was a large sum. Allen paid all the big things first, including giving Ann and I our $5,000 for working all those months on the tape project on the farm and in New York. We took it to the Wells Fargo bank in Chinatown, where all the counters had an abacus. The tellers used them too, rapidly clicking away, faster than an electronic calculator could be operated. Allen sent Barbara Rubin money as a wedding present, and operating money to Gordon Ball on the farm. Cheques went to Herbert Huncke, Gregory Corso and Harry Smith.

One of Allen's boyfriends got some but Allen still had a lot left. He set off down Telegraph Avenue, Ann and I accompanying him to make sure he didn't just give it all away and have no money to live on until the next cheque. At a Tibetan-Nepalese import shop Allen bought a huge two-foot-high shiny brass Nepalese figure of Buddha. He returned later in the day and picked up a Wheel of Life in the form of a shiny brass plaque and an outsize ritual *dorji*. All this stuff appeared with him on stage along with flowers and incense for a benefit for Tarthang Tulku's Nyingmapa meditation centre, as if Allen were himself some kind of religious guru. Allen was becoming increasingly interested in Tibetan Buddhism and soon made it his religion, but not as unthinkingly as many of the other post-sixties drop-outs who browsed among the increasingly crowded shelves in California's spiritual supermarket. At the Tarthang Tulku benefit, a friend of Allen's called Joel Findler announced onstage that the Chinese had killed 'millions of lamas', getting ever more excited until Allen restrained him and pointed out that the total population of Tibet was only two million and would Joel be precise if he had any information to give.

One day someone knocked on our bedroom door at Woolsey Street and walked in without waiting; a middle-aged man in a suit and tie, clean shaven and with a large smile on his full moist lips. He said nothing. I was astonished; he was a stranger, yet his smile suggested that we knew him. I just couldn't place him though his smile certainly looked familiar. His silence bothered me, then Ann said, 'Haven't you got it yet?' Allen laughed; he had shaved off his beard, had his hair cut short and bought an armful of $5 suits, white shirts and terrible ties at the local thrift shop. It was Chogyam Trungpa's idea. The Tibetan Buddhist teacher told Allen that he was hiding behind his beard and that his beard, long hair and dark work shirts were scaring people; that he would have better communication if he dressed conventionally. That evening Allen went out to the gay bars and was shunned by everyone. When he asked whether he could join them they cried, 'No, no. We're expecting more people!' They only wanted attractive young men to join their tables. Allen relished the anonymity, at least at first.

It was not an image that suited him. In 1979, when he and Peter were staying with us in London, he told me he thought that being clean shaven made him look like 'Old liver lips!' He had long hair at the time and the results were a little unfortunate as the long hair, without the balance of the beard, drew attention to the balding pate. Eventually he adopted the same neat small beard he wore in Mexico in 1954 when he looked like 'a German professor'. His sixties image of long beard and ringlets made him look like Karl Marx; he finished his life looking like V. I. Lenin.

In the hall at Woolsey Street there was a plywood noticeboard hanging from a piece of knotted rope with a colourful logo of a bird leaping into the air from a skull surrounded by flames and the name KALI FLOWER. Attached to it were two clothes pegs where the latest issue of *KaliFlower* was posted each Thursday. At the bottom was a short section of bamboo where you could post any contribution, manifesto, poem or free advertisement you wanted to see in the newsletter. It was distributed free to about three hundred communes in the Berkeley area from the KaliFlower commune run by writer Irving Rosenthal, an old friend of Allen's from the early sixties.

Rosenthal had been the editor of the *Chicago Review*, which had been suppressed by the university authorities because of the chapters from *Naked Lunch* he published. Rosenthal had resigned and started *Big Table* magazine, the first issue of which published ten further chapters from *Naked Lunch* (as well as Kerouac, et al). Rosenthal had moved to San Francisco in 1967, towing his printing press in a U-Haul trailer accompanied by Peter Orlovsky and George Harris, the anti-war activist in the now-iconic photograph of a demonstrator pushing a flower into the barrel of a National Guards-man's rifle. Rosenthal was one of the key Beat Generation members to cross over into the inchoate hippy movement.

In San Francisco, he set up the Sutter Street Commune, and in early 1968, with the help of two of the Diggers, he set up the Free Print Shop just as the Communication Company had been inspired to provide a free printing service two years before. Once they got the offset litho press up and running they distributed a flyer that read: 'The Sutter Street Commune invites you to submit manuscripts, drawings, manifestos to our Free Print Shop. Free distribution guaranteed for whatever we print.' Then, in April 1969, the Sutter Street Commune began publishing *KaliFlower* as a free weekly intercommunal newspaper. Everything in it was anonymous; even the poem that Allen gave to them.

Eventually the Sutter Street Commune became so identified with KaliFlower that it became known as the KaliFlower Commune. They were very ideological with strong beliefs about not participating in the money economy. They believed that everything should be free and should be bartered or exchanged according to need. As well as providing free printing and the newsletter, they were dedicated to distributing free food and to creating free art and theatre. Their clothes were shared, with drawers of large, medium and small underwear, large, medium and small T-shirts and so on. The bedrooms lacked doors and free-sharing sexuality was the norm.

At the KaliFlower Commune, young George Harris grew his hair long, put on a dress and became 'Hibiscus', an extremely flamboyant gay actor, singer, drag artist and experimental theatre director. Irving Rosenthal was the unofficial commune guru and theoretician, and Hibiscus provided the razzmatazz, the theatrical and dramatic activity that made it an exciting place to live. Though many members of the commune were gay, the majority were heterosexual, though these definitions didn't mean much in the ever-changing relation-ships between gays, straights, transsexuals, cross-dressers and out-and-out queens that constituted the commune. There were children there, for instance, in one case conceived by a straight woman with her gay husband.

It was at KaliFlower that Hibiscus formed the Cockettes. Named after the Radio City Music Hall chorus line the Rockettes, the Cockettes were a cross-dressing alternative. They first performed in 1969 at 'The Nocturnal Dream Shows', a weekly series of weird, eclectic and experimental films that showed at midnight at the Palace Theatre. Hibiscus and his friends climbed onstage and did a hilarious chorus-line version of 'Honky Tonk Woman' dressed in wild costumes. The audience loved them and the Cockettes were born. Hibiscus was one of the people who delivered *KaliFlower* to Woolsey Street on Thursdays. He was a colourful visitor with his moustache covered in glitter dust, his rose rings, black-painted toenails and feather boa. He and Allen had been on-off lovers in New York but now they renewed the relationship. Allen was always complaining that the glitter got everywhere, in his mouth, up his arse; it was like fucking on the beach, he said, and getting sand everywhere. He would try to shake the sequins and glitter out of Hibiscus's sheets but he was never able to get rid of it all and sometimes Allen would have a few stray bits in his own beard.

The Cockettes' early shows such as 'Paste on Paste', 'Gone with the Showboat to Oklahoma' and 'Tropical Heatwave/Hot Voodoo' had no proper narrative, they were mostly in the form of revues with creative spontaneity reigning supreme and everyone making their own costumes. But then came 'Pearls over Shanghai', which had original script, lyrics and music and coordinated costumes. They rapidly became an underground theatrical cult; with shows like 'Tinsel Tarts in a Hot Coma' they were the *Rocky Horror Show* years before its time.

But success meant money, previously anathema to the Kali-Flower commune, and in August 1971, Hibiscus left to form his own purist group, The Angels of Light Free Theater, untainted by commercial success, who put on such audience favourites as 'Flamingo Stampede' and 'The Moroccan Operetta', described by

Hibiscus as being like 'Kabuki in Balinese drag'. Allen made an appearance at the first Angels of Light Free Cabaret, a show called 'Earthquake' to commemorate the sixty-fifth anniversary of the San Francisco quake.

Allen performed onstage before 2,000 people in what the *Berkeley Barb* described as a 'Yiddisha Momma in acute drag' and sang Blake's 'Songs of Innocence'. Dressed in a green wig, heavy rosebud lipstick, enormous drawn-on eyelashes and with a third eye in the middle of his forehead, he pumped away at his Indian harmonium and gave a convincing performance. He said he had always been afraid to go in drag for fear it would bring out something in him that he didn't want to see but, having already cut off his beard, this was just a further change of appearance. 'It felt very gay to do, a gay liberation assertion, also liberation from identity.'

We visited a number of the local communes. There was one that had a very large kitchen where people hung out. Though the communards had the long hair that was common at the time, they did not look particularly like hippies. In fact several worked at a local hospital and in social service jobs. We were sitting at the table, talking to some of the residents, when the woman who lived with the man we were talking to came in. She bent and kissed him, said hello to us and went to make herself a cup of tea. As she stood at the sink, a man walked in wearing a bathrobe, his hair still wet from taking a shower. He went to the sink to get a drink of water and the woman making tea casually opened his robe and fondled his penis, holding it in her hand like a fledgling bird. It was done just as someone might lay their hand on someone's arm, just a gesture of friendliness; she was not looking for sex. It seemed very natural and her boyfriend, if he saw it at all, did not register it. Though they lived as couples, the commune practised free love and sometimes had orgies. Allen missed it and was most intrigued when I told him about it afterwards. He loved sexual gossip.

Allen was keen to resume his live recording projects and wanted to tape more Blake songs as well as some mantras. For this we needed musicians, and Allen made contact with a Japanese tantric Buddhist sect, known for their choir and instrumentalists, who lived in San Francisco in an old house at 2362 Pine. They were called Kailas Shugendo (Yamabushi) and practised fire-walking. Their leader was a stocky Mussolini-jawed Russian who spoke perfect English and claimed to have been in Tibet, though he was unwilling to tell me exactly where in Tibet or to name any towns when I asked him. His followers knew him as Ajari or Vajrabhodi, but he went under the name of Mr Warwick in the outside world (later Dr Warwick).

Their religious practices included running an ambulance rescue service that specialised in fire-related incidents like getting people out of plane crashes, as well as mountain climbing, playing country and western music and daily fire rituals of several kinds. Twice a day they performed Homa, a fire ceremony in which they chanted mantras and Ajara did his thing. Once a week they did a fire purification, or Hiwatari, for which Ajari donned his priestly garb: baggy Indian trousers, a short gown and an oversize white skullcap on the front of which was a large woolly bobble. Four more large bobbles adorned his waistcoat and he held the usual Buddhist beads. He chanted while his followers, dressed in more traditional Japanese outfits – also with bobbles – sang or played instruments. Then they would approach a large pit, about six feet long and filled with burning logs, and Ajari would lead the others in walking 108 times across hot coals while chanting mantras.

Ajari led the way, placing one foot on each log, moving quite rapidly across to the other side. This was usually done on some remote beach. In Japan Kailas Shugendo are called the Mountain Climbing Sect and Ajari's group also performed Shugo, in which they climbed the mountains outside San Francisco while chanting mantras. They took part in, and may even have originated, the annual Circumambulation of Mount Tamalpais. They also walked under ice-cold waterfalls and hung each other off rocks. It seemed a rather masochistic set of practices to me. One thing I liked about them was that they actively discouraged people from joining their group, which never numbered more than about thirty-five adherents.

A number of Dr Warwick's followers lived in the house with him. There were too many for comfort and there was clutter everywhere: walls covered with chakra charts, house rules, posters and religious objects. There was an overfull glass-fronted bookcase and lots of chairs stacked in the living room to be used at meetings. One room was so full that the student who slept there could hardly use it during the day; he had made a narrow corridor between stacked music stands and storage boxes leading to his bed. There were speakers, amps, a cello case and fire-making equipment, including a huge cauldron in the fireplace. There were far more men than women – I understood that Ajari came on much too strong for most women, and those that were there were coupled up with men in the group. Allen asked one of them whether they had sex. She was driving us back to Grant and Columbus at the time. She turned her head from the road and looked Allen coldly in the eye and said, 'Well, it's tantric Buddhism so it's tantric sex, you know.' Allen was very intrigued by the whole subject but her attitude showed she was not interested in saying any more than that. Allen nodded knowingly, though he didn't know and wanted to very much.

I was always surprised to see them out on the street; they seemed so unworldly and incompetent. Ajari was a man of monumental egotism and they were cowed by him, being mostly of a nervous disposition. There was one monk who really couldn't function in the outside world, large and fumbling, good natured but really suited only to a monastery. Several of the others were so seriously involved in their religion that the outside world rarely penetrated their lives. The most active was a younger, more energetic cello-playing adept called Jigme, whose real name was Arthur Russell. Arthur was very shy, probably because he had suffered a bad attack of *acne vulgaris* when he was an adolescent, which left his cheeks badly scarred. One time Allen and I took him to Enrico's coffee house and bar at Kearney and Broadway, where he sat in awe, looking round wide eyed like a country hick. 'I suppose you're used to places like this, aren't you?' he said. None of us understood what he could be talking about. Then we got it. 'Are they all like this? Would you say this was typical?' He had never been in an upmarket bar before, even though the front of Enrico's was open and he must have walked past many times.

Jigme had been at Kailas Shugendo for more than two years but was beginning to resent Ajari's authoritarianism. He had obviously gone along with it at the beginning but by the time we met him they were at loggerheads. Ajari would demand something and Jigme would ask why, and question the reasons. This infuriated Ajari, who roared and bellowed and leapt across the room to hit Jigme on the head, or to sometimes only pretend to do so. It was done in a playful, half-joking way but in reality both sides were deeply serious.

Jigme played cello for the recording I made with Allen at Pacific High Studios and later, when Ann and I were in England, Allen flew him out to the Record Plant in New York to play with him and Dylan. It's no wonder Jigme left Ajari. Jigme reverted to his real name of Arthur Russell and joined Jonathan Richman's proto-punk band the Modern Lovers. After this he became a central figure in the New York gay disco scene and made a number of disco records under his own name featuring his amplified cello under layers of echo and reverb which revolutionised dance music. Tracks like 'Is It All Over My Face' and 'Go Bang' became great favourites both at Studio 54 and of composers such as Philip Glass. Allen Ginsberg said, 'He kept saying he wanted to write Buddhist bubble-gum music.' Arthur died of AIDS in 1992.

Ajari found it difficult to be around Allen because he was used to being the complete centre of attention. In a room with other people, whenever Allen was telling a story or imparting information, Ajari could never wait more than ten minutes before doing something to attract attention to himself, and if that didn't work, he would usually fake an errand for the most absorbed member of his group. We had them along to make a recording of some Buddhist chants. Since it was Allen's recording, Ajari was placed in the chorus. He made a terrible fuss about being sidelined and particularly objected to being told what to do by Ann, who was assisting in the production. He cheered up only when he was given a Tibetan thigh bone trumpet to blow. His disciples, except Jigme, seemed not to notice his posturing and egomania. It's hard to say whether they got anything from it; it was certainly not equipping them for life and they didn't look enlightened, but then, nor did he.

6 1971

big sur

Living in Berkeley was fascinating: the university was enormous and supported dozens of student cafés and bookshops: places like Moe's Bookshop on Telegraph Avenue sold all the sixties counter-cultural publications, there were record shops selling bootleg albums – Beatles, Stones, Dylan, Zappa – at about one quarter the price they would have been in London. I bought dozens. There were vegetarian restaurants and juice bars, head shops and craft centres. It was as if the sixties revolution had actually happened!

Work on the tape project went slowly, partly because Allen was getting very involved in the many attractions that the newly emergent gay scene in San Francisco had to offer. Allen was very aware of his tendency to become distracted and suggested that we leave the city for a bit in order to concentrate entirely on the work. Lawrence Ferlinghetti offered us his cabin in Big Sur, which was quiet enough for recording, and had no distractions to prevent us from editing the tapes. I was very enthusiastic because this was the famous cabin where Jack Kerouac came down with the DTs; the subject of his book *Big Sur*. Lawrence and Shig Mureo, the manager and co-owner of City Lights Bookshop, drove Allen, Ann and me down in Lawrence's big VW microbus. Shig was the one who sold a copy of *Howl* to an undercover detective, thus launching the 1956 obscenity trial that was to make the book, and Allen Ginsberg, famous. Shig was a Japanese-American and had been interned during the war when he was a child. He proudly wore a long oriental-style goatee and in the evenings liked to play Zen flute.

The cabin was in Bixby Canyon, a thousand-foot slash in the rocks made by tiny Bixby Creek, which meandered gently along the bottom. The Cabrillo Highway spanned the canyon by means of a mighty single-arch bridge. In fact it was not the cabin in the book. Ferlinghetti's original place, where Kerouac had stayed, was farther up the valley, near the gate leading into the private canyon with its cattle crossing that scared Kerouac so much when he fumbled his way down from the highway in pitch blackness. Lawrence showed it to us. It was a basic wooden structure, very small, little bigger than a potting shed, with a sleeping pallet and a small pot-bellied stove. Standing near by was the wooden privy with Kerouac's graffiti still on the walls: 'The rain, the rain, falling into the sea' in his distinctive script. Surrounding the cabin was a lot of poison ivy, which I still never recognise, so I walked with great caution.

Lawrence showed us yet another plot of land that he had recently bought which had building permission. James Laughlin at New Directions had sent him a royalty check for $12,000, which he signed over to one of the landowners, buying a small field in the canyon, not far from his land but a little farther upstream. Then, farther down the private track towards the sea, we reached his second cabin. This larger building began with nothing inside except a fireplace. Lawrence had slowly added modern conveniences: electricity, a refrigerator and a modern bathroom with hot water. You still had to cook on a fairly smoky pot-bellied stove, though I think there was an electric kettle for heating water.

The cabin was pretty. Shut off from the track by a high fence and locked gates, it was not likely that anyone would stumble upon it. The gates were kept shut because anyone sunbathing naked could be seen from the track as the front porch was on that side of the house. Trees grew close around and there was no garden, just a front yard. A huge iron bar hung from a tree to the left of the gates, used as an entrance gong as in a Japanese temple. Steps led up to the porch from the left and a door in the middle of the front wall took you to the living room. The house was built around the huge stone fireplace, made from rough-hewn rocks from the cliff-side and built on a large stone platform. To the right of the fireplace was the bedroom. To the left was the kitchen, which could also be reached from wooden steps outside. A fridge stood outside the kitchen door at the top of the steps. There was a bathroom behind the fireplace, between the bedroom and kitchen. The window above the bath looked out of the back of the house through close-growing saplings to the river, giving a beautiful moving green light as you sat in the tub.

One incongruous thing about the cabin was that it had a telephone, but it was disconnected because Lawrence used the cabin to get away from it all, which for him meant Kirby and the family. Things were not going well for his marriage. Even in the familiar confines of his cabin, Lawrence seemed a little lost and fumbling. He and Allen discussed the role of poetry as a public art form, with Lawrence stressing the importance of performance and designing the poetry to be read aloud. It was sometimes quite cold at night; nonetheless, Shig liked to sleep outside whenever he was there. Lawrence did also, but only when it was a warm night. Lawrence and Shig returned to San Francisco the next day.

I was determined to get a lot of work done, that late spring. We had our tape recorders there to listen to versions of poems and to record some new ones, including 'Hum Bomb'. To get different acoustics, we recorded both inside and outside the cabin; the Electrovoice microphones had very long leads. I set up my editing suite in the right front corner of the living room, hanging the take-up reels, the leader tape and edit reels on the shelves from nails. I arranged the two tape recorders, an editing block, splicing tape, single-sided razor blades and I had a studio. A uniform edition of the classics, including Sherlock Holmes and *Dr Jekyll and Mr Hyde*, sat on the shelf above. These were the same small-format hardbacks in red bindings that Kerouac described reading in *Big Sur* during his sojourn in the old cabin, still there.

One day I put on a master copy of Allen reading 'Iron Horse' for him to hear and then went outside to chop wood in the yard in the damp fresh May air. A morning mist often hung in the valley till the sun 'burned it off', as Lawrence called it. Swinging the axe the way I was taught by my father was exhilarating, then suddenly Allen appeared in tears, the rendition of the poem having been too much for him. I knew how he felt, having had watery eyes myself the first time I heard that particular recording back in the dusty living room in Cherry Valley. That was why I was outdoors chopping wood, which we needed anyway for the fire that evening.

The poem was written in July 1966 on the same Sante Fe Super Chief on which Ann and I had travelled across America, only Allen had been going in the opposite direction: from San Francisco to Chicago. The poem juxtaposes his daydreaming thoughts, memories of lovers and friends sparked by the places the train passed through, sex fantasies and idle mind chatter with the evidence everywhere in the passing countryside that America was at war: airfields, factories ablaze with lights, newspaper headlines, radio and TV reports, the carriages filled with drafted troops on their way to basic training before shipping out to Vietnam, others returning from a tour of duty: 'Soldiers asleep, rocking away from the War.'

He reports actual conversation, overheard in the restaurant car: 'We're fighting the communists, aren't we? Isn't that what it's about?'... 'So I sat and I listened, / and I brooded in my beard.' His attempts to question their support for the war met only the knee-jerk responses: 'It's my country, better fight 'em over there than here.' He mixes radio news – '600 Cong Death Toll this week' – with memories of his mother's old boyfriend, Dr Luria, Jack Kerouac, Peter, Julius, old friends – even Ferlinghetti's dog Homer makes an appearance in his stream of consciousness; a long, thoughtful meditation on the horror perpetrated on the world by America in the name of 'freedom'. Allen, at this point, thought America was doomed to be destroyed by its own bad karma for causing so much death and destruction on the planet.

After dinner we would sit around the fireplace, on the stone platform, drinking wine, and Allen would reminisce about his early days with Neal in Denver, or visits with Kerouac in Lowell, or just recount the saga of the Beat Generation. Sometimes we all three went for walks, exploring the valley up past the rusted-out sawmill and the ruined lime kilns deep in the wood-covered valley. I loved the precipitous brown banks, everywhere covered by trees. It was a hidden valley, secret, you couldn't see the mountain-side and no one could see you for the tree cover.

Ann wanted to meditate down by little Bixby Creek as it gurgled past our cabin. There were lots of nice places to sit on the bank surrounded by trees where you could see the small fish darting in the clear water in the soft green light. Allen and I walked to the beach. In retrospect you can see how Kerouac found the canyon claustrophobic; the thousand-foot walls climb steeply, sheer rocky bluffs with pines clinging to whatever foothold they could find. The thick tree cover down in the narrow valley was damp and very green. It was hard to imagine how long it must have taken this innocent little trickle of water to cut such an incredible gorge.

There were a few houses to pass before we reached the beach. The valley widened a little and someone had built a ranch-style house set back on the other side of the stream. In the yard the vegetarian-vegan freaks were grooming their horses. We first met them by chance, leaning against the 'Private Property' sign on the beach. Then we walked past their driveway and the one on a horse saw us and waved. It was very hard to talk with them: 'This is a great place to get it together,' said the one who made periodic runs to Canada for organic vegetables by the truckload (probably a drug dealer, thought Allen, when we first met them, and I agreed).

'Get what together?' asked Allen, exasperated; they mouthed this phrase all the time.

'Why, uh – to get your shattered head together of course!' he said, with a beatific grin, stroking his waist-length hair.

'I sometimes wonder what we all started,' said Allen, once we were out of earshot.

A few days later I was walking past their house and saw in the yard a slim young woman wearing just a cowboy hat and boots, her skin tanned the colour of her tooled cowboy boots. She quickly hurried indoors out of sight. A Cat Stevens album played loudly through the open windows.

Past the house on stilts, the canyon-side to the south rose steeply so the path often had a sheer bank on that side, fern covered among the tree roots. The track was just wide enough for a car to drive down and there were a few tyre tracks where one had passed, some time before. Allen was laboriously taking notes, having hurt his finger while leaping from rock to rock during a walk upstream where the valley widens out. He was writing a nature poem in the grand tradition but we neither of us knew the names of many of the plants. Some reminded me of British plants so he would write, 'little British chickweed...' A brilliant sun shone through to the bouncy moss in the leafy glade like a Dulac drawing of fairyland.

I also wrote down my own impressions, about six pages of manuscript. It was interesting to see how much Allen's poem changed from the original nature notes taken on the walk, and how his vision differed from mine. We came out from the leafy glade into the sun and a gentle breeze. The trees were bleached out and ice plants and wild flowers grew all around. A bare cliff face suggested the proximity of the sea. We could hear the distant whisper of the waves. Trees gave way to bushes and undergrowth, stunted by sea storms. High, 1,000 feet above, the single span of the Bixby Creek Bridge curved over us. The creek widened out and meandered its way through yellow sand to its final destination, its course ever changing. As we watched, its shallow banks crumbled away and new ones were cut. A car engine stuck up out of the mud near the cliff-side, rusting away, corroded like a giant meteorite or a lump of iron ore. Sometimes buried, it was slowly sinking lower and lower into

Miles Collection

The Bixby Creek Bridge. Kerouac found the canyon claustrophobic

the primeval mud layer beneath the sand. It was there in Kerouac's time. In *Big Sur* he describes sea-eaten tyres and the remains of old car seats, their stuffing spewing out. The beach stretched away, a few hundred yards to the south, to a blocked sea cave that he also described.

Millions of years ago, Bixby Creek must have tumbled, a windswept wisp of a waterfall, off the cliff edge of Big Sur into the Pacific. Now it has cut a gorge down to sea level. Great ropes of kelp twisted round each other were heaped on the fine sand. Offshore some rocky outcroppings stuck up as islands and to the north side of the beach there were caves from which the sea never retreated and was constantly roaring into, crashing the great pebble bank; you could hear millions of pebbles grinding together after each breaker. The terrific wave swell tore up kelp from 50-foot-deep tendril root-ends and threw it in a writhing tangle on the beach. As we looked out to sea, an old sea head poked up from the waves and stared at us; a sodden head, ancient eyes, wrinkles and tusks. It looked a million years old. When we returned to the cabin our first words to Ann were, 'We saw a seal!' in unison.

I settled myself at the table with a gallon flask of Red Mountain wine and transcribed Allen's spidery notes on to the typewriter; just making notes had made his broken finger ache so he had written it using his left hand. He wanted to transcribe them as soon as possible as he was unsure he would be able to decipher them in the future. He told me how many spaces to indent and I typed it out for him exactly how he wanted. It was quite an epic, of eight pages or more: 'Bixby Canyon Word Breeze'. I felt ambivalent about it. Some passages were very good but it was not his greatest work. I liked the way he incorporated the words from a scrap of paper he found blowing about just as we reached the beach.

A year later, Allen and I were eating in the twenty-four-hour French restaurant on the corner of 2nd Avenue and 65th Street after a long day of receptions and book launches when he delved into his shoulder bag like Santa Claus and handed me a copy of his *Bixby Canyon Ocean Path Word Breeze*. Published by the Gotham Book Mart, it was one of the twenty-six signed hardback copies. 'It's your book,' he said. I opened it and was thrilled to see my name on the dedication page. He had signed and dedicated it to me. I was particularly flattered because Allen had also dedicated *Ankor Wat*, his Cambodian journals, to me back in 1965. It was a beautiful production with a small colour reproduction of Emile White's painting of Big Sur pasted on the front.

A few days after our walk we did some recording down at the beach with Allen's new portable Uher (replacing the one stolen at East 10th Street), sitting on rocks in the white sand with waves breaking in the distance. We recorded a Big Sur poem for the album but it took many takes because of the wind blowing on the microphone; we had no wind guard. I had great difficulty in making the hiss of the waves sound like waves and not simply tape hiss. It was a beautiful place to record, though; a vast bright blue dome of sky, the Pacific Ocean with white frothy waves stretching out to the horizon. Suddenly there came the crash of jets, horribly near, three flying in close formation only a hundred feet or so above the waves. Silver and red markings, then gone. So fast that if you had happened to be blinking you would have missed them. Even here in paradise there were reminders of America's military might.

Lawrence and Shig came down for the weekend. The sun had already set spectacularly into the Pacific and it was dusk as Allen, Lawrence, Ann and I were driving along the Cabrillo Highway towards Bixby Canyon, when Allen suggested dropping into the Esalen Institute to use the hot baths. There was a large 'Members Only' sign but both Allen and Lawrence thought that they might be honorary members so we turned into the drive anyway. The road dropped steeply to a long plateau hugging the cliff, high above the ocean. There was a group of long wooden bungalows, a row of trailer homes, a swimming pool and a lawn. In the distance stood a large old house surrounded by trees.

We were all feeling really hungry so we first went to the café, but it had just closed for the day and all that was left was horrible instant coffee in polystyrene cups. Everyone there seemed to know Allen and Lawrence and someone managed to come up with a sandwich. It was already dark by the time we reached the baths. The big house had been constructed by an old country doctor who had moved to Big Sur for the natural hot springs, which he considered health-giving. As the Coast Highway had not yet been built, he had the huge outdoor bathtubs brought to the bottom of the cliff by boat and then hauled up the cliff by breeches buoy. The tubs steamed in the night air and the view out over the ocean was spectacular.

Lawrence told a story of going there once with Kerouac and how Jack freaked out at seeing sperm floating on the water. I examined the water more closely. It looked kind of cloudy. I decided that I didn't want to use the tubs and went to look at the bookstore while the others immersed themselves. The store was closed but had some interesting notices in the window. One of them read: 'Esalen photo-graph. Tuesday morning; 10.30 with clothes. 11.00 without clothes. Please be prompt.' Another, which advertised one of Fritz Perls' books, said, 'All the girls know that Fritz still knows how to kiss!' Fritz, the co-founder of Gestalt Therapy and director of the Esalen Institute until his death in 1970, beamed from the cover of his latest paperback, long white beard and twinkling eyes like the original Mr Natural. I sat on a stone wall next to a carefully tended lawn and smoked a cigarette while watching the waves break in white lines on the rocks hundreds of feet below. The sound was distant and peaceful. Though the setting was marvellous, there was something creepy about Esalen.

On the way back to the canyon we stopped at the ocean, where we encountered a girl wandering along the beach wrapped in a brown blanket but otherwise naked. She told us that she had a history of mental instability, but several years before Fritz Perls had given her acid and then fucked her. She was later found out of her mind and eating her own shit. She apparently lived at Esalen and had simply wandered off, and no one had been watching over her to prevent her leaving. She seemed rational enough and told us her story in a matter-of-fact, casual way, as if such events were perfectly normal. Of course, it may not have been a true story at all. At Shig's suggestion she spent a night with us at Ferlinghetti's cabin and the next day he drove her to Carmel, where she had friends.

Lawrence, Allen, Ann, Shig and I visited Emile White, for many years Henry Miller's secretary. He was a friendly white-haired old man living in a small villa on the coast road at Big Sur. The front gate was high, like an enclosed French garden, but vigorous tugs on the bell-pull summoned Emile. He had a laughing voice, twinkling eyes and was clearly delighted that Allen and Lawrence wanted to visit. He seated us all and produced red wine, pâté and biscuits for everyone. One complete wall of the double-height room was covered floor to ceiling with books, and the shelves extended to adjoining walls. This was his Henry Miller collection; Miller was in every one of the browning magazines, anthologies and first editions. Miller's paintings were also on display, but most of the paintings were White's own colourful amateur landscapes, which reminded me of Alfred Wallis, the Cornish primitive.

A noticeboard had snapshots of Miller with his new Japanese wife and Henry's latest letter was proudly passed around for all to read. With all this Milleriana it was surprising that White's presence wasn't overshadowed by his old friend's invisible ghost, but White had a great deal of vitality of his own, and welcomed the visit as an excuse to gossip with Lawrence and Shig about Big Sur residents, the latest scandal at the Esalen Institute and who had bought which plot of land. Allen loved gossip and listened eagerly. Ann frowned at the small colour snaps that Emile had pinned up and at the pre-women's-liberation attitudes he expressed in the way he discussed women, plenty of whom he still seemed able to pick up and bring home to his bed. He did the painting of Bixby Creek Bridge that appeared on the cover of Allen's *Bixby Canyon Ocean Path Word Breeze*. He was fascinating to meet because he seemed to know exactly what everyone was doing within a ten-mile radius and was filled with insights into the life of the Big Sur community.

On another day, we all drove high up the mountain to see a group of people living communally in a historic concrete house where the poet Robinson Jeffers once lived. Allen's friend, the artist Bob Brannaman, had lived there previously and some of his calligraphy was still pinned up. The view was astonishing, with the mountain falling away steeply at a 45-degree slope to the Pacific. There was a long meadow ending in trees below the house that was too steep for anyone but the children to play on. We all sat on a balcony and watched the sun dip into the silver pool of the sea. We were so high up that the curvature of the earth could easily be seen and the waves were like tiny wrinkles on its immense surface, like the shifting textures on a blob of mercury.

Allen slowly chanted the *Om ah hum vajra guru padma siddhi hum* mantra, accompanying himself on his Indian harmonium. He stopped singing once the last fiery arc disappeared in the direction of Hawaii, and there was a profound deep silence as we sat quietly, backs to the great rock heart of the mountain, huge volumes of air in front of us, high above the Pacific. Even the children appreciated this special moment in their idyllic life on the side of the mountain.

Allen, Lawrence Ferlinghetti and I made a shopping run into Monterey, whirring up US1 from Big Sur in Larry's VW bus. After stopping in Carmel, we decided to go on to Monterey to eat. The route we took seemed to miss the town, just huge curving spurs of freeway running across vacant lots scattered with rotting clapboard houses, rusting autos and scrubby vegetation. A huge freeway sign pointed to Cannery Row, confirming that Steinbeck's days must be well and truly over. Still, sea birds curved in the air, white clouds scudded in from the sea, and the California sun made the water sparkle.

Cannery Row was as I had feared: rusting metal-sided ware-houses, empty lots and railroad tracks gave way to boutiques, leather shops and head shops as we neared the ocean. Hippies sat on the sidewalk smiling and laughing in the sun. Allen and Lawrence were immediately recognised in a hip paperback shop by the young owners. I checked the shelves and they had two or three copies of each of their books. One antique shop featured as a tourist attraction an old steam locomotive parked outside, complete with cowcatcher and hooded chimney to catch sparks. Some very trendily dressed people were strolling about.

Lawrence told us that he knew of a great fish place and we finally parked beside a converted cannery built on a jetty out over the ocean. Small boats were pulled up to its road frontage and large fishing nets gave an illusion of a fishing port. The dining room looked straight out to sea – or rather, out over about 100 feet of scum glistening with strange chemical colours; froth and foam from another planet. Bits of broken wood, empty bottles and cans bobbed up and down in the wavelets. The restaurant had a large hole in its floor, which was glazed over so that one could see the sea hitting the barnacles and encrustations on the wooden piers below. From the window you could see rows of such buildings, jetted out over the water so that loads of fish could be winched straight up into the building without the need of cranes, docks or beaching. We all ordered fancy fish dishes that were very good. Lawrence asked whether the fish came from Monterey. 'Gee no!' said the waitress, aghast. 'The sea here is too polluted. We get them flown in from New Jersey.' Allen laughed. The irony of it, having to import fish 3,000 miles when your restaurant is built to winch fish up from the ocean itself. Lawrence, who had been extolling the advantages and wonders of California and the west coast, seemed chagrined.

Back in Berkeley, we were almost finished with the tape project; there were just a half-dozen poems that we had no recordings of, for the most part long, difficult poems that were not well suited to public performance. For the sake of completeness we decided to record them. Richard Friedman had a late-night radio show at KPFA-FM but he and his girlfriend were going on a trip to Los Angeles to interview Anaïs Nin, among other things, and so I took over his programme for him. We had in a few guests, people like Michael McClure and Freewheelin' Frank from the Hells Angels, and if the listeners' phone calls dried up or I ran out of things to say, there was always the row of Dylan bootlegs or the live Lenny Bruce tapes.

Allen came on the show a number of times and we used the occasion to slip in those poems he had never read live before. It was fun doing the show, which ran until about 2.30, or whenever I wanted. Then all I had to do was call the guy at the transmitter to tell him I was closing down, remember to turn off the Pultech compressor that punched our FM signal across the bay, and lock up. Compared to all the fuss and bother at the BBC, the men in white coats and assistants with clipboards, it was a breath of real freedom. I always felt that freedom of the press should be extended to the airwaves and deeply resented the control over broadcasting the state exercised in England.

The reason I got to do the show was that we were now using

KPFA's Ampex tape machines to edit the tapes, as it was no longer convenient to do so at Fantasy. We would arrive around 10 p.m. when the machines were no longer in use and spend two or three hours there each night before calling a cab to take us home. The cab company was a wonderful Berkeley hippy institution. There was a strict fifty-fifty ratio of men and women drivers, and the cabs themselves were painted in psychedelic colours, with exploding mushrooms across the doors and weird third eyes on the boot. The main problem was that the drivers tended to have friends with them and sometimes we would have to try to squeeze in with two other people and possibly the driver's dog. Allen finally exploded with exasperation after an enormous German shepherd dribbled all over the new trousers he was going to wear to a reading the next day. 'Let it all out, man,' said the driver infuriatingly. 'Let it all come out!'

We completed the project in August and handed sixteen hours of tape to Fantasy Records for the proposed box set. We also gave KPFA a set of tapes, and that October they held an Allen Ginsberg day and played all sixteen hours of recordings. (It was a tradition of theirs to have theme days; they held a Gertrude Stein day, and once a year they played the complete *Ring Cycle*.) The box set was ultimately not released, but many of the tracks finished up on the *Holy Soul, Jelly Roll* CD box set that Allen released many years later on Rhino so the work was not wasted.

7 1971

desert days

In August, Ann went away on Buddhist business. She
was becoming more and more involved with her medita-
tion teacher and went on retreat at his centre. I flew down to Tucson,
Arizona, to visit my friend Walter Bowart, the founder of the New York
underground newspaper *East Village Other* (EVO). I had been their
London correspondent. He was now married to Peggy Hitchcock,
sister of Billy Hitchcock, who owned Tim Leary's headquarters at
Millbrook. I first met her when she was going out with Tim. Peggy
and Billy were the heirs to the fabled 'Mellon Millions' and between
them sank many of these millions into Leary's operation.

Peggy and Walt lived in a relatively modest mansion in the desert
outside Tucson, though it was still big enough to require a staff.
They had servants; 'wetbacks', they called them, the two young
Mexican boys having swum, or waded, across the Rio Grande. The
staff lived in a large corrugated-iron shed in the grounds which
had an enormous air-conditioning unit perched on its roof. One
of the boys was singing a Mexican love song as he worked in the
garden. An old Mexican gardener wearing a cowboy hat sat under
a tree near the front drive. A Mexican maid dressed in black moved
silently around the house. Peggy and Walter were living in the guest
house in the grounds as their rooms in the main house were being
rebuilt and the other guests were living in other guest houses or in

the apartment above the printing press.

I was given a room in the main house which was lined with books, mostly comparative religion, including all the standard texts on Sufism and the *Great Books of the East* series. There was a good selection of modern literature, poetry, drug culture and popular culture. Curiously many books were present in duplicate or triplicate but very few of them showed any signs of ever having been read. During my visit I was able to read a biography of Howard Hughes, Colin Wilson's *Poetry and Mysticism* and a few other volumes; it was wonderful to feel relaxed enough, and to have time enough to just sit and read all day, something I hadn't been able to do for years. My room had an en suite bathroom beautifully decorated with Mexican tiles, and across the corridor was an oak door leading to a walled courtyard, dominated by a huge palm tree which, with all its undergrowth, separated the courtyard effectively into two sections: one side was in the sun and the other was shaded by the meeting of two wings of the house. The shaded side was used for outdoor eating and furnished accordingly.

There was another walled garden, surrounded by an adobe wall and accessible only from inside the house. This was where Walter grew his marijuana plants. 'How are the houseplants doing? Yuk! Yuk!' he would laugh, and slap the old Mexican gardener on the shoulder. The old man's face cracked in a barely perceptible smile, more of a rictus really. The plants were about seven foot high. Two huge saguaros grew outside one of the living-room windows so the view was almost completely filled by the spiky trunks that reached all the way to roof level. The cacti had holes in them where birds had penetrated their spiky defences. In among the spines were the homes of spiders. Everything was decaying: the palm in the courtyard was skirted by a waving mass of dead fronds, hanging 10 feet down its trunk. In the desert outside, the rains had brought out the flowers; intensely coloured cacti blooms, visible for miles.

Sunsets were viewed from the flat tiled roof of the house and were magnificent, maybe the most beautiful I have ever seen: an oriental fan of magenta, rose madder, mauve and pink; a Technicolor-neon aurora borealis as intense as the flash of a parrot wing. We used to get *Arizona Highways* magazine at my local primary school in Cirencester – a gift from the local USAF base at Fairford from the Cold War days when there were more than a hundred American bases in Britain. I was used to the watery Cotswolds, and never believed that the colours could be that strong; but they were. The mansion was built in the middle of a forest of giant saguaro cacti that grew as high as the house, and as twilight fell, their bulbous shapes grew dark, then black against the night sky. A mature saguaro can weigh 10 tons, depending on rainfall. Too much rain and they burst open and die. Thousands of them stood like sentinels on the rocky hill outside, stretching away to the horizon of cut-out mountain ranges. Amazing to think that Geronimo once knew these mountains.

Dinner was rather more formal than at the Woolsey Street commune. Both Peggy and her friend Alexandra changed for dinner and stood wearing floor-length gowns that caught the last vestiges of light from the sky. One of the other house guests was a Mr Vestal, the executor of the Mellon Foundation, the source of Peggy's wealth. He was a silver-haired old Texan gentleman with every hair perfectly clipped and in place and a heavy watch-chain that he fingered constantly. He wore highly polished steel-rimmed spectacles. He rambled on about old Paul Mellon and the old days when the Mellon family owned most of Pittsburgh. He was charming with the ladies and had elegant manners. He was not fazed in the slightest when Walter explained that it was a family tradition to hold hands around the table after dinner and say 'Om!' As the last traces of the sun sank beneath the cacti-covered knoll to the west, he confidently assisted the ladies down the stairs leading to the living room. The air was still and warm.

One day I forgot to tap out my cowboy boots when I got up. A tiny red spider bit my foot, causing intense pain that took most of the day to go away. Nonetheless, the power of nature here was stimulating. I loved to walk along the dried washes and see the crisscrossed animal tracks, perfectly preserved in the fine white desert sand, where they would last until the next rains came, a day or maybe a year. Big mountain lion tracks crossed tiny spider prints and the cross-hatch of hopping birds, all frozen in time. There was still water coming off the mountains. A powder-dry wash that we had crossed the previous day was now a boiling torrent of thick muddy water. There was still rain about. Clouds piled up over the Superstition Mountains, miles away, looking exactly like the Hopi symbol for rain. A misty column in the darkening air showed a storm 10 miles away over the open desert.

We drove out to see some friends of Walter's in the desert. They had sent directions on how to get there, which included making a left turn off the highway past Benson, and driving 30 miles up a dirt track. The track wound its way across vast shallow valleys with wonderfully subtle changes of hue and colour. Again and again we crossed washes, bone dry now but probably running with furious water the day before. A few times the track was covered in a layer of deposited sand several feet thick, and once we got quite badly stuck while trying to cross a wash that was about three times wider than the track. On another occasion we stopped to allow a scorpion to cross the road, its delicate footprints tracing its path.

Walter's friends lived in a hand-built, free-form adobe house in a grove of stunted trees by a deep-running wash at the foot of an extraordinary cliff wall. The cliff was over a thousand feet high and several miles long. The wash was fast flowing and deep brown with topsoil. The hippy commune had a thriving pottery industry and a very large kiln. The house was an assembly of railroad ties and adobe. Wine and beer bottles had been embedded in the mud walls to give a stained-glass effect inside. The buildings surrounded a central pond with a fountain and a cactus garden that included some remarkable saguaros. Along the eaves of the building were amusing clay portraits of its makers. Life was lived primarily out of doors, which was good because there were great holes in the building's walls and often the windows did not fit or contained no glass;

however, the house withstood the few rains which occurred at this time of year. A huge black raven sat outside the kitchen window, croaking to itself.

The commune seemed rather lethargic and hierarchically organised. A group of older men, in their forties, were in control and acted out all kinds of male fantasy roles while the women were younger, subservient and mainly concerned with food and 'earth mother' mysticism. The older women ordered around the younger women and the only area where there was any equality was in the endless discussion on the effects of and uses of drugs. Despite claiming to be democratically organised, they employed a couple of Mexican gardeners to do the heavy labour and were surprised when I asked why they were not also invited to become members of the commune. When we arrived they were digging irrigation ditches at the command of the eldest commune member, a man with a drawn face, wrinkled skin, a long beard and a Zapata moustache. He wore a long ponytail down his back and looked as if he had lived like this for many, many years. He was the king of his mini-kingdom. One of the Mexicans showed me a snake swimming in the irrigation channel he had just dug.

Another day, driving to Phoenix, we stopped at Tom Mix Wash, where the twenties movie-star cowboy met his death by drowning in the middle of the desert. The highway runs straight to the horizon in both directions so he must have seen the wash running and tried to ford it. His car was swept away and he drowned. A cut-out metal silhouette of a grazing horse marks the spot, its reins dragging on the ground. It reminded me that Frank Zappa told me that Tom Mix's horse was supposedly buried in the basement of the log cabin that Mix built on Laurel Canyon, where Zappa lived in the mid-sixties. (I later found out that the horse outlived Mix by two years and went to the usual place dead horses go.) In the distance were the Superstition Mountains, where prospectors looked for gold and Geronimo made his last stand.

Walt and Peggy took me to visit another friend in order to see his house, which was built into the side of a narrow canyon, surrounded entirely by rocks and cactus. He had a large outdoor terrace, and when it got dark we gathered there for drinks. He turned off the house lights and switched on infrared spotlights positioned on the other side of the canyon, about a hundred feet away. Soon two mountain lions warily approached, fully illuminated by the lights; we could see them using special glasses. The house owner had placed several large slabs of fresh raw meat on a platform and soon the lions were tearing into it with enthusiasm. It was the most extraordinary sight to have right next to your living room.

Peggy and Walt's own living room was huge and the house guests gathered there to avoid the heat of the day. I sometimes listened to the radio there; I loved the ads on the local stations: 'His prices are very reasonable and I'm not saying this just because he happens to be my dad, as many of you know.' Even the national ads were strange: 'Like an eternal blue spirit: Levi's!' There were several other house guests. One evening Billy Hitchcock wandered into the room with Peggy when we were in the middle of a conversation about radio-activity. 'That's very interesting,' he said. 'I think I own a uranium mine. I must look it up on the list.' This was the life of the seriously rich. One of his companies had manufactured a machine that registered your alpha, beta and theta waves at the flip of a switch. It could display them on a dial, or if you preferred to sit with your eyes closed it would bleep with a different tone for each. Everyone sat around with the terminals taped to their heads, trying to get a level alpha. I found that it wasn't too difficult to maintain once you got there. 'Would anyone like to help me take the helicopter back to New York?' Billy asked casually one day. 'It's going to take days!'

Walter, Peggy and I drove out to visit Arcosanti, the Italian architect Paolo Soleri's experiment in organic architecture about sixty-five miles north of Phoenix. Proper building started in 1970, but a year later there were already quite a few structures. Walking through the tunnels and alleys, it was impossible to know whether we were on the roof or in the basement. It was architecture of surprise and humour. We peered through strange joke periscopes down into cool underground rooms, which looked shady and pleasant, and walked through corridors which had the sloping walls of Egyptian burial chambers, a distant light source flickering ahead. It was a surprise to turn the corner in a dim corridor and suddenly encounter a shimmering rooftop swimming pool, part shaded by a huge futuristic roof slab on columns, wind-bells hanging out over the water. It had little ropes to guide children to shallow pools and overflows. Soleri's students and assistants had dug themselves in near by. A chimney and periscope window stuck up out of the earth near a large cactus, like something built by the Professor in the Rupert Bear stories. A short search revealed a part-hidden stairway leading down into the earth and also another nearby dwelling. The whole place was like a children's fantasy story with doors in the roots of trees, doors in the desert floor itself.

Soleri's settlement is still growing now, almost forty years later. It is really one huge building designed to grow organically into an actual city. It is not a commune; it is an educational facility that teaches ideas of sustainable urban living. Arcosanti is a high-density residential environment, it is compact, it stresses culture and urban living rather than dissipation into the suburbs, it deals with efficient, sustainable land use and self-reliance: from the very first they used solar power as their chief form of energy.

When we were there a new section was under construction, even more decorative than the first; the older buildings used unusual ceramics and gentle curves whereas the new addition featured a huge barrel-vault roof with a Romanesque feel to it. We met Soleri, a small, deeply sunburned, muscular sixty-one-year-old Italian. He was determined and youthful, with a refreshing no-nonsense approach to his work. Despite having discussed his ideas a thousand times before, he talked enthusiastically about medieval Italian hill towns and the commune concept of Europe, not a hippy concept but the ancient civic pride and social responsibility of the village dwellers, a respect for privacy and a sense of security. None of us wanted to leave the site; the curves of the poured concrete were so pleasurable and the underground caverns so cool and inviting in the desert heat, like limestone grottoes. Arcosanti is an obvious model for 'green' development, decades ahead of its time.

My friends Ken Weaver and Betsy Klein had moved to Tucson from their slum apartment in Alphabet City in New York. There was a wistful, friendly sadness between Ken and Betsy, who no longer lived together. Behind Betsy's small house was a little one-up, one-down detached building with an outside staircase. Ken lived upstairs behind a wooden door that he had covered entirely with the silver tabs from flip-top beer cans like chain mail. The dull shine gave a weird medieval quality to the building which was in every other way unremarkable. Ken was from El Campo, Texas, half Irish, half Cherokee, and though not a member of any particular chapter, he could be easily mistaken for a Hells Angel. He was well over six feet tall, powerfully built with a huge mane of black hair extending below his shoulders and a full Santa Claus beard.

I first met him when he was the drummer with the Fugs, that anarchic meld of poetry and rock 'n' roll. Ken had originally got a job digging drainage channels for Peggy Hitchcock but now he was working out at the Desert Museum, looking after the animals. We drove out there with me riding pillion on his Harley-Davidson chopper, roaring through the open desert past the cacti stands, Ken's long hair tied up so as not to hit me in the face. Ken stood in the 95-degree heat under a cloudless sky, spraying water at the bears with a high-pressure hose. They waved their paws at him in slow-motion pleasure, moving their huge bodies to take best advantage of the spray.

One rose up from its artificial pond, stood on the concrete rocks and pointed his muzzle to the sun, water running from his jaws. Ken imitated the gesture perfectly, his beard jutting to the sky like the engraving of Tennyson on Beachy Head. The mountain lion purred as Ken tickled her. He was fearless in the lion cage, even though one of them had recently clawed him. A lioness had jumped up and

THE FUGS FIRST ALBUM
WITH SIZZLING ADDITIONAL TRACKS FROM THE EARLY FUGS

Ken Weaver, centre, author of such Fugs' favourites
as 'I Couldn't Get High' and 'Slum Goddess'

put both paws on his head, digging her claws in. She was just being friendly but it hurt him badly. He hauled her off and punched her in the mouth with a right hook and was able to make his escape. He told me he understood their feelings about being in captivity, he had often felt that way himself. He had felt a bit that way when he was in the Fugs, which was why he wouldn't allow any Fugs albums into his apartment.

Ken, Betsy and I piled into a battered pick-up and set out for Kit Peak. We stopped for some six-packs and ice lollies at a seedy truck stop but no one gave us any trouble for having long hair or anything. The mountain was always there in the distance as we drove along the highway, growing bigger and bigger, rising a sheer 4,000 feet from the already high desert floor, to over seven thousand feet at the solar observatory at its peak. The hairpin bends on the way up gave incredible views of sheer tree-studded cliff-sides with puffy clouds floating by, jumbling up the perspective so you couldn't tell what was up or down. The mountain is in the middle of the Papago Indian Reservation but they permitted an observatory to be built on top, and a perfectly maintained blacktop with bright yellow stripes takes you all the way there in a triumph of road-building. A cluster of domes and telescopes crowded the peak but we wandered away and smoked a little dope while leaning on a parapet and admiring the view.

Eighty miles away was a mountain range looking like flat

cardboard silhouettes. About a hundred feet below us was a vultures' eyrie; a dozen or so huge black birds with a couple of messy twiggy nests visible among the boulders. They stretched their wings and flapped them at the sun. Ken explained that the sun baked away any germs or bacteria that might attach to their beaks or heads when they were foraging, which was the reason they were bald. After a few tokes on Betsy's brass pot pipe, Ken began to flap about over the rocks. 'I feel like – going like – T-H-I-S!' as he imitated the huge birds' intuitive response to the sun's reappearance from behind clouds. Beautiful Alpine flowers grew among the rocks and boulders. The observatory's normal operations were suspended because there were clouds during the brief Arizona rainy season, but the public was still allowed in and we got to see the solar image, reflected on to a huge viewing plate. The image was weak because of water vapour in the air.

On the way back, near Ken's house, we encountered a pick-up truck driven by a local farmer. He had shotguns mounted on a rack behind the driving seat and his two dim-looking overweight sons stood in the back, shotgun in one hand, the other on the handrail. The farmer seemed to know Ken so we chatted a little. Finding out that I was English he felt obliged to tell me his concern that the British did not have the right to bear arms. 'In fact,' he said in a slow drawl, 'Ahh think that it's every man's right to own his own, person-aaal, nu-cleeaar device!' His sons glared at me, brows furrowed, as if I might disagree. 'That's very interesting,' I said, lamely. I could not help but think of *Dr Strangelove*. Maybe it was time to go back home.

8   1972

with william seward burroughs in st james's

Ever since my days at the Indica Bookshop in the mid-sixties I had been toying with the idea of compiling a bibliography of the work of William Burroughs. I needed to return to London, and having completed my work with Allen Ginsberg, this seemed a suitable next project.

I had first corresponded with Burroughs in 1964, when he was in Tangier, and we became friends when he moved to London in the latter part of 1965. I first published Bill in an anthology I edited called *Darazt* in 1965, and he was a frequent contributor to *International Times* throughout the sixties. Towards the end of 1965 Burroughs returned to London from New York and moved into the Rushmore Hotel at 11 Trebovir Road, a converted Regency town house in Earl's Court. Then, in 1967, he moved into Dalmeny Court at 8 Duke Street, St James's; a deal arranged for him by his friend, the film-maker Antony Balch, who already had a flat there.

St James's was the perfect place for William to live; discreet, safe, anonymous, an area catering very much to the needs of gentlemen. In fact it is still something of a last bastion of male privilege with its all-male gentlemen's clubs, service flats and traditional bachelor housing like Albany, running between Piccadilly and Vigo Street. St James's specialises in men's outfitters – Savile Row is just across Piccadilly – wine merchants and cigar shops, shops selling sponges, loofahs and shaving brushes. When Bill lived there one could spend the night in the Turkish baths on Ormond Yard. There was also nearby Piccadilly Circus with its population of male hustlers, known in the trade as 'Dilly boys', who gathered at the 'meat rack' outside the Regent Palace Hotel on Piccadilly. If this was regarded as too indiscreet (which it often was), there was the garden in the centre of Leicester Square, a short walk away, where wealthy older men picked up rent boys.

Dalmeny Court was a purpose-built block of luxury service flats occupied mostly by men. Access to the flats was by a slow-moving elevator with a sliding-grille door, unusual in London at the time. The St George's Gallery was on the ground floor, run by a highly refined Frenchwoman, selling oil paintings suitable for the library or dining room and with a discreet line in erotica in the basement. Next to the Checkers pub, filled with louche art dealers, an archway led through to Mason's Yard, home to an electricity generating sub-station in the centre of the square, with a celebrated gentlemen's public convenience built against it that was much used for cottaging.

Across from this was the old Keyhole Club, which from 1965 until 1972 became the Scotch of St James's, a trendy, exclusive rock 'n' roll in-club catering to the music business. In the seventies it reverted to its role as a hostess club, now called the Director's Lodge. Across the corner from the Scotch stood the Indica Gallery, where John Lennon met Yoko Ono and Mark Boyle had his first gallery show. I was co-owner of Indica and when we first started in 1965,

Miles Collection

WILLIAM SEWARD BURROUGHS

8 Duke Street, St. James's,
London S.W.1.   Telephone: 01-839 5259

Burroughs quickly adopted the protective colouring of a St James's resident: shoes from Lobb, hat from Locke and a visiting card it was Burroughs' then boyfriend, Ian Sommerville, who wired up the gallery and installed spotlights. The bookshop moved to South-ampton Row in 1966 and the gallery continued until 1967 before closing. Bill could see it all from his back window and had been a frequent visitor.

In all his years in London Bill never learned the street plan of anything other than his immediate environment; everything he needed was there within easy walking distance, including, of course his Senior Service unfiltered cigarettes, 'The only service you get in England, hyuh! hyuh!' His local shops were Jackson's of Picca-dilly and Fortnum and Mason's, where, in the early seventies, the assistants always looked around carefully for your servant before they handed you your purchase to carry. Bill was in every sense the St James's man, right down to his beautifully tooled shoes by John Lobb on St James's Street, made to fit his unusually long thin feet. Lobb had his hand-carved wooden last on file. Bill had a neat small-brim fedora and wore a Monte Cristi panama from Locke's of St James's in the summer.

He was very knowledgeable about panamas, and assured me that this was a very good one, hand woven in Ecuador from tequila-palm fronds. It was a wide-brim folder and he liked to demonstrate how he could roll it up and put it in his pocket and how it would snap back into shape when he pulled it out. This was all protective colouring; you would not give him a second glance as he walked down St James's.

He was always good at blending in. When he was in Tangier, Bill wore a burnoose and often carried a shopping bag containing a few oranges, which showed that he lived there and was not a tourist. He became so good at it that in Morocco the Spanish boys called him *'El Hombre Invisible'*; no one saw him glide down the street and into Dean's bar. In the eighties he lived in Lawrence, Kansas, where he wore work overalls or jeans and a peaked cap with the name of a seed company written on it. He looked like an old farmer, come into town for supplies. I was once in a coffee shop in Lawrence with him and James Grauerholz, having breakfast, when he noticed thick black clouds heading our way. 'Jess look at those thunder-heads,' he drawled in the local accent. 'Sure as shootin' a tornado's heading our way.' At the other booths several people followed his gaze, looked at his wise demeanour, got up and quickly drove off in their pick-ups, convinced he knew what he was saying. William gave a satisfied grin. The clouds soon cleared away.

In London I once asked him about this desire for anonymity and at first he shrugged it off, almost contemptuously, as if it was blind-ingly obvious. When he saw I was indeed being thick he explained: 'When one has certain, um, interests, it is better not to advertise the fact. I prefer to fit right in and not to draw attention.' He referred, of course, to not being identified as being homosexual. Bill was fifty-eight but he looked ageless. His wispy hair still had a sandy hue but in his neat three-piece Jermyn Street suit and tie he could have been anything from forty to sixty-five years old.

Bill was interested in Beau Brummell and his sense of refined dandyism; wearing understated but well-fitting clothes, so perfectly turned out that no one would notice him on the street (as apposed to the later, more flamboyant, foppish dandyism). William was even more invisible on the streets of St James's than in Tangier. It was for this reason that he was horrified when his friend John Giorno visited on his way back from India, wearing a see-through Indian cotton shirt open almost to the navel and adorned with various necklaces, amulets and bracelets.

We all went to dinner – at one of William's least favourite restau-rants – and on the way out of Dalmeny Court, William whispered to me: 'Pretend he's not with us.' William engaged me in intense conver-sation, and as there was not room for three people to walk abreast down the street, John had to walk in front. This was when it really sank home to me that William's main fear of persecution was not as a drug user, but as a homosexual. I now understood his distress when Antony Balch camped it up in La Capanenna for the waiters or Alan Watson, Ian Sommerville's boyfriend, paraded down the street, hand on hip, casting seductive glances at William from beneath lowered eyelids. William had always cultivated the lowest possible profile.

Flat 22 had two bedrooms and a good-size living room. There were a number of Brion Gysin's paintings displayed on the walls, including a superb large desert scene above the settee. One day in March 1972 I visited Bill and found he had traded in his old television for a new colour model, adjusted to a very red colour bias. 'Once you've seen a riot in colour, it's never the same in black and white,' said Bill, looking up. 'The films of Belfast are tremendous!' This led to a discussion about revolutionary violence, and I remarked that the Italian publisher Feltrinelli had just been blown to pieces, supposedly while planting a bomb at an electricity pylon outside Milan. 'I admire Feltrinelli,' said Bill, lighting another Senior Service; 'after all, he didn't forget about the bombs! Most revolutionaries, they get rich and comfortable and they forget all about the bombs! I haven't seen Genet, Jean Genet, hustling in the streets for a long time. And me, ha-ha, I just should go back to rolling drunks!'

In July 1972 Bill moved from flat 22 to flat 18, a smaller, cheaper one-bedroom flat on the top floor, high in the eaves of the same building. He looked out east over Mason's Yard and the back wall of the London Library at the rear, and out over the rooftops of St James's and down Ryder Street from the front of the flat, a view that he photographed scores of times to use in his collages and scrapbooks. Brion Gysin arrived from Paris to take over the larger apartment and live there while he worked on the screenplay of *Naked Lunch*, one of William's many projects at the time.

Bill shared the flat with John Brady, a Dilly boy from Piccadilly Circus. It was not a sensible arrangement, as Bill was the first to agree, but he was often lonely and appreciated the company. Johnny described himself as 'black Irish', and said that his black hair was the result of the Spanish blood introduced into Ireland at the time of the Armada. The Spanish fleet, having been blown anticlockwise down the coast of the British Isles, had stopped off at various promontories for water and supplies and to drop off their sick and wounded. The sailors fathered a few children on shore leave and that accounts for the strain of dark curly hair in Kerry and Cornwall. He was a country boy, barely literate, trying to get by. Bill liked to get him to describe his experiences with 'the little people', and if he was in a good mood Johnny would oblige: 'To be sure, it was raining at the time and I was walking down the lane and there he was, sitting on a leaf, just like that...' He seemed genuinely convinced of their existence. I asked whether he had read any of Bill's books. He lowered his eyes and muttered, 'I do intend to. They're very thick books and there's a powerful number of them.'

Sometimes he would bring girlfriends back to the flat and I was working there one morning when Bill encountered a naked girl, coming out of the bathroom. He was shocked and embarrassed and after she left I heard raised voices from the front room. Most of the time, though, things were calm. Bill gave Johnny £5 a day – some days £4, others as much as £10 – and he presumably made himself available when he was needed. William showed me a sequence of photographs displaying increasingly large wet patches on his progressively more rumpled red sheets. Johnny was usually there for drinks at six o'clock because that was when he received his daily allowance. Johnny rarely stuck around if Bill had someone else there to spend the evening with. Sometimes, if he felt that he had been neglecting Bill and thought he might move on to someone else, Johnny would bring home a friend for a threesome, but this was rare. More often it was Johnny who was sulky and difficult and it was Bill who had to do the mollycoddling.

When he was first seeing Johnny, William encouraged him to display all the things he had stolen from his clients on Piccadilly on a coffee table against the wall. John was a skilled pickpocket and the table usually had a good selection of Ronson lighters, wallets and expensive gold-nibbed fountain pens, which would mysteriously disappear a few days later. Burroughs undoubtedly got the idea of displaying the booty from Jean Genet and delighted in pointing it out to his guests.

Bill's bed was in the living room, covered with a red blanket, and Johnny slept in the bedroom, which was used mostly for storage. There was a four-drawer file cabinet in there, jammed with folders. Bill's ex-boyfriend Ian Sommerville had once attempted to organise Bill's papers: 'He has two hundred files and a hundred of them are labelled "Miscellaneous",' said Ian, despairingly. Many of the folders were still carefully labelled in Ian's flowing calligraphy, but most were in Bill's spidery handwriting and called things like: 'Pages to cut-in'; 'B & M – Egyptian Dog Tag Number Diary Switch'; 'District'; 'Materials Dream File We are the night family'; 'Wild Boy film ideas. I first discussed project with Terry Southern. Later with Fred Halsted. Project given up as 6,000,000 spectacle. File under Coum.'; 'Children story letters'. My personal favourite was called: '? Yes. Very good. Very good. Everything out of sight. Material to be retyped for finished file'. It was, of course, impossible to organise these files alphabetically.

There was a bathroom next to the bedroom, and a kitchenette next to the front door. Bill used the kitchen only to make tea or bread and jam; he ate all his main meals in restaurants. The kitchen cabinets were filled with boxes of books and magazines. In the living room Bill sat at a wooden office desk with his back to the window. A large hole had been crudely cut in the desk to allow the electrical cord for his typewriter to come through. There was a file cabinet to his left filled with manuscripts in progress with a vase of flowers on top and to his right was a low bookcase with sliding glass doors, its shelves thick with dust. About half the books in it were by him: foreign editions, different paperback editions, anthologies containing his work; most of the others were sci-fi paperbacks.

Pride of place went to a copy of the full-colour illustrated edition of *The Report of the Commission on Obscenity and Pornography*, given to him by Terry Southern, which, as it was a US Government report, and the illustrations an integral part of it, Bantam Books had cleverly published in 1970 without having to worry about the obscenity laws. The pages illustrating gay sex were well thumbed and in many cases loose in the binding.

On top of the bookcase sat a bottle of whisky and a Philips portable cassette recorder. Against the wall stood a small brassbound seaman's locker with a handle at each end and a broken lock. This had been used by Brion Gysin to preserve Bill's manuscripts when he would precipitously up and leave the Beat Hotel in Paris for London or Tangier, leaving his papers to be stored, stolen or thrown away. Brion would usually retrieve them in time. At the other end of the room was a narrow double bed covered with a red blanket that was used as a settee. Above it hung Brion's large painting of the Sahara desert.

Bill was short of money; his books were not selling very well and so he had decided to sell his papers. Brion Gysin was in a similar situation, and they decided to combine their archives and sell them as one lot to an institution. Though Brion's archive was much smaller, it contained a lot of letters from Paul Bowles, Alice Toklas and the like, and so was about equal in value. (Bill had not kept his correspondence until the sixties; all his letters from Kerouac and Ginsberg from 1944 until then had been thrown away.)

Bill and Brion commissioned me to describe the collection and sell it on their behalf, so in June and July 1972, I wrote a preliminary description of the contents to show to the Butler Library of Columbia University in New York, which had previously bought all my letters from Burroughs and at that time were holding Allen Ginsberg's archives on deposit. They expressed great interest and so I set to work. Though Bill had found quite a lot of material for me to describe in my initial inventory I suspected that he had things stashed all over the flat as well as in storage with friends in New York, Athens and London. Virtually every day he found something new in a storage cupboard in the kitchen or stuffed behind the filing cabinet. Clearly it was going to be quite a job just assembling the archives, let alone cataloguing them.

Now that I had a good idea of what Bill and Brion were offering for sale I took my notes to New York and we discussed how Columbia wanted the material catalogued so that we could agree a price. I also used the visit to contact the various people who were still holding things for him. Bill had sublet a New York apartment at 333 Park Avenue South, the old Tiffany Lamp factory, for the summer, but now decided that he didn't want to leave London after all, so Ann and I took it on instead. It was a nice loft and belonged to a young woman who imported Moroccan carpets to the States.

William had suitcases stored with a number of people, including the painter David Budd, a minimalist who burned his canvases so that little was left except the wooden stretcher, and with another painter who stuck the paintbrush up his arse and made Zorro-like marks on the canvas. One of the boxes that a friend had so loyally stored all those years contained little but old New York newspapers and used paperbacks, but another revealed treasures such as a copy of *APO-33* in the original Fuck You Press edition.

Bill had given the book to Ed Sanders to publish when he was living briefly in New York in 1964/65 and had stopped by the Peace Eye bookshop to see how it was going. Ed published the Fuck You Press books on a mimeograph machine 'at a secret location in the Lower East Side', but there was a problem with printing *APO-33* because it incorporated a number of illustrations. Ed had devised a solution by having electronic stencils made of the illustrations, then cutting them out and pasting them in at the appropriate places. Unfortunately the cutting and pasting was done by Peter Orlovsky, high on speed, who smeared the paste everywhere, stuck the pictures on top of the text or in the wrong place, singing and yodelling at the top of his voice. When Bill saw the result he first thought it was some sort of mock-up. When Ed told him that was it, that was how it was going to look, Bill was aghast and refused to allow him to make any more. He gave the book instead to Claude Pelieu and Mary Beach, who published it in a facsimile offset edition distributed by City Lights Books. About fifteen copies of the Fuck You Press edition did get made, and Ed sold some of them to institutions, making his edition the true first.

I returned from New York to find that Bill had set up a number of new files, including one labelled: 'Letters I do not have time to answer preparing the archives which answer such letters'. He had also found a huge block of manuscripts, about eighteen inches high and tied up roughly with string. In black magic marker, scrawled across the top page, was 'Bottom of the Barrel'. I was to find wonderful things buried in there, including about half of *Queer*, a book that he had sometimes refused to acknowledge even existed. Cataloguing a writer's manuscripts can sometimes be difficult. Unless they keep an accurate record of which draft is which, you have to compare each page and look for changes. Bill's work was particularly difficult because he was still using the cut-up technique on his manuscripts, so a large number of pages were missing altogether because he had thrown away the cut-up pages after using them. As he told me: 'My writing technique, as you know, doesn't allow for corrected drafts. I work from a first draft, uncorrected, typing the second one straight on the typewriter. Then I will work again from that, just as it is, without correcting any typing errors. It's only when I have arrived at the final form that I will correct the errors. In the final draft. Of course, I may later cut that up and from it may come other final drafts.'

I sorted the manuscripts first by page size – American, A4 or quarto – then by typewriter face and paper type before trying to decide which pages belonged together. Bill rarely numbered the pages. He sat at his desk, typing, while I spread the manuscript pages across the floor. He was at work on his latest book and I usually set problem pages to one side so as not to interrupt his work. Towards the end of the afternoon I would present him with a number of questions, usually concerning the identity of a correspondent or asking him to confirm my identification of a manuscript, and I would also show him any new files that I had created that day. More urgent clarification – anything that might hold up a large sequence – I usually asked him about when he took a break. The files sometimes threw new light on his manuscripts and he would sometimes remove a few

Barry Miles

William Burroughs at Duke Street, St James's, working on *Exterminator!*

pages to incorporate into whatever he was then working on. Other times they would give him an idea for a title for the folder which he would then write on it. I kept track by numbering all the folders. Though he was not actively engaged in organising the files – he created only a handful himself – it was necessary for him to be there to answer innumerable questions and he had to cancel a planned trip to America because of it.

Many of his characters came to him in dreams. Bill told me that he always woke up about ten times each night and immediately wrote down anything that seemed at all promising. The piece 'They do not always remember', for example, was a direct transcript of a dream, written with very little modification, straight into his notebook. He had always slept like that and so it was not a problem for him: 'I remember one time, my wife and I were asleep on separate mattresses about eight feet from each other and I was awakened by the smell of burning. In fact it was her mattress on fire but she had not noticed it. I did, even though I was some distance from the smouldering. I always wake up, an unusual noise in the street, a key in the door...'

He told me the dream he'd had the night before. He was at James Pringle House, the clap clinic on Charlotte Street, a building he was very familiar with, and just as he was having some blunt lubricated instrument shoved up his arse, he happened to look out of the window and saw the Queen and Prince Philip visiting the place. Prince Philip entered his cubicle and enquired politely, 'And how did you catch the clap, my man?' William went on to discuss the psychic disadvantages of the monarchy, that the population regarded themselves as subjects rather than citizens, but most of all he was aggrieved by the unfairness of people with titles getting preferential treatment in restaurants.

Working on the archives gave Bill some amusing ideas: 'We could check everyone in with an e-meter test: "How do you intend to use these files? Do you intend to steal any of them? Are you telling the truth?" Specially trained dogs to sniff out anyone with the wrong intentions.

'We could spend millions of dollars housing the archives. Rebuild all the sets here. Have Arab boys as librarians: "You want see nice layout books, meester?" Have computers retrieving material relating to particular characters.' The discussion drifted on to the size of the property needed to satisfactorily house such an archive, leading Bill to remember large mansions: 'John Paul Getty Junior managed to sell his house in Marrakesh for two hundred thousand dollars, which was a miracle. It was as big as a city block and every time you turned round, part of it fell down behind you!'

We discussed the desert town houses I had seen in Arizona

and William began to explore the possibility of fortified castles to house the archives, 'with a moat all around full of piranha to eat the children that fell in and then later to eat as food, if needed'. He warmed to the subject: 'with a big radar tower and gun of some sort in the centre to get plenty of advance warning of anyone approaching to try and catch the fish'. The conversation continued to examine the possibilities of crossbows in the conditions of limited warfare such as that which would occur with a breakdown in the communications systems in the USA.

We talked about the huge files that the FBI, CIA, MI5 and so on keep on everyone. Bill chuckled and said how funny it would be if there was someone else with the name William Burroughs and Bill's activities were being added to his file. 'Maybe there's a sixty-year-old grocer in Connecticut…' He laughed. He said he had always disliked his name and would like to change it to Lee. 'In England it is not so bad because Burroughs is a more common name, but in France…!' He imitated various French attempts to pronounce his name. 'I would like a name which everyone will get first time on the telephone.' This was not likely to be a problem in London as William had only an unlisted number and that was to the telephone in flat 22, where Brion now lived. To reach William you had to call Brion and make an appointment.

Ann decided to stay on in New York and look for an apartment while I returned to London to continue work on the archives with Bill. I would get to Bill's apartment around 10 a.m. and usually stayed on to have dinner with him as he hated eating alone. At lunchtime Bill always said the same thing: 'Would you like some milk and a pretzel, Miles?' and I would stop for a break. 'I really enjoy a salted cracker with milk,' said Bill. 'I've cleaned Jackson's out of Saltines, you know Saltines? Jackson's never restocked.' Jackson's on Piccadilly was one of the most expensive food shops in Britain.

At exactly six o'clock, after many impatient glances at his watch, Bill would reach for the bottle of Johnny Walker Red Label and pour us two enormous whiskies. Sometimes there would be other visitors and a sociable evening would begin, but most of the time it was just Bill and me. He told so many interesting and amusing stories that even before spending the summer in New York I had begun excusing myself to visit the bathroom and quickly scribble notes of the things he had said. My first notes were on 3 July 1972: 'I've always had terrible trouble from the neighbours. In Mexico City they used to call me *"El Vicioso"*, the vicious one. That's the Mexican word for dope fiend. In Tangier, Ian and I were in a villa for fifteen dollars a month, a real slum. The neighbours really hated us. They threw rocks through the skylight and it got so bad that Ian and I used to draw straws to see who was going out for kerosene! Run the gauntlet of old orange peel and garbage. The Arabs really know how to harass you: they'd get some rotten old beggar to bang on the door at six in the morning. I guess they thought we were just a couple of long-haired fairies.'

After a couple more industrial-size whiskies, we would set out to eat. There were hundreds of places within easy walking distance. Bill's ideal restaurant was one that was completely empty. The Scandia Rooms on the top floor of the Piccadilly Hotel at the end of Bill's street usually fitted this description. It was a huge room, often quite empty, and Bill liked to sit at the far side of it so that the waiters had to make a long trek across the carpet to bring us our aquavit. Another deserted local place was the Icelandic Steakhouse on Haymarket. The two rows of booths rarely had any customers as most people didn't understand what an Icelandic steak would be like, nor were there enough Icelanders to fill the place. In fact it was a perfectly normal steakhouse, with not even any special drinks to recommend it. The only Icelandic connection seemed to be the service, which was glacially slow. For French food there was Rowley's on Jermyn Street, where they served wine in litre carafes. This was where Bill usually ate with Antony Balch; it was rather more trendy and noisy than he usually liked but it suited Antony perfectly and it was just around the corner from Dalmeny Court. Bill loved caviar, and if he was eating alone he would sometimes treat himself to a meal at Prunier on the corner of St James's Street and Piccadilly, the finest Russian caviar house in London.

Bill liked Chinese food so we often went into Chinatown, where he knew many of the restaurants. His favourite was the Kow Loon on Gerrard Street. It was not much frequented by tourists and we were often the only non-Chinese there. 'I've always found Chinese society quite impenetrable; "Velly solly, Chinese only!" It's really quite refreshing,' he told me. One time in the Kow Loon I was surprised when Bill remarked on the beauty of a Chinese girl who entered the restaurant, mentioning her not once but several times, noting the colour of her blouse, which was revealed only after she removed a striking red satin jacket. 'She's stacked,' he said appreciatively, a phrase I had previously heard only in forties American films.

Sometimes William visited Francis Bacon at the Colony Room on Dean Street; he had known Bacon from Tangier and enjoyed discussing art with him, something Bacon rarely did with his friends. Bacon told him how little abstract painting meant to him and that even the best of it seemed to him to be nothing more than superior decoration. He found the work of the super-realists 'equally dreary'.

If Bill was feeling more sociable and wanted a restaurant with people in it, we would visit Capaninna on Romilly Street, Soho, a very festive eatery with bells hanging from the artificial rafters which the waiters rang exuberantly when they were particularly astonished by a customer's witticism or by the outstanding size of his order. For some reason the waiters there thought Bill was called 'Mr Albert' but he never attempted to correct them. We often went there with Antony Balch, who was having an affair with one of the waiters, the cause of much ringing of the bells when we entered. At one meal, with Claude Pelieu and Mary Beach, Antony managed to silence the entire restaurant by announcing, halfway through his Dover sole, 'The trouble with fish is that they're so *fisheee*!' Bill pursed his lips; there was no answer to that one.

Antony had directed Bill's films *Towers Open Fire* and *Cut Ups* and he, Brion Gysin and William had a company called Friendly

Films, set up to make a film of *Naked Lunch*. Brion was supposed to be writing the script, but this was posing problems, largely because William didn't like Brion's treatment but could not bring himself to tell him so. Brion had unaccountably written it as a musical with some truly awful song lyrics, presumably some sort of throwback to his days with John laTouche working on Broadway musicals. Meanwhile Antony had sketched out four thick volumes of shooting script with pans, zooms, close-ups and tracking shots. There was a certain uncomfortableness whenever the project was mentioned. Antony, however, didn't seem to be bothered. He had a new boyfriend in San Francisco and jetted in and out, somehow overcoming massive jet lag, overjoyed by the new atmosphere of sexual freedom in San Francisco.

One day he burst into Bill's apartment, fresh off the plane, wildly excited. He had seen icebergs on the way out and had a spectacular view of the aurora borealis on the way back. He said the prominent colour was lavender and the shapes and colours moved very quickly. Apart from a slight overexposure to 'Have a nice day' he had had a fabulous time, and was even talking of moving there. I thought William looked a little jealous of his friend's happiness. In 1971 William and Antony had been working on a film called *Bill and Tony*, an experiment in overdubbing and superimposition in which a talking-head shot of Burroughs spoke, but Antony's voice, perfectly synchronised, came from his lips and Antony spoke using Burroughs' voice. The film was in colour and used a script made from a cut-up of a Scientology routine and the script from Tod Browning's 1932 film *Freaks* which Antony was screening at the Times Cinema; the origin of the line that William drawls: 'She was once a beaut-I-ful woooo-man'.

In the course of our aperitifs and dinners together, Bill told me quite a bit about his life. He described the suburban upper middle classes in St Louis in the twenties and thirties and the hatred between the generations. 'Staying at Rex Wiesenberger's family's house was something. Where he was quite likely to have two sailors for breakfast and his parents frowning over their coffee and orange juice as if to say, "You know what happens to people who go out with sailors" and him saying, "If you cut off my allowance, I'll get in and cut the legs off that goddam antique chair!" And they all just HATE each other.' The memory made Bill crack up with laughter.

Another time he reminisced about his time in Chicago during the war when he worked as an exterminator, the longest time he ever held down a proper job: 'I'd go to the apartment and yell, "Got any bugs, lady?" I used to bang on the door real loud, hoping to attract the neighbours so that she might lie and say she didn't have any, and she would sign my book and I would get through my list early.

'"Ssh! Ssh! Come in, come in." The old Jewish woman would try and pull me in the door real fast, and there it would be, her bedroom with the covers all pulled back.

'"Can't spray beds, lady. Board of Health regulations."

'"Oh. You vant some more wine? It wasn't enough before?" and she'd pour me another glass of horrible sweet wine. So I'd hold out and eventually she'd hand me a crumpled dollar bill.

'Of course, in the Negro district it was different. I didn't come the Board of Health regulations there. I used to carry a gun. You never knew what might happen if one of those spade pimps woke up off the nod: "Hey, what's this white boy doing in the apartment?"

'"Shaddap, he's the exterminator!"

'I can go into an apartment and I know where ALL the roaches are. I also know where ALL the bedbugs are. I used to have a spray gun and I could adjust it from a fine spray to a stream, and go in a room and get a bug, Phattt! From across the room, like that. With sulphur or cyanide you have to be careful to seal the room because there's been dozens of deaths from cyanide seeping through into other neighbouring apartments. And if you have to enter the room, it's no good taking a deep breath and running in to open the windows because that stuff will attack your eyes and blind you before you even get there. You have to wear a gas mask or else open the door and let it escape first. I never have any roaches. I just go in there, to a new apartment, and give them a spray with pyrethrum powder and they all rush out and die instantly on the floor. You have to get a broom to sweep them up. It's a great sight!'

Bill had a good memory of events, even from many years before. He told me about a party he went to in Harlem in the early forties with Herbert Huncke and another friend: 'There were two queens there and one of them starts jumping up and down and shrieking, "I'm a man! I'm a man!" and this black chick with huge muscles on her arms – she was much bigger than him – starts beating him up. And the other queer, who's bigger, gets involved and the woman from downstairs is screaming and accusing someone of running a whorehouse for whites. She'd called me a white motherfucker on the way in and hit me with her elbow. And there you are, a race riot! When she stepped in I thought, "No good will come of this." Then someone broke a chair over someone's head and I knew it was bad news and I was out the back door and over the wall. I mean, the cops would soon be there. Huncke stayed till the end as usual, but I usually managed to get out before the stabbing or the cops arrived.'

One of his favourite subjects of conversation was guns; it was something he never tired of talking about. In London, of course, he was not permitted to own one, though he did have a legal Webley air pistol that had such recoil that he almost broke his finger on it and had a large bruise on his hand for weeks. He grew up with guns: 'You forget America has a gun culture. It was founded on the gun. When you are a child you are given your first air rifle at a certain age, then a .22 repeater. And all the time you get revolvers and pistols. I used to be able to shoot the flame on a candle out from across the room. I had a gun one inch long and at one point I had a .43 Russian pistol with a nine-inch barrel. Of course, there is a point when a pistol becomes a rifle, you understand. So I was brought up to know about these things, how to make a gun, how to make powder.

'I used to go out duck shooting with the old man and the president of the First National City Bank and the owner of the *St Louis Post Dispatch*. And you have to be up real early, six o'clock, to catch the ducks. All in hiding in this marshy ground, and we would put out decoys and then as the ducks came in, all these fat old businessmen would stand up and blast away at them. We had a retriever dog to collect the ducks. I used to really enjoy it.

'There was a family in St Louis and the kids weren't content with just guns, they had to have a cannon. They used to get real plastered, leap in the cars and drive on out to shoot the cannon. The tenants all muttering, "Oh no, not the cannon again!" So I suggested to the boy that he should get some explosive shells so he could see where they landed on the other side of the valley and I went away thinking, "Oh my, what if the shell explodes in the barrel. There'd be some nice casualties then!"

'I used to carry a gun in Mexico City. You never know when a bunch of guys are going to close in on you and beat you up. When you pull your gun they back away into the night...' Bill grinned, making a waving motion with his hand. 'I was going into a pissoir in Mexico City when this guy tried to elbow his way in front of me. I just...' Bill pulled his jacket open and demonstrated reaching for his weapon, a smile on his face, 'and he just backed away. Best goddam piss I ever had.

'You never know with Mexicans. A guy was standing on a street corner and up comes this other person and asks him directions how to get somewhere. Well, he doesn't know, but he thinks he ought to tell this other fellow something so he starts to tell him about all sorts of things, this and that, and then he realises, "What am I telling this bastard all these things for?" So he picks up a rock and beats the other fellow's brains in. That's the kind of city Mexico City is.

'There was another case of this fellow who comes in from the country and he's standing there with his machete waiting for a bus. And along comes another guy and stands there waiting when suddenly the first fellow ups with his machete and cuts the other guy's head off. "Well, he was looking at me so dirtee..." It has the highest homicide rate of any city.'

Bill was very knowledgeable about the old West, in particular about the types of guns the cowboys and lawmen used: 'Wyatt Earp had a special gun with a twelve-inch barrel he used to shoot with. It came right down to his knee. He went after the terrible coward who had gunned down his brother and when he caught him the guy said, "But they gave me twenty-five dollars to do it!" And Wyatt said, "It was the twenty-five dollars that really burned me up, so I said, 'I'm going to count to three, real slow, and then fire. You can draw and fire anytime.'" "Uno!" and the guy goes for his gun. "Dos!" and he's still fumbling with it, trying to get it out. "Tres!" and Earp's first shot got him in the stomach, the second in the chest, and the third right between the eyes. "Earp! Earp! Earp!" Remember, it's not who shoots first that counts, it's who hits first that's important.' I heard Bill tell this story several times and he liked to demonstrate Earp's moves by dancing in a decidedly campy way across the room, then pulling an enormously long imaginary weapon from a holster and firing away, a huge smile on his face.

'Jesse James was a morphine addict. They used it to kill the pain from gunshot wounds. Used to administer it by hypodermic syringe, or maybe by dipping cotton in it and placing it beneath the tongue. It was quite legal then, of course. Even in the 1920s every American town, even small towns, had an opium den. Those who couldn't afford it used to be given the opium ash left over from smoking as a free meal, so to speak. The ash, of course, has a high percentage of morphine in it. All the best people did it. Society ladies used to send each other jewel-encrusted hypodermic syringes as gifts. Can't see anyone sharing a needle there. Get out your jewel-encrusted syringe and the morphine, "Do come in, my dear, and close the door!" Not going to pass it round. That was in the 1840s, they had very elaborate ones, very streamlined. Of course, a lot of them didn't even know they were addicted. They would just feel ill and run down to the drugstore to get some morphine to make themselves feel better.'

Bill's constant talk of guns inevitably led to me asking about the death of his wife, Joan Vollmer, whom Burroughs shot in the middle of a drinks party when a drunken game of William Tell went horribly wrong. 'It was insanity,' he told me. 'Even if I had shot the glass off her head, there would have been shards of glass flying across the crowded room.' He said, 'Not one day goes by that I don't think of her.' Her death was a constant factor in his life.

Bill's old boyfriend Michael Portman came to visit. He was an idle young man, given to borrowing people's clothes and not returning them, burning holes in the bedding and forgetting that he had a cab waiting outside until the driver appeared, sometimes hours later, to demand his money. Like many rich people, Michael never seemed to have any actual cash on him for meals or drinks. He was just back from Morocco and was complaining that the hotels in Tangier and Marrakesh would not let him take back any 'Moroccan trade'. Bill sympathised: 'There was a time when a London fairy could take off for Tangier for a month and catch up on his sex. Tangier wasn't really on the tourist route then, that was one of the features of the place. Now it's packed with tourists, even in the winter. They just want to get them there and take their money from them. They don't want Europeans who are a bit weird. There are a few old queens still in residence, of course.'

Michael had become rather ill in Morocco, something that he attributed to the fact that the Johnny Walker whisky sold there was really hooch. William said that it was really something called Dutch Scotch that they slapped a label on and sold as Johnny Walker for $1 a bottle. He smiled. 'But these are the kinds of things which you expect to happen if you drink for two weeks, Michael.' Apparently Michael was so drunk that they wouldn't allow him on the plane when he tried to leave. Michael had an addictive personality; if he wasn't strung out on heroin, he was a shambling alcoholic. He took a number of cures but none of them worked for long.

Inspired by his visit, Bill found some letters from Michael to put in the archive: Michael Portman to his mother, the Hon. Mrs M. Portman, Portman Lodge, Durweston, Blandford, Dorset. [c.1963] 'I just got your letter today. It was a very nice letter, mummy, and made me feel good all day. As to plans. I have been very lazy about writing to the bank for money. And have rather enormous debts. I will write...'

There was an undated letter from Michael to Bill describing a party on a yacht belonging to an American millionaire called 'Junkie' Fleischman, who was a delegate of the Ford Foundation and the Congress for Cultural Freedom, the CIA front organisation that covertly funded *Encounter* magazine: 'Stephen Spender was there like a big poodle eyed nanny...' William enjoyed this vicarious connection to the world of power and corruption because it enabled him to speak knowledgeably about it at dinner. Unfortunately Bill's best opportunity to glean some insider gossip came when he dined with Miles Copeland, the head of CIA Europe, whose son later managed the Police, but he had been so drunk that the next day he had no memory of meeting the man at all.

Sometimes Johnny Brady came to dine with us, though he rarely said much. I sometimes wondered what his real feelings were towards Bill as they obviously had no intellectual contact and Johnny's actual sexual preference was for women. One day, when Bill was out, I asked Johnny what he liked about Bill. He told me he loved the way Bill walked round corners. And it was true, it *was* great. Bill would move swiftly down the pavement, often jostling passers-by, who looked round in astonishment at the retreating figure in a black overcoat, his hat worn dead centre. At a corner, up would go the inside shoulder and 'Wheeee!' he pivoted round on it in a camp imitation of a 1920s gangster hugging the wall. One of Bill's few breaks with anonymity. In every other way he looked like a respectable middle-aged man, hurrying down the street, holding his hat against the wind, not the sort of man to slither round a corner as if he had a Thompson machine gun in a cello case, though this was one of his models. How William loved the film *The Godfather*, he talked about it all the time. Bill was delighted to see that one of the young men he used to sell heroin to in New York played a minor role in the film: 'Nice to see one of my old customers getting ahead in the world... yuk, yuk!' This naturally led on to a fond remembrance of how he and Bill Garver used to cut the heroin they were dealing by 50 per cent; and yet they still gave the best deal in town.

One evening Bill, Antony Balch, Johnny Brady and I went to La Capaninna to eat and Bill sped on ahead, leaving the rest of us a half-block behind. When we caught up with him at the restaurant he grinned: 'It's amazing what I am able to do with my super O-T powers!' 'O-T' meant an 'Operating Thetan' in Scientology jargon. Antony laughed; he had reached the clear stage in Scientology too, before giving it up. Scientology was something Bill had been toying with since 1959, though he had been thrown out of the organisation in a 'condition of treason' for running 300 hours of 'squirrel techniques' on himself – self administered e-meter tests. Bill was interested in their systems and programmes but regarded L. Ron Hubbard himself as a complete charlatan.

Bill was first introduced to Scientology by Brion Gysin who had known some of the early Scientologists in Tangier in the late fifties. This involvement had unfortunate results. A Scientologist called Mary Cooke arrived from Algiers with her husband and 'invested' in Brion's restaurant, 2001 Nights. 'Those bastards, they took everything I had and then threw me out without a penny!' Brion shouted. I asked him why he thought William was so interested in Scientology; he had been running auditing sessions on himself for months. Brion said, 'Ian Sommerville says Bill is interested in it because he wants to have power over people.' But Brion didn't think this was the case; to him it was a typical Burroughs investigation, unplanned, poorly organised, sloppily conducted but done with such thoroughness that he inevitably got results and learned from it. He said Bill had done exactly the same with mirror-gazing and with cut-ups.

There were some areas in which William and I did not agree; the principal one being the newly emergent women's movement. Burroughs was famously misogynistic but I found that his position changed from day to day, depending on who was there. Around Ian Sommerville, for instance, he was vehemently anti-women, whereas with me he was prepared to discuss his position. His upbringing in pre-war St Louis society led him to assign gender roles and to believe in certain stereotypes as fixed, rather than changeable. He told me: 'If Women's Liberation are in favour of what they say they are then I'm for them one hundred per cent but my experience has been that women just want everything they can get. In fact, almost as a definition, women want it all: "Give me everything!" I'd be happy if I never saw another woman in my life...'

It was not that he regarded women as inferior; only the day before, Bill had said, 'Mary McCarthy is my spiritual sister,' and told me that he regarded Jane Bowles as one of the finest fiction writers of the century. It was a question of behaviour. In his youth William had a number of girlfriends and after the war, when he was hanging out with Kerouac and Ginsberg, he continued to see women, even though his preference was for men. I asked whether he ever had a scene with Kerouac and he said no: 'Jack wasn't a real homosexual though he did have relations with a number of men such as Allen and Gore Vidal.' I got a sense that William was not attracted to him. In William's opinion, Kerouac didn't enjoy sex and never had a good time: 'Jack would suggest we all go out and try to get laid, but often as not he would go home alone. Sexually he was a failure.'

9 1972

a condition of treason

In 1972, when I was seeing a lot of Bill in London, he was doing quite a few experiments with photography – a continuation of the superimpositions and collages he did in Tangier in the mid-sixties – and continuing his experiments with Scientology techniques. Both of these were frequent subjects of discussion over drinks and dinner. He had been working on Scientology e-meter routines with John MacMasters, the neat, silver-haired Englishman of a certain age who helped Hubbard found the Church of Scientology, and who was the world's first clear. Clears are those who have completed the first level of Scientology processing. An auditor reads out a series of long questionnaires while the student holds the terminals of an e-meter – a galvanometer which measures the change in the electrical resistance of the skin caused by emotional stress. If a question gets a reading then it is explored over and over until it results in a floating needle. When all of the questions are dealt with, the student is then 'clear'. Clears were numbered chronologically, beginning with MacMasters.

He and Hubbard had since fallen out and John was being subjected to harassment by Hubbard's organisation. I often ran into MacMasters at Bill's apartment as he frequently came over in the afternoon to assist Bill with his scientology auditing while I was working on Bill's archives. One time he told us that he woke up one morning lying on the floor of his bedroom, covered in marks and bruises. He claimed that this was the result of a psychic attack by the Sea Org. (It couldn't have been a physical attack as Sea Org is a Scientology abbreviation for Sea Organisation, which at that time was moored off Casablanca protecting Hubbard's yacht.) 'If only I had been there to save you with my karate, my dear,' sympathised Bill. Bill was practising karate but had a few problems with it. The instruction book said that he should obtain an ironing board to practise chops on but he bought a metal one from Fortnum and Mason instead of the wooden one required and bruised his hand.

Bill described his experiences at the Scientology World head-quarters in Saint Hill, East Grinstead, where he took an advanced course. He was almost caught snooping round Hubbard's house armed with a camera; he had been intending to claim he was a plumber if caught. 'I sat there in Saint Hill and I didn't tell them the biggest withhold of all, that was, "I hate your guts, you pink sons of bitches." One of the auditors caught me in the closet and he said, "Have you had any bad thoughts about Mary Sue Hubbard?" He said, "I'm getting a strong reading."

'Boy, that was made to get a reading! So I said I was jealous because she was so good looking and he said, "You're getting a floating needle."' William gave a big grin. 'I don't know what that was supposed to mean, whether that was in sympathy or what!... All that time I didn't know how I managed to avoid getting a withhold on hating Ron Hubbard's big fat face. I would be sitting in a reception room and some shiny-faced new pre-clear would say, "What do you think of Ron's new directions?" and I'd say, "Oh, I'm sure he knows what he's doing. Heh! Heh!"' Brion said that William was the only person he knew ever to have come out of Scientology with more than he took in. He used their question-and-answer e-meter routines as the format for many routines of his own and his short story 'Ali's Smile' was based on his experience at the Scientology centre. He used it as a chapter in *Exterminator!* The 'Dead Child' section of *The Wild Boys* was also written at Saint Hill.

Bill loved to talk about snakes, particularly puff adders and black mambas and said that his favourite was the spitting cobra. When John MacMasters said that he had been spat at by one Bill was ecstatic: 'All my life I've wanted to meet a man who's been spat at by a spittin' cobra! Did it getcha?' John said it fell short by about twelve feet but that had been close enough for him. Bill went into tremendous detail about the two darts of blinding spittle that the snake aims at its victim's eyes. This naturally led to Bill telling us about another of his favourite snakes, the King Cobra. 'I've never heard of a King Cobra on a psychiatrist's couch saying, "Oh, Doctor, I do terrible things to everyone, I just feel poisonous!"' Much laughter. Bill quoted a passage from *African Genesis*, which showed how death only comes from individuation and that all pre-individuation creatures such as the amoeba never die; they exist for ever by cell division unless the lake dries up. 'The introduction of form is the introduction of death!' said Bill in a sonorous voice. That pretty much wrapped up the evening.

One evening we were dining at La Cucaracha, the Mexican restaurant on Greek Street, with some other people when, after many margaritas and jugs of sangria, John MacMasters leaned over to Bill and in a stage whisper said: 'I have never told you this before, Bill, but I feel that I really should let you know.'

Bill looked slightly uneasy: 'What's that, John?'

'In my previous life, the previous one to this one, I was Rudolph Valentino.'

William pursed his lips in his guppy imitation and twitched a couple of times: 'Really, John? Most inneresting.' One could see Bill's respect for MacMasters melting away, like a snowdrift in a rainstorm. Rather than ask him what it had been like to play next to Gloria Swanson, Bill changed the subject by summoning the house guitarist and asking him to play 'La Cucaracha' for the millionth time. Bill sang along in a cracked voice and tipped the man a pound, but complained that he had left out the verse about smoking pot. Bill then loudly sang the missing verse, which caused a few looks in our direction from other tables.

Whereas the Scientologists had publicised the fact that Burroughs had become a clear, they said nothing about the fact that they had now placed him in 'a condition of treason' for 'squirrel techniques'. Bill got so fed up with their criticisms that he decided to mount a sound-and-image attack on their London headquarters at 37 Fitzroy Street in Bloomsbury. This was a technique he had written about quite extensively and was a frequent subject of dinner conversation.

After attending the Democratic Party Convention in Chicago in 1968 as a reporter for *Esquire* magazine, and witnessing the police riot there, he became interested in the more practical applications of cut-ups as weapons. He approached the idea initially through his experiments with tape recorders: 'It's more of a cultural takeover, a way of altering the consciousness of people rather than a way of directly obtaining political control… simply by the use of tape recorders. As soon as you start recording situations and playing them back on the street you are creating a new reality. When you play back a street recording, people think they're hearing real street sounds and they're not. You're tampering with their actual reality.'

His experiments suggested to him that by taking photographs and making recordings in or near someone's premises, then returning to play back the previous tape and take more photographs, he was able to disrupt the time–space continuum enough to cause some change in existing reality: 'I have frequently observed that this simple operation – making recordings and taking pictures of some location you wish to discommode or destroy, then playing recordings back and taking more pictures – will result in accidents, fires, removals, especially the last. The target moves.'

He headed for Fitzrovia and took photographs and made tape recordings, returning week after week. Sure enough, within a couple of months the Scientologists moved to 68 Tottenham Court Road. Encouraged, Bill stepped up the pressure, taping and photographing their new centre, but this time without success. They still occupy

Barry Miles

Bill Burroughs shooting at targets in his St James's flat, 1972. The gun is a Webley air pistol

the same building today. Bill wondered whether maybe they had countered his attack with a defensive move of their own.

He was, however, encouraged by the Scientologists relocating, and continued with his experiments. This time he turned his weapons on an easier target: the Moka Bar at 29 Frith Street, Soho, London, London's first ever espresso bar. The reason for the operation was 'outrageous and unprovoked discourtesy and poisonous cheese-cake'. Bill began the attack on 3 August 1972, making no effort to disguise his activities. 'They are seething in there. The horrible old proprietor, his frizzy-haired wife and slack-jawed son, the snarling counterman. I have them and they know it.' Bill returned every week to play the previous day's recordings on his Philips cassette machine and take more photographs – usually only one or two on each reel. Their business fell off and they kept shorter and shorter hours. On 30 October 1972, the Moka Bar closed. Later the premises were reopened as the Queens Snack Bar – a name that gave Bill a certain degree of satisfaction.

Brion Gysin flew in from Tangier on 6 September to work on the script of the *Naked Lunch* film, bringing with him his own papers for the archive. He moved into flat 22, which had been empty and waiting for him for some months. While we were waiting for Brion to arrive – he came on the 10 p.m. flight – I asked Bill whether he had heard about the massacre of the Israeli team at the Munich Olympics the day before, but his only reaction was to look up and say: 'Oh yes, some Arabs killed some Jews.' The next day he told me that eight people had been murdered on a golf course, thinking perhaps I was interested in this type of day-to-day news. He went on to say that he didn't know whether this had occurred in Addis Ababa, Bangkok or wherever; it turned out to be the Virgin Islands. William did later remark, however, that he was not surprised that, when the Israeli reprisal raids killed 300 civilians, including women and children, these deaths were downplayed in the newspapers, something that he attributed to the power of the Jewish lobby. Bill was a cynic, he didn't expect things to get better: 'If everyone had a little tenderness in them, we wouldn't have any problems in the world. But as you know, we have problems. Do you think Nixon has any tenderness? Or Kissinger? They have NO tenderness at ALL!'

Brion arrived full of good humour and, for once, no complaints about his travel arrangements. He wore a brown Moroccan waistcoat and had allowed his hair to grow into ringlets. Despite his public-school accent, and being born in Taplow, right on the River Thames, I always found it difficult to think of him as being English. To me Brion was Continental, a citizen of some unnamed Mediterranean country like Monte Carlo or San Marino, somewhere with a casino and a lot of very old money. Brion, for his part, always maintained that he had been born the wrong colour, in the wrong place, at the wrong time. There had been some mistake. In his novel *The Process* he turned himself into a black. It was always wonderful to see Bill and

Brion together. Brion regarded Bill as the acknowledged master and deferred to him as such; Bill had the highest regard for Brion's intellect and reacted to any praise from him with ill-disguised pleasure.

It was good to have Brion working on the archives because he saw immediately what I was trying to do, whereas Bill had spent much of the time pulling things out from the folders I had established and starting new files for them, using a very different system of classification. Bill was in fact still using the files, and it might have been better if he had not had to sell them. As it was he eventually removed a certain number of pages, and I catalogued the rest. Brion's contribution to the archives was very easy to classify and describe: mostly letters from William – providing both sides of the correspondence – and letters from Alice B. Toklas and Paul Bowles. He brought with him a large number of photographs, some going back to his days on Broadway. One folder turned out to contain a thick pile of eight-by-ten-inch glossy prints of naked Moroccan youths. He had not intended these to join the archive and was rather relieved that customs had not gone through his things as many of them were most explicit. He removed them for his personal use, but not until he had gone through them all, telling me their names and pointing out their best attributes. He placed them in the drawer of his bed table.

In one of Bill's unmarked folders I found some texts in French, obviously typed by Bill, and as Bill was out I asked Brion whether they were in fact Bill's. He said they were. He told me that Bill had a large vocabulary but his accent was so dreadful that he was frequently misunderstood. 'The funniest thing is being in a cab in Paris with Bill and the cab goes past where you want to get off with Bill yelling, "EEcy, goddam it, EECY!"' That evening, after a few drinks, Bill showed Brion all the various things he had written since they last met. Brion remarked how prolific a writer Bill was. William smiled and said: 'I am one of the few writers I know who can say, "*Je suis un homme de lettres*!"' and laughed.

One day Brion came in very upset and flustered because he had been stopped by an elderly woman on Jermyn Street who told him, 'You have a purple nose and it's easy to see the kind of life you lead. You should be ashamed of yourself, young man!' He had been too astonished to reply. Brion's nose was an unfortunate feature, being rather red and bulbous. Brion hated his looks. In his mind's eye he saw himself as suave and sophisticated, a debonair man-about-town, but he was born with his father's Swiss peasant looks: big boned, sandy haired, red faced with large features. He compensated by adopting a rather grand manner. Though permanent lack of funds meant that he could not afford to live luxuriously, he insisted on the best within his limited price range. Thus he had special bread from Jackson's and the strawberry jam was from a certain small village in France. Only the best Earl Grey from Fortnum and Mason could be drunk and, when possible, the restaurant was also first class. He befriended as many rich people as possible: 'Brion's princess set' Bill called them behind his back, and Brion's conversation was peppered with 'I must call the ambassador...'; 'The princess told me...'; 'The minister is expecting my call...'

He did not always behave like that, only when he was trying to impress. There were many sides to him, including the one that was the campaign manager for a black woman union activist who was running for office as a union president on the Brooklyn water-front during the war. 'I show people the side that they want to see,' he confided to me. 'I like to be the person they want me to be. It makes life *sooo* much easier that way.' Thus he was a woman-hater in high queen company, yet his best friend – after Burroughs – was Felicity Mason, his soul sister. He was an artist, filled with art world gossip in the rue de Seine and Cork Street, and became a writer with strong opinions on the avant-garde, and an encyclopedic knowledge of who was sleeping with whom, whenever in the presence of the London literary set. He moved effortlessly from the Joujouka music of Morocco to 'Mick is getting back to me about doing the music later in the week' in London. Needless to say Jagger decided against writing the music for the *Naked Lunch* movie. Brion told me the reason was that Antony had made an ill-advised attempt to proposition him, though it seemed to me more likely that Brion's lyrics were simply not up to scratch.

With Brion's arrival, the quality of gossip improved enormously. Even when discussing the architecture commissioned by Catherine de Medici, Brion made it sound like hot gossip that he had just heard from a courtier. It inspired Bill to recall the European glitterati he had known through Brion. One day, with the files tidied away and the first drinks of the evening poured, Bill sat at his desk, his lips barely moving, his body absolutely still as he told an extremely funny story of how Helena Rubinstein hid her money in her palatial bathroom.

It seems that she had a safe in there which had drawers filled with emeralds and drawers filled with rubies and so on which she would fondle fetishistically while sitting on the toilet. The safe also contained large quantities of money, wrapped in bands. One day she was in there and one of the drawers stuck. She gave it a wrench to free it and tipped over the whole cabinet. The drawers and $20,000 fell on top of her, almost dislocating her shoulder. She shouted for Patrick Higgins, her secretary, to come and assist her. Bill rocked backwards and forwards in silent laughter at the thought of all the money falling on her. Later that day, at a reception, Higgins was steering her through the crowd using one finger on her shoulder to point her towards the most important people in his practised way. She wore an apron of jewels and had a black eye. 'Madam's money hurt her,' explained the implacable Higgins. The way in which Higgins manipulated and directed Madame was always regarded with amusement by his friends, who saw him as a puppet-master.

Brion joined us during the telling of the story and described a party at Barbara Hutton's palace in Tangier. 'All the international set was there in their tiny bikinis with big straw hats pulled down over their faces. Enter Helena Rubinstein guided by Patrick Higgins. Then came a disembodied voice from under one of the hats; no one knew which one: "I always say that Patrick Higgins is the cleverest

Barry Miles

Bill in his seventies flares on
Duke Street, St James's

toymaker of them all." Madame raged.'

Bill laughed and said, 'She left him very little money, of course, because she knew that if she left him a lot he wouldn't have to write a book about her.'

Talk of Tangier led the conversation to Paul and Jane Bowles. Bill recommended Jane Bowles' *Two Serious Ladies* to me with great enthusiasm saying it was one of the best novels ever written. I had not read it and at that time I knew very little about her or her husband, though I had read several of his books, recommended to me by Ian Sommerville. The Paul Bowles cult had not yet started and they were not well-known characters outside Tangier. When Bill told me that Jane had been in a mental institution for years, I asked whether Paul Bowles had other women. Bill and Brion found this most amusing and Bill expressed doubts that Paul Bowles had ever had sex with a woman in his life. 'Jane Bowles was a lesbian of no mean achievement who was brought up by her family to marry a millionaire. She had the petulance of a rich person.' Bill said that she married Bowles when he was an impoverished composer in order to spite her parents. For his part, 'He married her because his parents didn't like Jews.'

One of Brion's better-known projects was the Dreamachine (he spelled it as one word); the only work of art you look at with your eyes closed. Brion had tried, unsuccessfully, to market it through Helena Rubinstein's showrooms. It consists of a cylinder with holes punched in it that rotates at such a speed as to imitate the flicker effect of driving past a row of trees; the alpha rhythm of the brain. When the correct speed of between nine and thirteen flickers per second is attained, the viewer sees geometric patterns, including crosses, even though it is an entirely drug-free experience. Bill had spent hours using the dreamachine and was a great advocate of it. One evening I asked him whether he had ever met Dr W. Grey Walter, the discoverer of the effects of alpha-rhythm flicker. Bill said he had: 'I attended a lecture by Grey Walter in which he was describing a case of a young woman who had an aura, as you do before an epileptic attack. And she was visited before each attack by this very personable young man who was in every sense tactile to her, tactile to the extent that they were able to have completely satisfactory amorous encounters.

'Then there was another woman patient who was visited regularly by the devil, who was very leathery and had a long tail. So Grey wired her up, got the terminals stuck on her head and pressed a few buttons. What happened was that the devil appeared wearing a homburg hat. Walter pressed a few more buttons and the devil tipped his hat to her and disappeared for ever. All this is caused by the application of the correct electrical impulses to the brain. Now what is the point in spending years in meditation to try and conjure up a phantom when science can give you one in seconds?

Any mental state can be induced instantly electrically... This new interest in Eastern religions which is sweeping the States is no different than the wave after wave of strange Eastern religions which swept through Rome just before the collapse of the empire. Fashionable society ladies vying with each other over holy men.

'I read of a Tibetan who walled himself up away from the world and had food pushed through a hole in the wall and eventually he was able to manifest a completely tactile phantom. So obviously he had it made, he just stayed there and played with his phantom for the rest of his life. I mean, what else do you need?' This was an old theme for Burroughs, who had written about it as far back as 1960 in *The Exterminator*.

One day in September I brought in my camera to take some photographs of him. He sat behind his desk after placing the typewriter in the absolute centre. He pushed his hands forward and opened his eyes wide in a sinister stare. It was an image which suggested coldness to most people but which came partly from nervousness, a dislike of small talk and a painful sense of self-awareness. This produced awkward silences in those people who liked to chatter on. If a silence occurred, I noticed that Bill rarely heard what you said when you first broke it, he became so completely absorbed in his own train of thoughts and associations. I took some photographs of him fooling with his air pistol and he explained the feelings of security he got when he was armed. 'There is only one freedom and that is freedom from fear,' Bill told me. 'You are scared to walk the streets of New York, so you get a couple of bodyguards to walk with you and it's much better. A gun can make you feel a lot better, knowing you can deal with trouble. Two skinheads start to make trouble with you in the street; you pull out your gun and blast them in the belly. Now if two bodyguards make you feel good, what if you have a million? Stalin had it made, man! All this shit about rich people being lonely and everything. They have got it made! The richer people get, the more alike they get. People with a hundred million dollars or over are virtually part of the same organism. . .

Buried under layers of grey shale.' This was a good theme and he soon developed it: 'I think rich people develop this green fishy aura around them! "You like to be a feeshee, mister? Grow nice gills?"'

William spent the second half of the sixties writing *The Wild Boys* and *The Job*, and he had so much material left over that it overflowed into *The Revised Boy Scout's Manual*, *Ah Pook Is Here* and *Port of Saints*, which is really *Wild Boys Part Two*. William used his scrapbooks as a way of developing the characters in his own mind, selecting pictures of boys from newspapers and magazines who could play Wild Boy roles, including photographs of boys he knew. One narrative, the 'Frisco Kid' section in *The Wild Boys*, was suggested by an 1882 photograph of Front Street, Nome, Alaska. On one occasion William asked me to take some photographs of him and Johnny 'coming in the door'. Five or six times he and Johnny walked into the room and I took a picture. Some of them were pasted into the scrapbook and contributed to the composite character he was building at the time.

Many of these images had strong meanings for William; when I was working on the description of his archives there were several instances where folders just had photographs on the front and William insisted that the picture was the name of the folder, which was fair enough but it did make filing a bit tricky. Burroughs regarded the illustrations as integral to *Port of Saints* but the publisher, Covent Garden Press, which was also the printer, was nervous about sending out some of the photographs of naked young men to have screen prints made. Fortunately my friend, the designer Pearce Marchbank, now living with my ex-wife Sue, had his own PMT machine and was able to make PMTs (photo-mechanical transfers) of those images of naked young men that a conventional print shop might find questionable. PMT was a process that converted a normal photograph into a grid of dots that could be printed by photolithography. Covent Garden Press did not have a PMT camera, which was a huge apparatus, taller than a man and requiring a darkroom of its own. William had revived the cut-up technique for *Port of Saints*, written in the early seventies, and sometimes, as I was sorting through his papers for the archive, I would surreptitiously watch as he cut pages of typescript into quarters and moved them against each other, typing up any new lines that he liked.

William needed someone like Ian Sommerville around to do basic secretarial work; a role I sometimes performed as Johnny was clearly useless at such things. William was short of money and needed to put another book together as soon as possible. He decided to assemble a collection of existing pieces and somehow link them. He found manuscripts and tearsheets from magazines and put them in rough order. I took them to the stationer's to be copied. Though copy shops did not yet exist, there were a few Xerox machines available, but they were very expensive so we made a careful selection before investing in copies. I was critical of some of Bill's choices for his new book; for instance, he was going to call it a novel and yet one of the pieces he chose to include was a factual report on the 1968 Democratic Party Convention called 'The Coming of the Purple Better One' that originally appeared in *Esquire*. To me it didn't belong, but though William reluctantly agreed, he couldn't find anything better so this strange mixture of pieces was packaged up and sent off to his agent. It appeared in 1973 as *Exterminator!*, which he subtitled: 'a novel'.

This was the last book Bill wrote in England before returning to New York in 1974. By then he was thoroughly fed up with London. He hated the fact that he could not get a meal late at night; he hated the absurd licensing hours which deprived him of an afternoon drink; he hated the miserably small measures of spirits and their exorbitant prices and the publican bellowing 'Time, gentlemen, please!' at 11 p.m. when in New York the bars closed at 2 a.m. He hated the surly shop assistants who referred to each other as 'my colleague'. He hated the rotten weather and the fact that central heating barely existed; his flat came equipped with night storage heaters that gathered heat at night from cheap-rate electricity and gave it out in the morning and afternoon, leaving the flat cold in the

William Burroughs playing the President of the United States in David Z. Mairowitz's 1971 play
Flash Gordon and the Angels

evenings. These eventually broke completely, and he told the janitor
to tear them out and get him some regular electric bar heaters. He
hated the titillating yet prudish attitude of the tabloid press and lack
of any real pornography. 'Never go too far in any direction is the
basic rule on which Limey Land is built. The Queen stabilizes the
whole stinking shithouse...' he wrote in *Exterminator!*

Only two years before he had written that he could not stand
New York and could not possibly live there; now he found London
to be even worse. When Allen Ginsberg arranged a teaching post
for him at New York University he accepted immediately. I helped
him to pack his things and arranged for storage at Harrods, which
shipped them to New York when he found an apartment. He sorted
which manuscripts to store and which to take with him. After he
left I sold his furniture for him and threw away everything that we
couldn't sell. I missed him.

10 1973

a visit to wilhelm reich's orgonon

When I was at art college in the early sixties I was very intrigued by the work of Austrian psychoanalyst Wilhelm Reich. As a Marxist he was in the spearhead of the fight against fascism in the thirties, but his analysis of the sexual disfunctioning of the masses resulted in him being expelled from the German Communist Party and his books being banned. Ironically, at the same time Hitler personally put a price on his head for the devastating psychoanalytic study of *Mein Kampf* in Reich's book *The Mass Psychology of Fascism* and had his books burned.

Reich had been the longest-serving member of the Freud seminar, and his book *Character Analysis* made a number of contributions to standard Freudian analytic practice. It was when he took Freud's ideas about sex to their logical conclusion in his book *The Function of the Orgasm* that problems began to develop. Reich believed that neurosis was caused by a blocked sex drive, and in the course of developing techniques to free up 'locked-in' sex energy he thought he had discovered a new energy form that he called 'orgone' energy, which was the life force itself. Shortly afterwards he developed a method of concentrating this energy in what were known as 'orgone accumulators'. If you sat in one of these and got charged up, you were on your way to recovery. In the 1940s orgone accumulators were very popular in intellectual circles in New York, particularly among the members of the Beat Generation, when Reich's books were a major subject of conversation. His sex theories formed the basis of much of Beat Generation attitudes and Allen Ginsberg told me a number of amusing stories about people getting charged up in orgone boxes before an orgy.

William Burroughs usually had an accumulator unless he was living in a very small apartment. In fact the last orgone accumulator I sat in – in the early nineties – belonged to Burroughs; he had it in his backyard, next to the goldfish pond, at his small wooden house in Lawrence, Kansas. It was home-made, with a circular window in the door, and had been invaded by big black spiders. He liked to smoke a joint in there and get himself charged up with that good orgone energy. Sitting in there, I felt the usual slight tingling sensation that I had experienced back in the early sixties when I built my own box, but whether this was imaginary or caused by focusing my attention on my body I can't tell. Burroughs firmly believed Reich's orgone theories and had done so since the late forties. Over the years he wrote a number of pieces about accumulators and Reich:

...the orgone box does have a definite sexual effect; I [...] made a little one from an army-style gas-can covered with burlap and cotton wool and wrapped around with gunny sack, and it was a potent sexual tool. The orgones would stream out of the nozzle of the gas can. One day I got into the big accumulator and held the little one over my joint and came right off. That used to be one of Cocteau's party tricks – take off all his clothes, lie down, and come off, no hands.

William Burroughs: from My Experiences with
Wilhelm Reich's Orgone Box

Brion Gysin told me that he met Wilhelm Reich a number of times in 1946 at the house of a woman who ran his Children's Institute in Greenwich Village. Brion distinctly recalled that they were all crazy and that there appeared to be special classes in masturbation, which were kept rather a dark secret. Anything to do with sex was regarded with opprobrium in those dark days.

Reich's belief that blocked sexual energy caused anxiety had led him to develop a system of massage – he believed the blockages were manifested physically in a rigid musculature and could therefore be broken down: a system he called vegetotherapy. Out of this and his massage theory came Carl Rogers and the Encounter Movement, EST, Arthur Janov and Primal Therapy – the scream therapy that John Lennon found so fulfilling – Ida Rolf's deep massage, Eric Berne and Transactional Analysis, Fritz Perls and Gestalt Therapy, and many others. All have their origins, to a greater or lesser extent, in Wilhelm Reich's vegetotherapy. Reich was caught in the all-American consumerist, conformist, Cold War fifties. He was obsessed by flying saucers, atomic energy (Death Orgone Radiation) and Stalinism.

To give proper credence to his ideas and to maintain a respectable public persona, Reich applied scientific method to even his craziest schemes with carefully documented archives. All his findings were published in scientific looking papers complete with the requisite amount of new terminology and acronyms – HIG, DOR, Melinor, Uror, Or, Orgone, Orgonome – just like the work of the Scientologists of a later era. In the fifties Reich was reinforced by a group of believers also in retreat from the horrors and sterility of mechanistic McCarthyite America. Possessed of sufficient funds, isolated in a distant natural setting of great beauty, Reich prepared the perfect conditions for himself and his followers to go logically right around the bend.

Despite his more recondite ideas, Reich's theories of the importance of regular orgasms were a vital part of the sixties sexual revolution. Reich's ideas – or in many cases a travesty of Reich's ideas – were a major part of the theoretical basis for the free love movement, for sex orgies and 'swinging'. The hippy slogan 'Make Love Not War' meant literally that: a belief that a peaceful world would result from making love to as many people as possible.

The Wilhelm Reich Museum is in Rangeley, Maine, up by the Canadian border, but it was open only two days a week, on Tuesdays

Wilhelm Reich in 1944. In August 1956 the American authorities burned several tons of his books

and Fridays during the months of July and August. My old friend John Howe was visiting from London and this seemed like a good trip to make from New York to enable him to see something of the American countryside. My friends Rick Fields and Sara Vogler also wanted to come. Ann, unfortunately, couldn't take time off work. We set out, stopping for a picnic lunch in Annandale-on-Hudson on the campus of Bard College. Students sat around on the grass in the bright sunshine, looking out over the Hudson. One of the co-eds got up from her group of friends and walked over to ask casually whether she could have one of our sandwiches. She was completely naked. John was not used to this sort of thing, even though he lived in Notting Hill. The English hippy scene never involved much nudity; we haven't the weather for it, and it never entered the college lifestyle in the way it was absorbed in the States.

The liberal New England colleges had come a long way in the previous decade. This same casual attitude prevailed when we arrived with no prior warning to visit a friend of Sara's, who lived in the woods near Brattleboro, Vermont. She seemed unsurprised to see us, took us to a nearby lake for a skinny dip and easily made space for us all to stay over. She would have come with us, but she was in the middle of a firing. Her home-made kiln stood next to the wooden cabin, filled with her pots and plates. We made an early start out across New Hampshire the next morning. The farmland gave way to huge pine-covered mountains crossed by unsurfaced roads and fast-flowing streams filled with pebbles, and everywhere was the penetrating fragrance of pine.

At the end of the last dirt road we found the Rangeley tourist office. Orgonon, the man said, was up the road a-piece. The nearest bar was down the road a-piece. The bar was in a huge log cabin filled with loggers in plaid shirts and baseball caps, and despite our long hair everyone was friendly. The toilets were designated as 'pointers' and 'setters'. Moose heads hung on the walls and Sara got her finger nipped by a caged mongoose.

A large wooden sign with white lettering indicated: ORGONON. The drive wound through scrub and trees; it must have been so familiar to Reich the years he lived here. We arrived at a large clearing and found a chain across the road. They were closed for lunch, so we sat eating wild blueberries and taking photographs of each other standing under the 'Wilhelm Reich Museum' sign until 2 p.m.

The museum opened on time. Someone took the chain down and drove off in a cloud of dust. The first building we came to was the students' laboratory, where much of Reich's research work was done. I had a sense of déjà vu, having seen faded photographs of Reich in his white lab coat bending over the microscopes surrounded by attentive students when I first read his books. I recognised the room, now empty, with dusty long bare lab tables. The only thing in the room was the wooden prototype DOR-buster that Tom Ross built for Reich. These were supposed to break up clouds and produce rain; DOR was bad orgone energy: Death Orgone Radiation. It looked like a 12-foot anti-aircraft gun only with lots of barrels and a hose leading from each one to the base, where it would have been connected to an accumulator. The strange bits of plywood hammered together looked like a Louise Nevelson sculpture. Mr Ross was Reich's handyman and had built the orgone accumulators for him. Across the road I saw the outline of another DOR buster through the dirty glass of a locked storage room. Everything was locked and closed.

The road climbed steeply through trees. I remembered Peter Reich's autobiography and how he ran frantically up the hill to warn his father that the Food and Drug Administration men had arrived at last to arrest him for building orgone accumulators in defiance of an FDA ruling. We took a final sharp left and the buildings come into view, once again familiar from the illustrations to Reich's books and Dušan Makavejev's film *W.R. The Mysteries of the Organism*. There was the observatory building. We parked in the lot as directed by an elderly man. It was Tom Ross himself. 'Do you want to see the house first or the grave?'

I had expected to find the place overgrown, with strange rusting orgone guns sticking up through weeds, rotted smashed accumulators slipping into the edge of the lake; instead it looked like a National Trust property with neatly clipped lawns, flower beds and wooden park seats. Reich's death suddenly became real to me. When we had to decide between first viewing the grave or the house, it made me realise he had become a part of history. The Reich that lived on in the counter-culture with his guilt-free sex and massage techniques had very little to do with anything at Orgonon, at least for me. Mr Ross said that they had a particularly good cloudbuster down by the grave which we could get a close look at, so we decided to see the house first as it was open only for two hours.

Towering over the parking lot was a multi-barrelled cloudbuster surrounded by a neat hedge. Reich used it to break up thunderclouds by draining them of orgone energy and depositing it in the water table to which the barrels were all 'earthed' by metal tubes. It had a stopper on each barrel. In Peter Reich's *Book of Dreams* he described them using the cloudbuster to chase away a flying saucer. Reich

Orgonon, Maine, 1973. The lab and living quarters

saw a lot of flying saucers; he thought they were powered by orgone energy. He believed George Adamsky's books about flying saucer sightings and was convinced that the occupants of the saucers were ill intentioned. He also thought that Eisenhower was protecting him by flying air force jets over Orgonon and was convinced that Ike was going to come and stay one day. A room was prepared in anticipation. Sad to say Reich sent the only plans of his orgone engine to the Pentagon, where they were never seen again. A. S. Neill said that he saw it in operation. It is hard to believe that this is the same Reich whose *Mass Psychology of Fascism* helped inspire the 1968 French revolution and whose books – bootleg copies of *The Function of the Orgasm* – were used to bombard the police during the Berlin University riots.

The building was very 1950s modern and solid, all balconies and Bauhaus plate glass. A local girl from Rangeley charged us $1 each and we began the guided tour. Reich was always called 'Dr Reich' and great reverence was given to all artefacts connected with him: 'This is the carved cane given to Dr Reich by the anthropologist Malinowski.' A very nice one it was, too.

'This is the mail-order catalogue which Dr Reich ordered most of his furniture from.' Amazing! A well worn catalogue with Reich's familiar impatient scribble encircling chairs, coffee tables, rugs… And there they were, a museum of 1950s Americana: a giant settee, huge blockbuster armchairs, heavy square shapes. An enormous battleship-sized television set, a weighty hi fi, lamp stands, coffee-tables, everything. 'Nothing has been touched since Dr Reich left here,' she said. No mention of where he went to when he left.

In a small exhibition room various models of the orgone accumulator were on display. They still couldn't bring a real one on to the premises because of the 1956 FDA court injunction that had declared most of Reich's books advertisements for 'a worthless medical device' and ordered their destruction in the last old-style book burning in the United States. The trustees of Orgonon were worried, probably unnecessarily, that the authorities might do it again and didn't want to run the risk of the file copies in their library being burnt.

At the head of the stairs an alcove contained many photographs of Reich from his cancer research days in Scandinavia. And there was Reich's desk by the window, with several high powered microscopes, slides and, neatly folded on his blotter, his glasses, as if waiting his return. Corny yet evocative. Here was an orgonoscope: a modified Geiger counter to measure orgone levels. Here photographic enlargements of microscope pictures labelled in German, a large X-ray photograph of the orgone field between the palms of the hands and, on the wall, the famous signed dedicated photograph of Freud, the old man himself looking stern. All the illustrations familiar to me from Reich's books, the drawing of adolescents from

Wilhelm Reich: 24 March 1987–
3 November 1957

People in Trouble, and Reich's paintings: crude, expressionistic daubs after Edvard Munch; I never thought I would see the originals. All my impressions of Reich gathered over the years fell into place like a jigsaw puzzle.

Naturally we wanted to see Reich's bedroom but all felt slightly embarrassed, as if we were intruding, for here if anywhere his theories were put to the test. What kind of orgasm did the author of *The Function of the Orgasm* have? He was married to Ilse Ollendorf until they decided to separate in 1952. This was where they slept. A double bed, a simple pallet against the wall. It was such a symbol of Reich's subversive ideas that vandals broke in and took a shit in the middle of it. The wall behind was covered in a huge, crudely executed painting of a leaping man painted by Reich himself: a flat white mural with a huge red naked figure, five feet long, with a big red erect cock like a cave painting. It was called 'The Messenger' and represented Mercury-Hermes. I could imagine Reich dancing about as he slapped the paint on and stood back for a better view. There was a small bronze, cast from a clay model by Reich, of the same subject.

On the windowsill stood a small framed reproduction of Rodin's 'The Kiss' and a Japanese woodcut. The walls were three-quarters glass, opening out over a wide balcony on the roof of the floor below. Here he would walk at night, looking at the millions of stars, or in the day, even in bed, he could see out over the lakes and mountains, an endless view. A plain bare room, vibrant with light and the wall painting.

The library contained many interesting works: leather-bound collected works of Freud in German, *Das Kapital* and other works by Marx, two volumes of Kautsky. The standard modern authors, Hemingway, etc. One whole bay had nothing but Reich's own works, including of course all the rare ones: the two volumes of *Conspiracy*, bound volumes of the *Orgone Energy Bulletin* and *The International Journal for Sex Economy and Orgone Research*. The shiny white 'scientific' bindings looking so official and proper, as Reich liked it. In the hallway hung a pen-and-ink drawing of Summerhill by its founder, A. S. Neill. Neill, after all, remained loyal to Reich the man, if secretly sceptical about Orgonomy. He took the easy way out, claiming that it was all too scientific for him.

The top room of the observatory contained, naturally, the telescope and other weather measuring equipment, wind vanes and the like. Paintings were piled up everywhere. Reich painted up here at night after he'd done everything else. He slept little. Once again, the amazing view out over the mountains and lakes, mountains and more lakes. A view one could never tire of. He claimed he saw orgone energy flickering over the lakes. It would be dead easy to see orgones from here; little white flashes, friendly little blue orgones!

Old Mr Ross took us to see the grave with its well-known bust by Jo Jenkins on top: a photograph of it is on the cover of *Selected Writings*. It stood in a small clearing on a rocky bluff surrounded by thick woods on three sides, looking out over the lakes. Next to it stood a DOR-buster; a strange science fiction instrument pointing down at the grave, at Reich, its tubes corked. The whole thing looked like a Flash Gordon movie set mixed up with a Richard Stankiewicz abstract expressionist sculpture. Reich had painted this one flat black and signed it WR in big white letters, so even he regarded them as art objects. Mr Ross admitted that he touched the paint up now and then to keep it fresh. A bronze plaque on the side commemorated the discovery of orgone energy.

John asked Mr Ross whether he realised that Reich was a great man when he first met him. 'Oh yes.' He smiled quietly. 'I felt that!' Now he just tends the lawns and trees philosophically, the excitement of the fifties long gone. 'We used to follow the spaceships with the cloudbuster,' he said. 'It made them go away!' He said that Reich gave him credit in his books as an Orgonometric Technician but he didn't feel he deserved it. He just designed and built such machines as Reich requested, and didn't fully understand all the scientific theory behind it. One could tell that he was proud, though. Did he get on with Reich? 'I wouldn't have stayed around here ten years if I didn't!' He laughed.

What to make of it all? There is no doubt that Reich became delusional and paranoid later in his life but who can blame him? He wasn't protected enough for such a venture. The bearers of the 'emotional plague', in the form of the Food and Drug Administration, came and seized him. They burned his books, smashed his equipment and threw him in jail. And on 3 November 1957, Reich, white haired and frail, died in Lewisburg Penitentiary of a broken heart. I think he was poetically correct about many things, even though a lot of the theories were crackpot. The Nazis burned his books and Hitler put him on his personal hit list. The Americans burned his books because they advocated complete sexual freedom. To get up the nose of both the Nazis and the American authorities means he must have been doing something right.

11 1973

harry smith at the chelsea

One of the first people I got to know at the Hotel Chelsea back in 1969 was Harry Smith. Harry is perhaps the only genius I've ever met; he was talented in so many areas that he had a whole series of parallel reputations in different subjects. As an ethnomusicologist he was renowned for compiling the *Anthology of American Folk Music*, the standard collection upon which the sixties folk music revival was based, whereas to film-makers he was an award-winning auteur who invented several forms of animation, coloration and screening techniques and whose abstractions connected America with European modernism; in the art world he was an influential painter, much of it based on Kabbalistic themes; in the world of the occult he was respected for his knowledge of the work of Aleister Crowley as well as the tarot and for his concordance of the Enochian language; to anthropologists he was famous for his recordings of Native American peyote ceremonies, his collection of Seminole Indian patchwork, his catalogue of Ukrainian painted Easter eggs, and his method of scoring the working of string figures or 'cat's cradles'; in fact there were very few areas where Harry did not display dazzling erudition. He could also be very rude, drunk, abusive and even violent.

Harry was tiny, thin and hunchbacked. He hid a weak chin with an untrimmed, unkempt beard and his grey hair was a tangle of dirty locks, roughly pinned in a tangled bun at the back with stray strands falling around his face; he was an early example of a white man wearing dreadlocks. He seemed to be shrinking; his cheap work clothes big on him.

His interest in Crowley was personal as he sometimes claimed to be Crowley's illegitimate son and had lots of his notebooks and paraphernalia. Harry sometimes tutored some of the richer ladies living in the hotel in the magical arts, for which he charged a substantial fee. When the Jefferson Airplane lived in the hotel, Marty Balin spent hundreds of hours talking with Harry, whom he regarded as his teacher. Some years later Harry presented him with a bill for several thousand dollars. The guitarist was horrified; he had thought they were friends. Harry rarely left the hotel. Mostly he hung around in the lobby asking people for money. When he had enough, he would film a few more minutes of his latest film, *Mahagonny*. Jonas Mekas, the head of the film-makers' co-op who also lived in the Chelsea, regarded Harry as a genius. When Harry introduced us, he claimed that Mekas, who was Lithuanian, did not speak English. Mekas grinned and kept silent.

I would often visit Harry in the mid-afternoon at his room in the Chelsea. That was the best time to talk to him because he hadn't yet taken the pills and vodka that would transform him into an ill-behaved gnome. Harry always had problems and I was always one to lend a sympathetic ear. He rather hopelessly discussed his finances and bleak future. He could not travel because of his two budgerigars. There was always something that stopped Harry from moving – before the birds it was Fishy. He once told me that 'Feeeshie', as he called it, was the King of the Fishes and had granted him three wishes. Fishy also used to answer questions by swimming a certain number of circles in his pottery bowl. According to Harry, Fishy once communicated to him the true value of π. Harry claimed that most conversation between fish consists of boasting to each other how good they taste. To this end they had even evolved a line down each side of their body to show where to fillet them. Harry also had a fly in his room, of which he was inordinately fond, and a mouse that he used to feed on Saltine crackers, but Fishy held the key to Harry's heart. Harry gave it toys to play with, talked to it and fed it morsels from his mouth. He gave it a large-scale model of its own brain to swim around. Fishy cost 15 cents from the corner dime store and Harry was most upset when it died. Not being able to afford a pet's funeral, Harry buried it economically by flushing it down the toilet.

Harry had a complicated relationship with nature, be it goldfish, birds or the meat on his plate. He came from the country near Bellingham, in Washington State, where, as a child, he saw moose, fox, even a huge brown bear catching salmon as they swam upstream to spawn. His mother worked on the local Lummi Indian reservation and the Indians had told him that he should eat the sacred salmon, that it was all right. There were complex reasons for this; some species had to go through a certain number of incarnations like this and were born to be killed. Harry gave cows as another example, saying that most of them would never have been born at all if mankind did not eat meat. They had a limited time to see the sun and breathe the air. Harry apparently had a friend who was a champion slaughterer and who travelled to international competitions in Europe to slaughter cows. Harry discussed those species of plants that were also dependent on man, such as corn, which could not propagate itself if not picked and planted by man.

As the budgies flew around the room, Harry and I discussed Aleister Crowley. Although I was not that personally interested in Crowley I had recently been in Sussex and visited the chalk cliffs at Beachy Head where Crowley practised his mountain climbing. I told Harry that in the Old Town of Hastings where Crowley used to live, the old people still remembered him. I had visited John Martyn, the folk singer, there, and several of his neighbours remembered Crowley, except that, inexplicably, in their memories he had been turned into a Negro. The transition from black magician to black person not being a very great mental move to them, I suppose. This

Barry Miles

Harry Smith screening film in his room at the Hotel Chelsea, 1970

story delighted Harry, who then recited, verbatim, a large chunk of *The Book of Lies* in Crowley's honour.

Harry told a lot of conflicting stories about Crowley, including the fanciful notion that Crowley might be his father, but the utter lack of a physical resemblance did not allow him to push that idea very far. One frequently told story was of a meeting on a beach that Harry recounted to many people in slightly different ways. He told me that he met Crowley when he was about four years old. His mother took him for a walk on an empty beach near Bellingham, where, obviously by arrangement, they met up with Crowley. He was a kindly gentleman who showed young Harry where to find the quiet rock pools that contained sea anemones. Crowley had quite the opposite effect on Harry's mother, however. She apparently had hysterics and became quite agitated. Harry owned one of Crowley's notebooks, which many of Harry's friends coveted. He destroyed some of the pages at one time in a drunken rage but it remained mostly intact though a little stained.

One of Harry's followers, a wealthy young man, became obsessed with Harry's stories about the mysteries of the Golden Dawn Society and persuaded Harry to lend him the notebook so that he could commission a copy of the magic sword described in its pages. Harry finally allowed himself to be persuaded, a process which no doubt involved a fee of some sort. After a year, the sword was ready, complete with the Enochian inscriptions down its blade, and the young man hastened to bring it to Harry for his approval. On the way over, the young man's motorcycle was involved in an accident and the magic sword was broken in half. There was a hard glint in Harry's eyes when he told this story.

Harry's approach to magic was very down to earth and American. When I asked what effect magic and the occult had had upon his life, he replied, 'Not as much as drugs and alcohol have!' Since I first met him, in June 1969, he had not to my knowledge been involved in any major magical experiments, though he did have one ongoing project. He complained to me about the enormous problems involved in acquiring enough sperm to make a homunculus, the stated aim of several of Crowley's magical workings. To this end he still masturbated daily, though of late he had complained about the size of emission and quality of orgasm. Since he lived entirely on Miller beer, pills and canned mandarin orange slices this was not surprising, and he was never able to fulfil his ambition.

Harry said Crowley did nothing after becoming a junkie and that his most important work was his magical battle with MacGregor

Mathers, the head of the Golden Dawn Society. He telephoned Rosie Gardner who lived in the hotel and who paid Harry for occult instruction and asked her to bring up a first edition of the third issue of Crowley's magazine *Equinox III* for me to see, and after about an hour she showed up. This was the issue in which Crowley broke his vow to the Golden Dawn and published their secret rituals, causing MacGregor Mathers to hurry over from Paris and issue an injunction against him. The court initially agreed with Mathers and prevented the publication, but Crowley won on appeal because, according to Harry, Crowley consecrated a special talisman to the judge, which made him favourable to Crowley's case.

Harry and I had in the meantime been discussing *The Yellow Book*, Beardsley's later drawings and Crowley's two masturbatory books: *Dew Drops from a Curate's Garden* and *White Stains*. 'His layouts were superb and as his money ran out, his production naturally became more lavish,' Harry explained. Harry's favourite Crowley book was *The Book of Lies*. Harry discussed Frank Harris, Oscar Wilde and whether or not Crowley was actually the author of the translation of *The Perfumed Garden*, which he had published as if it were Richard Burton's own translation. Harry was certainly a good advocate for Crowley and made me reconsider his work.

May 29 1973 was Harry's fiftieth birthday. I visited him in his room at the Chelsea and we sat around getting stoned, listening to Gilbert and Sullivan's *The Sorcerer*. Harry particularly liked the song about strawberry jam at the end of side four, which always made us feel a bit peckish. His birthday made him think about his parents, and he said he felt that he had let his father down badly by reacting to his mother's death by becoming a junkie in San Francisco. He felt that he had 'betrayed him'. After saying this, he left the room and spent some time in the toilet down the hall before returning, looking rather more composed. There was no en suite bathroom in Harry's room. He had probably taken some Desoxyn, his favoured amphetamine. The afternoon drifted into a classic Chelsea evening as a group of us went down to the El Quijote, the Chelsea's bar, then accessible with its own door from the hotel lobby and filled with the usual mix of long-term Chelsea residents and a few newcomers.

As usual Peggy Biderman was with us. Peggy worked as a street vendor in Greenwich Village and spent the mornings haunting the thrift shops on 8th Avenue for things to sell. Peggy was the Jewish mother to the hotel: she befriended newcomers such as Patti Smith and Robert Mapplethorpe and commiserated with the old-time residents when they found themselves locked out of their rooms for non-payment of the rent. She was full of life. She knew everyone and her engaging, friendly energy, sympathy and boundless enthusiasm for the residents' most far-fetched schemes made the hotel a better place. She had brought up two daughters at the Fontainebleau in Miami – pronounced by the locals 'the Fountain Blue' – and told me how there would still be gamblers sitting around the pool when she came out of the hotel to take her daughters to school. One morning there was a corpse floating in the pool; no one had noticed. She decided to move to the Hotel Chelsea. Peggy could afford only a single room, with a shared bathroom down the hall on the second floor, but she decorated it with shells and coloured glass found on the beach at Fire Island, and with postcards from the Museum of Modern Art, where for many years she worked in the bookshop.

She was Harry's best friend: she put up with his rudeness, his taunts and tantrums. She had a mole right between her eyebrows that Harry always referred to as her 'third eye'. Harry had a very deep awareness of other people; he seemed able to identify their anxieties and weaknesses as well as their strong points and could be guaranteed to home in on the one area that people did not want to talk about. When he was introduced to the teenage daughter of a friend of mine he immediately commented: 'I see you're old enough to grow a moustache.' The girl burst into tears. He tested everyone, and only after subjecting people to considerable rudeness, including very personal remarks, did he feel secure enough to allow a glimmer of friendship.

With Peggy he was constantly calling her a 'Jewish cunt' and delighted when she would finally crack and snap back at him. They saw each other every day but did not have a sexual relationship. Harry did not like to be touched but said that in his youth he was a very active bisexual. He appeared to have been a non-practising homosexual for many decades. I used to kid him about his relationship with Peggy and once persuaded him to get into bed with her so I could take their photograph together. Surprisingly he agreed, climbed into her bed and allowed me to take one photograph. It was a transparency and I gave it to Peggy, who was ecstatic. They were fully clothed, of course, but he did have his arm around her. There was a lot of genuine affection there.

When I visited Harry a few days after his birthday he was not looking too good. He had recently been hit on the head with a chair by a customer from another table at the El Quijote. 'I used the word "nigger" once too often and the chickens came home to roost!' he explained, chuckling. Actually he didn't know what caused the attack. Though he had used the word 'nigger', he was sitting with two black people at his own table who had not objected. But as Harry said, 'I was also making Mafia jokes, maybe he was one of them.' Now he felt nervous even in the hotel. He had been tipped backwards off of his chair and then hit over the head with it. 'I'm only glad they didn't hit my face.' Dr Gross thought that the wound on his head should be opened up in case some hair had been trapped inside and grew in instead of out. That operation was to take place the next week.

We sat in darkness with the air conditioner on full, surrounded by tottering piles of transparencies and index cards, each stack just waiting to fall over. Some of them appeared to be purposely stacked too high, and balanced right on the edge of the table. There were folders of Kirlian photographs showing the supposed aura surrounding objects, a subject that Harry loved to discourse upon: whether or not leaves really had auras; he thought they did. There were piles of coloured drawings and thick cards on which were mounted Eskimo string figures. Harry practised cat's cradles every day in order to remember them. It was wonderful to watch as he spread the string between the figures of his hands and explained what was happening: 'See, here comes the fisherman, and now he's digging a hole in the ice. And here he's raising his spear. Now he's caught a fish…' and you could see a diagrammatic plan of the action unfold before you as Harry grimaced and twisted the string around his fingers so that loops moved and closed and new lines and shapes were created. He had evolved a form of notation for them, similar in part to ballet scores, but still needed the various starting points for an action, thus the examples glued to pieces of card.

This was just one of his many anthropological investigations. Another was his collection of paper aeroplanes. He had gathered discarded aeroplanes from schoolyards all across the city, carefully noting the ethnic background of their makers and the school's location. They were no good unless he saw who made them. This activity was fraught with danger as he was constantly stopped by security guards, who thought he was a dirty old man; which was how he looked half the time.

His wardrobe bulged with Seminole Indian dresses, each in a plastic cover, so many that the door was tied only half shut with string to prevent it from springing open. The drawers were filled with examples of their beadwork and with other precious objects from Harry's various collections. His own clothes were thrown in a dirty pile on the floor in the corner. The Smithsonian Institute regarded Harry's collection as the most complete in existence, and he had examples of every type of stitching and pattern, each of which had a symbolic meaning. Harry told me he had got to know the Seminoles in Florida when he woke up one morning in the drunk tank along with three or four Indians.

Being Harry, he naturally addressed them in their own language and they got on so well that they took him to their reservation. There he made a film of their symbolic patchwork and typically he shot it in such a way that it worked best if shown against the reed walls of their huts. Periodically Harry would have an amphetamine or an

alcoholic breakdown and start smashing things. When this happened
the Smithsonian sent someone to take the Seminole Indian dresses
away for safe-keeping, giving him a receipt for them until he felt
better again. He was passionately interested in American Indian
culture and was now working on the sleeve for an album of Kiowa
Indian peyote rituals he had recorded back in 1964.

The fuse to the air conditioner blew almost every day and even
one light bulb could overload the circuit and blow it. 'If it gets too
dark I'll light a devotional candle.' Eventually he turned the AC
unit off and played Gilbert and Sullivan's *Iolanthe* and *The Sorcerer*
once more. Inevitably we sometimes talked about the *American
Folk Music Anthology* and Harry told me about the people on it. He
explained the methodology used when he designed the sleeves. The
colours were supposed to represent the four seasons but the manuscript of the sleeve notes for the fourth volume got lost so there were
only three released. Harry had gone on a drunken binge, smashed all
the records and lost the notes. The tape survived but he was unable
to identify all of the people on it and the task of reconstituting the
sleeve notes seemed so enormous that he just gave up on it.

It was late afternoon at the beginning of October 1973 when
Peggy and I knocked on Harry's battered door; there was a large
crack in it where speed freaks had tried to break it down. Harry,
after first looking through the spyhole, let us in. He was wearing
a short-sleeve shirt and I noticed with a shock the limp, unused
muscles in his arms, flabby and of course pale white. He seemed
more unhealthy looking than ever – I had last seen him six weeks
before. He had gained weight but it had made his face puffy. His
untrimmed beard bristled out as ever. He described with sadness
how one of his parakeets had died recently. Like all his birds it was
called 'Birdy'. It had flattened itself against the side of the cage;
wings and tail feathers outstretched to give Harry a goodbye kiss
and peck his finger for the last time. Then a phone call interrupted
him and when he returned the bird was dead. Harry's eyes watered
as he spoke. He had lain the bird on a postcard sent to him by Allen

Ginsberg from Australia and faced the bird west, then at midday had faced it east. Finally he buried it in a secret place, as high as he could find so that the bird would be near the sky, and buried lots of seed with it for its journey to heaven. 'It died of grief. It wanted to build a nest and lay eggs and I prevented it. It also died of paint poisoning and plastic lodged in its crop as well…' Harry arched his eyebrows cynically. Budgerigar, in the South Australian Aboriginal language, means 'pretty bird' or 'pretty good bird for eating'. No one is sure which, as the tribe in whose language it originates was slaughtered by white settlers some time in the 1880s.

Film-maker Conrad Rooks, director of *Chappaqua*, had been to see Harry to give him the sad news that his wife had died. Harry told me about it when I visited a few days later, and this led him to reminisce about the man who first initiated him into the occult: Prince Felix Yusupov, whom Harry claimed was the father of Conrad Rooks' wife. Yusupov was a Russian prince of the royal blood, one of the richest men in Russia, who still had plenty of money even after fleeing the Bolsheviks to live in New York. When he was twenty-nine years old, in 1916, he and a friend had murdered Rasputin.

This event was so horrifying that even when the prince told it to Harry some forty years later, his voice cracked with emotion. The experience haunted him. He and his friend had prepared two bottles of wine filled with strychnine, enough poison to kill a village. They also doctored a plate of biscuits, adding so much poison to them that they turned green. Rasputin came to visit and they plied him with wine. He drank the whole of the first bottle and shouted for more. He also ate some of the biscuits. Horrified, they produced the second bottle, which he also drank. Then he finished off the biscuits and called for a third bottle. The friends consulted each other, then went upstairs and returned with a revolver. They fired six shots into Rasputin, who kept calling for more wine. By now, however, he was weakened from loss of blood, but the nightmare continued. They dragged him into a troika and took him to a bridge over the River Neva. They threw him over the side but, instead of landing in the water, he landed on an ice floe; it was 29 December and the river was filled with floating slabs of ice. In the dim moonlight they saw him borne away by the current, waving his fist and placing a terrible curse upon both of them. He finally slipped beneath the ice and drowned.

Harry had many Rasputin stories, gleaned from Yusupov, one of which was his ability to halt the bleeding of the Tsarovich by application of a preparation made from cobwebs and semen. He also told of 'indescribable orgies' held in the cellars of the Kremlin, in which everyone would drink, then Rasputin would announce: 'Away with accursed clothes' and they would all strip naked. He said that the prince showed him photographs taken of these orgies showing women with pinched-in waists and gentlemen with sharp little moustaches and pointed beards. The Tsarina was said to attend at times, dancing wildly in the nude while Rasputin rubbed his hands together with satisfaction. I was intrigued to find out more about the poisoning of Rasputin. I mentioned it to my friend the journalist Alex Cockburn, who said that his mother knew Yusupov in Paris before the war and that his Rasputin story was much exaggerated even then.

Harry had another occult teacher, Count Stefan Colonna Walewski, 'former Austrian ambassador to the USA who was suddenly out of a job when Austria turned communistic'. He settled down and opened a small store in New York called Esoterica selling fake Tibetan artefacts and quantities of unusual objects from the East. 'This was when Tibet was still there,' as Harry put it. Harry seems to have moved in with Walewski, possibly in a homosexual relationship. Harry said that the count gave him a little money from time to time, which was all he had to live on. The apartment was next to the store and the count kept all his more valuable objects there. There were sixty or seventy Tibetan tankas, of which Harry says he persuaded the count to give him the best ones.

There was a library of exceptionally rare and valuable books, including certain Crowley titles that were issued only in editions of fifty copies. Among other gifts Harry was given was Crowley's own typescript of the 5=6 ceremony. All these gifts he lost long ago when he was an alcoholic living on Gallo wine and pizza slices. Harry's total recall always amazed me – he was able to quote from memory long passages of Crowley's poetry or to remember all the details of some obscure tribe, complete with all their tribal names. He could never, however, remember the details of his notes to the fourth volume of the *American Folk Anthology*.

Walewski wanted Harry to protect himself against poisons by making three cuts on the inside of each thigh and rubbing in certain poisons, but he baulked at the idea and never got himself protected. Walewski's rooms contained a very disordered library and piles of ethnic objects. Tens of thousands of shabti figures, small Egyptian grave figurines, littered the floor, so many that you were forced to walk on them to get by, crunching them underfoot. A larger-than-life-size statue of Lon Nol riding a beast and using his flayed son as a saddle dominated the room. Rumour had it that Walewski used to somehow get inside this bronze figure as part of his own rituals, but this is unlikely as he was obese and could barely walk around his store. (Harry had introduced Trungpa, Allen Ginsberg's Tibetan guru, to his friend and pupil Rosie Gardner as Lon Nol. Trungpa didn't know what that meant until Harry translated it into Sanskrit. The incident made Harry regard Trungpa as a fake, however, and the ensuing argument was the cause of many rumours, all of them different. Harry always referred to Trungpa with disgust.)

The count used to eat potatoes and parsley that he chopped up vigorously on a medieval table in the living room and ate with his fingers. Harry one day went in search of a fork for himself. He noticed something boiling on the stove but it didn't appear to be a part of their meal. He opened drawer after drawer in search of a fork. 'They were all filled with human thigh bones. You see, he spent much of his time forging Tibetan artefacts and there was a certain demand for thigh-bone trumpets. He had a deal with a mortician or a hospital somewhere and that was what was boiling on the stove. First one had to boil off the flesh! This was before the "occult explosion", you know. Tibetan things came very expensive in those days. The Tibetans themselves, of course, were always traders. They made a million times more *dorjes* than Tibet itself could ever need. Everybody wanted one!' Harry often chuckled cynically about the young people who visited him who had all kinds of artefacts but no knowledge.

After playing 'The Titwillow Song' by Gilbert and Sullivan, he put on a 1936 recording of Yvette Guilbert, about whom he knew a great deal. Even the birds quietened and flew down to sit on Harry's head. All this time, of course, Harry had been drinking glass after glass of vodka and water and smoking joints. It was still afternoon when I left, about 5.30, and the beautiful young women of the hotel had begun flitting up and down the corridors visiting.

The experimental film-maker Shirley Clarke lived in the penthouse roof apartment at the Chelsea, where she had a roof garden. She arrived in 1965 and stayed for thirty years until her death. In November 1970, she decided that from that day on she would work only in video and gave her Bolex 16mm to Harry, who immediately began filming more segments of his magnum opus *Mahagonny*. Shirley helped him shoot some of the multi-frame sections, including one where Allen Ginsberg recites Blake's 'The Lamb' while hugging a child's woolly toy lamb on wheels. Patti Smith was later given this lamb and took it with her when she and Robert Mapplethorpe moved from the Chelsea to a loft a few doors down the street above the Oasis Bar.

Mahagonny called for four 16mm projectors in order to show four images at once, which would sometimes mirror each other, or be the same scene only with a slight delay. Harry had a projector set up and we would watch sections of it while he explained what it was all supposed to mean. It was hard to imagine what it would be like with four images but he rather condescendingly told us it would be like Michael Wadleigh's *Woodstock*, which sometimes used split screens, though not four equal-size images. Whenever he had the funds, he and Peggy would take a cab to Central Park and shoot nature sequences. Soon piles of film canisters began to fill his room.

Unfortunately Harry was in a terrible mood during much of this period; he was taking too many drugs and drinking too much, which made him irascible and difficult to deal with. Harry filmed Allen and me sitting side by side on a chaise longue talking in Peggy Biderman's room. It was a classic Harry set-up: even though the film had no soundtrack, he encouraged Allen to speak, but then slowly panned the camera round to face me. Allen, anxious to remain in the frame, leaned farther and farther into the picture until he finally realised what Harry was doing to him and straightened up, embarrassed. Harry made some typically cutting remark about Allen's ego.

He shot a series of what he called 'portraits' around the hotel. He shot his old friend Rosebud Felieu, also Robert Mapplethorpe and other Chelsea residents. I was in several of them, including one where I lounged on Peggy's chaise longue, drinking a cup of coffee, which I understand made it to the film itself as there is a still of me from it in *American Magus*, the compendium of articles and interviews by and about Harry.

Harry was well known in film circles but the public remained ignorant of him. When Jean-Luc Godard first came to New York, Harry was the only person he asked to meet. Fortunately a friend of Harry's worked in the French embassy and was able to organise it. Harry: 'A very gentlemanly sort of person. He spoke perfect English, which surprised me because I had attended a lecture he gave in which he spoke French and it was translated for him.' Harry assumed it was because Godard needed a little time to think things over before speaking in English.

In November 1973 Harry's new way of getting money, ostensibly to edit down the footage of *Mahagonny*, was to go into trances. His friend Rosie Gardner had given him $500 down and was to pay him $500 on completion for a course in Kabbalistic lore; she basically helped him out of charity, but to save face it was often structured as some sort of deal. In this instance Harry would go into a trance and dictate all this stuff to Rosie, who scribbled it all down. One of his things involved a set of ninety-six answers, any one of which fits any question.

Rosie: 'What is up?'
Harry: 'A door with a cardboard box holding it open.'
Rosie: 'What is down?'
Harry: 'Tweetie Bird!'

Peggy asked whether these daily trances were doing him any good. Harry replied characteristically, 'Well, I had a good shit today.' Harry did not look well and was periodically coughing blood, but he survived for another eighteen years.

12 1973

the mercer street arts theater

Denise Mercedes told me I must see the New York Dolls so I went with her to their all-night Valentine's Day 1973 party at the Mercer Street Arts Center. The Mercer Street Arts Center was in the back of the wonderful 1869 cast-iron Broadway Central Hotel at 673 Broadway. It was one of my favourite cast-irons with a huge out-of-proportion French mansard right in the centre of the roof. Though the hotel was pretty seedy, mostly single-room occupancy and welfare cases, there was a terrific café and artist's bar there called the St Adrian Company, named after a copy of Rembrandt's painting of the same name, which hung there.

When I wrote for the *East Village Other* underground newspaper in the sixties, I had been astonished to find that the staff could put drinks and meals on the tab there; clearly Peggy or Billy Hitchcock had guaranteed this luxury as the paper itself didn't pay much and operated in cruddy conditions from the huge room above the Village Theater, later the Fillmore East, on Second Avenue. The Mercer Street Arts Center was on the other side of the block, a theatre and performing arts complex started by Cynthia and Sy Kaback, consisting of two 299-seater and two 199-seater theatres, 'The Kitchen' video studio and performance space, a bar, a restaurant, two boutiques and two studios. I had seen several 'challenging' productions there. It was luxuriously appointed and millions of dollars had clearly been poured into the venture, but it is very hard to survive on avant-garde productions and the New York Dolls had originally been hired to fill the normally quiet Tuesday night slot in the Oscar Wilde Room, ideal for them as it had theatrical lighting and proper seating; it also attracted the uptown Andy Warhol crowd, who would probably not have gone to a seedy bar in the Lower East Side.

This was the first time I saw the full effect of glam rock on the New York underground scene. I switched to reporter mode and took notes so that I could write an article about it for *International Times*. The audience looked like the cast of *Satyricon*; not even the sub-zero wind could bring a glow to their deathly white faces as they tottered in on their three-inch platforms. The women wore thick white pancake make-up with vivid red lipstick and so did many of the men. It was a teen and early twenties crowd, some of them much younger than they looked. There was one Chinese-American wearing a diamond necklace and brooch, a Fu-Manchu moustache and a long, floor-length gown. I was admiring his outfit when a girlfriend of his arrived and they began to talk about classes and what a drag one particular teacher was. They were still in high school; maybe it was a false moustache. He had a wonderful seduction routine: 'Come over to my house, man, and we'll blow some grass, listen to some R&B and ball.' Sadly things were not like that at Cirencester Grammar School.

We went backstage, where Ruby and The Rednecks were getting ready. The Rednecks all wore little white satin majorette dresses and, were it not for the sinister look in their eyes, could have even been called 'cute'. Ruby Reyner was shrieking with laughter, she couldn't calm down because someone had used up all her Quaaludes. She flapped her arms hysterically, knocking over her portable dressing table and giggling, out of control. 'Get me,' she stammered, 'another large tequila. I've got to get this together.' Her hair was a giant orange backcombed balloon like some sort of extraterrestrial plant form.

Also on the bill was Wayne County and Queen Elizabeth. A girl on high silver platforms wearing a green lurex jumpsuit and orange lipstick came in the door: 'Sorry, Wayne, I couldn't get the dildoes you wanted.'

'Oh, that's all right, daarling! I'll get by!' he drawled in a Texan accent. He beamed archly at everyone. He was dressed as a drag queen in a huge Afro wig sprayed vivid green and pink, a black neck-ribbon and a diamond necklace. He had on black tights, which exaggerated his skinny thighs and hips, and over these wore a seven veils outfit so that he could do a strip during his act. As Queen Elizabeth kicked out a tight rhythm backing he tottered about the stage on outrageous high platforms, posturing and flapping his skinny bare arms in frustrated gestures. The overdone lipstick and weird snarling expressions showed that he was not impersonating the glamorous plastic *Playboy* image of a woman but some other tortuous image in his head.

He appeared to be sniffing coke right there on stage from a little tube he wore round his neck. The audience loved it. He dedicated 'Stuck On You' to the Dave Clark Five and did an awkward strip, finishing up in a pair of flesh-coloured tights with imitation pubic hairs stuck on the front which he combed and thrust at the audience. By now he had animated the crowd and had them laughing. Triumphantly he strapped on an artificial vagina: 'I'm ready any time you are!' he yelled, and, during a song called 'Dead Hot Mamma', which concerned someone's incestuous relationship with his mother's corpse, he went down on the silver-sprayed legs of a mannequin. This actually managed to shock some people; the woman photographer in front of me gasped and cracked up in hysterical laughter.

By now Wayne was drooling a bit and his lipstick was smeared. Ripping off his Afro wig to reveal his own matted locks sprayed with day-glo pink and green, he put his bra back on and continued with 'It Takes A Man Like Me To Fuck A Woman Like Me', a catchy, handclapping, hard-stomping number during which he played maracas, eventually thrusting one of them into his artificial cunt and waving the other above his head as he jumped about the stage in some kind of awful climax.

I thought that was it, but he continued with a rather touching little number called 'I'm So Confused' followed by 'I'm Your Wonder Woman', during which he used a huge double-ended limp rubber penis, which he sucked, drooled over and swung like a baton while strutting across the stage. He stuffed it between his legs, leered at the crowd and beat it on the floor. A lot of the high school girls in the audience became quite hysterical at this and even the group faltered in their heavy backing as they missed notes through laughing.

The audience could well have been in the group, they all looked like the Cockettes. One woman with black lipstick looked dead, many men wore full drag, including a man next to me with a full glitter-dusted beard who also disported a floor-length red ball gown and ethereal smile. Some couples wore unisex make-up and were hard to distinguish from each other in the welter of day-glo, lurex, tinsel, glitter dust on flesh, and clothes, studs, satin, silk and leather, lurid reds, pink angora tops, green boas and totally transparent blouses; and of course everyone had gained at least three inches in their multicoloured platforms. The total effect was a bit sinister after the lace and velvet of London. Afterwards Wayne told me that he was trying to raise money for a sex change operation; it was not just an act, he meant it.

When the New York Dolls came on I was struck by how much they had modelled themselves on the Stones; the lead singer, David Johansen, looked like Jagger, same big mouth, and lead guitarist Sylvain Sylvain was a bit like Keith; the black hair, five o'clock shadow; a terrible alter-ego Rolling Stones, come to haunt Mick 'n' Keith and the boys with an exaggeration of all that camping on stage. Johansen, in black tights, a tank top, diamonds and diamond rings, postured and imitated all of Mick's stage gestures and leaps. I thought they were terrific. Bass player Arthur Kane was large and looked like Richard Brautigan except with straw hair and a fetching white dress; he seemed very much out of it. All five balanced precariously atop outrageous platforms. They sounded more like the Move than the Stones.

DAILY NEWS.

NEWS photo by Anthony Casale

A panel truck is nearly buried by wood, steel, brick and mortar after the second section
of the hotel tumbled, leaving a gaping hole.

Four people died when the Broadway Central collapsed

When fans gleefully threw chocolate kisses at them they all
fussily ran and hid on the far side of the stage area, leaving only
Johansen trying to protect himself from the harmless sweets, pleased
at the attention. He pouted, bubbled, 'Bbbbbrrrrrr...' down the scale
then, hand on hip, turned his cute little nose up at someone in the
audience, who laughed. The echo of the Stones gave an eerie sense

of golems or doubles from a Gothic novel. The preening, posturing musicians actually played some pretty good heavy rock; a number like 'Jet Boy' really took off, and of course the group may have been camp, but they were not gay (though Johansen described himself as 'trisexual'). Not that it mattered. What I enjoyed was the way the high school girls knew all the words and sang along, just as fans of the Monkees knew all the words.

The vaudeville aspect of the evening was most present in Eric Emerson and The Magic Tramps, who featured, apart from Eric, an electric violinist with a touch of the gypsy in him. Eric looked as if he had just arrived from Muscle Beach; showing a lot of skin, covered with gold glitter dust and flexing his muscles to make little bits pop off while he gave naughty looks to the boys in the audience. He was a trained ballet dancer and a Warhol Factory regular. He was, notoriously, the one who sued Warhol when his image, as part of a projected light show, was visible upside down on the back of the first Velvet Underground album. It was removed at great cost. To front the MTs he wore a combination witch doctor and Captain America outfit complete with white feather headdress, white tights and a gold jockstrap. Waving bunches of feathers, he leapt in the air shrieking, coming down in a cloud of fluff and little feathers like a startled chicken. He rocked with 'Great Balls Of Fire' but couldn't stop his huge grin and limp-wrist action so it became a hard rock French cabaret act. Other notable numbers included the music from *Can-Can* in which Eric wore a delightful red flamenco dress, and the set ended with the theme from *The Lone Ranger*.

Bands were playing in three of the theatres and I missed some of them, including Suicide, but I was able to catch them a few weeks later: they were superb, musically the best of them all. What struck me was how American it all was; glam rock may have begun in England, with Gary Glitter, David Bowie and the rest, but this was the home of Hollywood glamour, and no one realises quite how tacky Hollywood actually is until they go there. This was real, a nation coming out from under ten years of unpopular war to greet

Pearce Marchbank

Allen Ginsberg in country commune attire of bib-overalls and workshirt on crutches after a car crash

four more years of Nixon with a feather and a limp wrist. It was a potent weapon.

I saw a number of bands at the Mercer Street Theater over the subsequent months but then, at 5.10 p.m. on 5 August 1973, the eight-storey façade of the Broadway Central and the rooms behind it collapsed on to Broadway, killing four people and injuring nineteen.

Decades of vibration from the subway and the heavy traffic on Broadway had fatally weakened the structure and the owner had systematically neglected critical repair work. The Mercer Street Arts Theater on the other side of the building was undamaged but never opened its doors again because the Kabacks thought no one would feel safe in the building. Had the accident occurred just a few hours later, the theatres and bars would have been filled with 1,500 people and the results catastrophic.

After seeing the Dolls play, Denise and I went back to East 12th Street, where she and Peter Orlovsky lived with Allen Ginsberg, to find Allen outraged by the press coverage of the Israeli shooting down of a Libyan civil Boeing 727, murdering 106 passengers. He was strongly anti-Zionist and thought that the existence of a Jewish state could mean only endless war in the region until the Palestinians got their country back. His solution was to make the Holy Land an international territory and move the United Nations headquarters there from New York. That way Jews, Christians and Arabs could live peacefully together. As far as Allen was concerned, the United Nations created the State of Israel and should address itself to this problem of its own making. This was not a popular view in New York and it was a subject that Allen rarely spoke about except to friends, knowing it was very controversial.

It was time to go back to Europe. Ann and I arranged that I would return first and ideally set up some kind of work for her, as I did not make enough to keep us both out of bookselling and underground journalism and we had depended very much on her job at a colour photographic lab in New York to pay the rent. I got her a job with the theatrical agent Clive Goodwin, a partner in a number of radical ventures, including *Black Dwarf*, the most political of the underground papers. Ann tested his left-wing credentials by immediately unionising his office staff – all three of them, including the cleaning lady.

13 1974

bananas

The cheapest way to get across the Atlantic in the early seventies was on Icelandic Airways, which flew from New York to Luxembourg, via Reykjavik. The stopovers in Iceland were scary as the plane landed on an icy runway, snowploughed only minutes before. There always seemed to be great snowdrifts right next to the runway. But they were experienced and there was never a problem. I arrived in Luxembourg on 1 January 1974, but this time, instead of taking the train or coach straight to London, I first went to Switzerland to visit Urban Gwerder, the editor of *Hotcha!*, the local underground newspaper; pretty much a one-man show and heavily biased towards his three main interests: Frank Zappa, Alfred Jarry and sex. I had contributed a long article on Frank Zappa to one issue, and as a member of the College of 'pataphysics since 1965, I was naturally interested in all the drawings and references to Alfred Jarry that appeared in its pages. As most of it was in German I couldn't read the content but graphically it was one of the most interesting of all the underground papers, with holes punched in it, odd-sized pages, and lots of graphics and photographs.

Urban managed to combine his interests in his own appearance: he wore his hair long at the back and sides in the manner of Alfred Jarry and sported a Zappa moustache and goatee. He got me a hotel room in the Schoffelgasse, a few doors from his own tiny flat. The bureaucracy was complicated and involved filling in many police forms. There was no sink in the room, just a large jug of cold water and a washbasin. There was a cold-water sink in the toilet down the hall. The rooms were above a lively café-beerhall and all the room keys lay in a jumble in the corner of the bar, mixed up with bottle caps, soggy beer mats and bits of bar equipment. The proprietor was pleasant enough, even though we spoke no language in common, but greeted me with a friendly '*Gruezi*' whenever I went in. The narrow lanes were thronged with hippies, many of them loud and belligerent, walking down the middle of the street. It was like being on Grant Avenue, San Francisco or St Marks Place, New York. Every town in the early seventies had a Hippy High Street.

It is always a wonderful experience to walk through a neighbourhood with someone who knows it intimately. I have experienced it with Jean-Jacques Lebel in Paris, Simon Vinkenoog in Amsterdam and Michael McClure in San Francisco. Here in Zurich, Urban casually greeted friends and acquaintances, pointed out the sights, and of course knew the best cheap places to eat. There was a growing movement to use Schweizerdeutsch, which was the language everyone spoke, instead of High German, which had dominated the media. Urban introduced me to several folk singers and rock musicians who were just starting to record in Swiss-German, something which was regarded as a radical new development.

In Zurich it was somehow astonishing to see the place where Dada was actually invented, a fairly ordinary-looking bar, originally of course the Meierei Tavern, now the Castel Pub on the corner of Spiegelgasse and Münstergasse in the Niederdorf. A little plaque on the corner of Spiegelgasse reads: 'IN DIESEM HAUS WURDE AM 5 FEBR 1916 DAS CABERT VOLTAIRE ERÖFFNET UND DER DADAISMUS BEGRÜNDET'. Just up the short alley, at Spiegelgasse 14 by the little fountain, lived V. I. Lenin, and it is interesting to speculate whether he ever attended the cabaret there; something Tom Stoppard would later muse upon. Could Lenin have met Tristan Tzara, Hans Arp or Hugo Ball? He enjoyed driving to the top of Zürichberg hill and lying in the grass with his wife and eating Swiss chocolate, so life was not all revolutionary study. Next door to Lenin, some years before, in 1836, lived Georg Büchner, author of *Woyzeck*. Now this celebrated alley was filled with shiny-faced men staring stupidly at the photographs of bare-breasted girls outside the nightclubs and strip clubs of the Old Town. Unfortunately the exchange rate was so heavily against me I could afford to stay only a few days and soon found myself on a train to Paris, intending to spend some time with Brion Gysin before finally heading back to London.

Back in November 1972 Brion had asked me to listen to some new tapes of the Master Musicians of Jajouka, recorded at Jajouka that summer by Mark and Joel Rubiner. The vocals were sunk low in the mix and were sometimes drowned out by the shrill pipes of the musicians. Brion wondered whether I could fix them. It was Brion who first introduced the Rolling Stones to the Jajouka musicians, and he accompanied Brian Jones to Jajouka when he recorded them. Brion wrote the sleeve notes to the album and Burroughs, when asked for a publicity quote, called them 'the 100,000 year old rock 'n' roll band', because he thought that their music was timeless. Together with Hamri, the head of the Jajouka musicians' union, Brion and I spent a day at Trident Studios in St Anne's Court, Soho, working on the tapes. Brion was very pleased because this was the studio where the Beatles recorded 'Hey Jude', and he always liked to be in the coolest place. I split the signal, and fiddled with the vocal, boosting different parts of the spectrum, until it was louder and clearer, then remixed it with the vocal in the centre of the stereo spread. Hamri and Brion both liked the results and it was released in 1974.

In 1974, Brion was living at the Cité Internationale des Arts, subsidised housing for artists at 18 rue de l'Hôtel de Ville, where he had a wonderful view out over the Seine to the Ile Saint Louis and Notre-Dame. Leases were only ever given for one year, however, and he said he would soon have to move on. He told me of his plans to get an apartment overlooking the Pompidou Centre, which was then under construction. He felt that if he made a series of drawings, collages and photographs documenting the erection of the building, as witnessed from his window, they would be more or less obliged to purchase them. This long-term planning astonished me. (The plan worked.)

It was always great to walk around Paris with Brion; he was so pompous and all-knowing about everything. 'And this, my dear, is absolutely the best Chinese restaurant in Paris,' he would say, indicating a mundane-looking Chinese engulfed in traffic fumes from a busy street that you would never think of trying out. He was always right. I remembered how, when he was living in William's old flat in London, Brion had always been so particular. He loved luxury, but having no money, he made do by buying only the very best in everyday fare: bread, unsalted French butter and jars of Fortnum and Mason's strawberry jam made from *fraises gariguette* in south-west France. At the Palette, on rue de Seine, he told me all the gossip. How Alan Watson, having split up with Ian Sommerville, was now living with Duchamp's widow and had become her principal confidant. Alan's new partner was Rudolph Nureyev, a move which, Brion said, made him very powerful in the international gay jet set. Brion adored court intrigue and was in his full 'princess mode', as Burroughs called it.

I visited him again in Paris in April that year, and he seemed in a great shape. His chef, Targusti, from the days when Brion owned the 2001 Nights restaurant in Tangier, was visiting and cooked us a delightful tagine which we ate with our hands, sitting on the rugs in Brion's living room. Just after Christmas 1974, I had lunch with Derek Taylor, the Beatles' old PR man who had helped promote the Jajouka record, who told me that Brion had just arrived in London. He had been referred to the Royal Free Hospital in Hampstead. We tried to reach him on the phone but without success. The hospital confirmed that he was a patient so I went to visit.

Brion had visited New York in late spring, and at a dinner party he had got up from a settee and, to his horror, saw a large circle of blood where he had been sitting. Unable to afford medical treatment in America, he flew back to Paris two days later. He was diagnosed with cancer of the colon and underwent months of painful radiation treatment, but to no avail, before being referred to the cancer unit at the Royal Free.

Brion had a gaunt skull face and was in the bleakest of depressions. He was recovering from major surgery, which had removed the colon and his anus. As Brion was a passive homosexual, this meant the end of his sex life. Strangely, he now found himself attracted to women, particularly his Jamaican nurse: 'the first woman I've ever had a crush on'. She had a jocular, easygoing manner and was very kind and considerate towards Brion, who introduced her to me as his girlfriend. It seemed to me that she didn't expect him to survive; she was just being a superb nurse, going along with his fantasies.

Visiting him was an ordeal. Brion was in great pain and as he spoke the tears ran down his cheeks. Brion had his own room, but conversation was not helped by the unearthly groans emanating from the room next door. On my second visit a young man wearing faded blue jeans and a denim jacket wandered into the room and sat on the end of the bed without even bothering to give more than a friendly nod in Brion's direction. The young man produced a plastic bag and began rolling a large joint, which he lit and passed to Brion, who sucked at it enthusiastically. The young man left and I asked Brion whether he wasn't concerned that the doctors might catch him. 'My dear, that IS the doctor!' Brion exclaimed, surprised that I hadn't realised. Marijuana was recognised as a very good painkiller and, rather than make a lot of fuss, some of the doctors in the hospital just went ahead and used it. To Brion's great relief the hospital waived his £3,000 treatment bill on the grounds that he was born in Britain and so was entitled to free healthcare even if he didn't have the correct paperwork.

······

One of the gifts I brought Brion was the first issue of *Bananas* magazine, which was launched on 2 January 1975 with a party at Emma Tennant's house in Elgin Crescent, Notting Hill. Emma was the editor and co-publisher with the designer Julian Rothenstein. I had become involved through my friend the architect Tchaik Chassey, who introduced me to Emma, who in turn had asked me to become involved. Most literary magazines at the time were very stuffy and extremely boring in their layout. Emma and Julian wanted *Bananas* to look as 'unacademic as possible', and so Julian designed it like a newspaper, so that the fiction and stories read like news. The large page size also meant that he could do more adventurous designs. I liked the newspaper format because it suggested a greater urgency and immediacy for the stories and think-pieces, and I saw my involvement with it as a natural progression from my days with the underground press.

I was assistant editor and an occasional contributor, which entailed spending time at the *Bananas* editorial office at 2 Blenheim Crescent, above the Dog Shop, a stereotypical Notting Hill head shop. This was a legendary underground address where designer Richard Adams had worked on the last few issues of both *Oz* and *Frendz* underground papers. It also housed *cOzmic* comics and the *Index of Possibilities*, a sort of English version of the *Whole Earth Catalog*. Richard Adams started the Open Head Press there together with Heathcote Williams. The building contained the headquarters of the Legalise Cannabis Campaign and, by the time *Bananas* moved in, was also the office of Heathcote Williams' Ruff Tuff Crème Puff Squatting Agency, which produced lists of people's second homes as an aid to squatters. Emma's friends always looked a little nervous around Heathcote, particularly when he showed an interest in the location of their country cottages.

Emma was only six years older than me but because of her aristocratic upbringing – her father was Lord Glenconner and she grew up in Chester Terrace, overlooking Regent's Park, and at Glen, the family's faux-Gothic castle in Scotland – her way of seeing things sometimes gave rise to amusing misunderstandings between us. Once we were talking about how useful it was to have someone with you when travelling and after talking a bit at cross-purposes I said: 'You know, like a roadie.'

'Oh,' said Emma. 'I was thinking of a chaperone!'

One side of Emma was faithful to her class origins. Emma had a live-in nanny who produced the children for inspection at the appropriate time and I once arrived fifteen minutes early for lunch and had to wait in the library until the appointed time; it wasn't done to arrive early. But Emma was full of surprises. One day she introduced me to Matthew Yorke, her eldest child, whose father was Sebastian Yorke and grandfather was Henry Yorke, the British novelist who wrote under the name of Henry Green. I said I liked Green's novels very much – *Living, Loving, Concluding, Back*, etc. – which prompted Emma to reminisce about a summer visit to Green at a rented villa near Gerona on the Costa Brava in 1957. She and Sebastian were not yet married and eighteen-year-old Emma was rather bored except in the evenings, when Sebastian went up to bed while she sat up drinking with Green and Terry Southern, another house guest, then still with his first wife Carol. Terry Southern was one of the funniest people I'd ever met, and the idea that he was friends with Henry Green was intriguing because, up until then, my literary connections in the US and in London had been like two different worlds with no overlap.

Emma's brother Colin inherited the castle and the money through primogeniture, something Emma felt rather badly about, and with good reason. She had a traditional upbringing and had come out as a debutante and did her best to make a sparkling career for herself, but her real passion was for writing. In the early sixties Emma held the wonderfully named position of Assistant Shoe Editor at *Vogue*. She published *The Colour of Rain* in 1963 under the pseudonym Catherine Aydy and had recently returned to her writing. When I first met her in 1973 she had just published *The Crack* with Jonathan Cape.

Bananas editorial involved many lunches, mostly at Emma's

Bananas was the liveliest literary
magazine of the Seventies

house. She also gave frequent dinner parties, often cooked by Luisa,
the Italian wife of Emma's father's chauffeur. Luisa's fame among
Emma's guests resulted in her being asked to cook for so many other
people in the literary world that she set up on her own, cooking
'Luisa's Literary Lunches' for such literary hostesses as Sonia
Orwell, with dishes named after her most famous customers like
'Oeufs Lacan', and 'Haddock Naipaul'. In the summer Emma held
'garden parties', which sounded grand but were really a buffet set
out on the large trestle table in the kitchen, where people helped
themselves and set out for the garden. I remember well the cases of
Good Ordinary Claret from Berry Bros. Many of Emma's guests were
her contributors: Angela Carter, Michael Moorcock, Jimmy Ballard,
Peter Wollen and Elaine Feinstein. Emma's best friend, Antonia
Fraser, was often there with Harold Pinter, whom she had just started
living with. Pinter seemed to me an arrogant fellow, interested only
in people well known in their field, and always very rude to the
staff. As someone whose parents were both servants I was always
very aware of how people treated the staff, particularly people who
claimed to be socialists.

Emma's ex-father-in-law, Claud Cockburn, father of Alex, came
from Ireland to spend a few days and was there for one of Emma's
dinner parties. I was there when he returned from a six-hour
interview for BBC television during which time he drank an entire

bottle of whisky and managed to persuade his interviewer to eat a banana on camera so that he could say, 'I say, that fruit reminds me of a literary magazine,' and give Emma's new magazine a plug. The taxi driver and a charming young woman from the BBC carried him to the door. He told the amused cab driver, 'I know that the scourge of your profession are drunks and that it must seem utterly unreasonable to request your assistance at four-thirty in the afternoon.' The lady from the BBC, who declined to come in, explained delicately that Mr Cockburn was feeling rather tired.

At 8 p.m. Claud awoke and we were all able to dine. He was very amused by my line, 'Which is my wineglass?' as a way of attracting attention to the fact that it was empty. When offered wine himself he inevitably responded: 'Just to the top.' He began to entertain us with his vast repertoire of stories. He was particularly pleased by Lord Longford's campaign against pornography which was dominating the press at the time. He said that Longford had problems stemming from his childhood. When a woman of Claud's acquaintance had visited the Longford country house as a child, when Longford was only fifteen years old, he showed the girl around the gardens. Claud warmed to his theme: 'It transpired that within the walled garden was another walled garden. This he refused to allow her to enter on the grounds that within, on a marble slab, lay the gardener's boy, stark naked, fucking his own sister. Naturally, as this was not an acceptable sight for a young woman, she did not enter. Later the girl found out that there was no gardener's boy in the household at the time and the whole thing was a fantasy!' He shouted with laughter. This led to a very amusing discussion of the Freudian significance of an English aristocrat having fantasies about lower-class incest in walled gardens within walled gardens.

Claud went on to talk about Stalin. He knew a number of journalists who had interviewed Stalin. One was Louis Fischer, who had achieved his interview by being very active in USSR support groups, though he was not a member of the Party. He was to do the interview for a small American newspaper with a circulation of about eleven thousand; he knew, however, that he would be able to syndicate it all over the Western world and make a fortune.

Claud: 'After a brilliant interview he was beaming, it was great. Then Stalin asked him if the interview would be read widely in the West. Caught off his guard he said, enthusiastically, "Read! Of course, it will be read all over the world!"

'"And how much do you think you might make for this?" enquired Stalin.

'"Uh, about 150 thousand dollars."

'"Yes," said Stalin. "That's about what we thought. Now we know that you are a great supporter of the cause, and you might have noticed that we relieved you of your passport and papers when you came in. Though I'm sure nothing would give you greater pleasure than to live here in Moscow with your comrades for the rest of your life, you might be able to support the cause better back in the West. So if you will just sign these papers giving us the syndication rights..."

'Fischer was right, it sold for about a hundred and sixty thousand and he made about five thousand dollars on it. All his friends couldn't understand why he didn't give a party to celebrate.' He told Claud his reason only later, in a foxhole, during the Spanish Civil War.

Raising the money to start *Bananas* had been difficult. Emma did the obvious thing first and approached her brother Colin and asked him to invest. He was not to become Lord Glenconner until 1983, but already had considerably more money than Emma. In 1958 Colin had bought the island of Mustique in St Vincent and the Grenadines, and in 1960 he very cleverly gave a wonderful plot of land at the southern tip of the island to Princess Margaret as a wedding gift. She built a villa there and Mustique's success as a fashionable resort was assured, though there was always the danger of that dreaded phone call to say that Margaret would like to drop in on you with eighteen people for dinner.

Bananas did not get enough advertising and with funds once

THIS WOMAN HAS CLASS.
SO DOES

BANANAS

The new magazine. Out January 1st. BANANAS is a monthly magazine that caters for the reader in search of lively, topical stimulating material. Interviews; articles on the issues of the day; photographs and rock music reviews and high quality fiction by world-famous writers; and all in a newspaper format that's easy to display and easy on the eye too. BANANAS will cost 50p. Should be displayed alongside Private Eye and Rolling Stone. Fully S.O.R. Usual trade terms.

Available through Moore Harness Ltd., 31 Corsica Street, London N.5 (Phone 01-359 4126)

The ad for the first issue
of *Bananas* playing on its
aristocratic origins

again low, in July I accompanied Emma to lunch at Bianchi's at 22 Frith Street with brother Colin. He looked around the Soho restaurant in astonishment: 'You always know the most bohemian little bistros, Emma,' he exclaimed. There was a lot of banter, during which Colin showed off his white sweater knitted from wool from his own sheep and bearing his monogram. 'Still living off the fat of the land,' he said, happily. Emma did her best to entertain him; she showed him the plaque which described how, in this very room in January 1926, television had first been demonstrated to members of the Royal Institution by John Logie Baird when it was his laboratory, and told him gossip about mutual acquaintances, but sadly the chequebook was not forthcoming. Fortunately Emma knew a number of other interested, wealthy people.

14 1976
rock 'n' roll

In London I began writing for *New Musical Express (NME)*, introduced by my old friend Mickey Farren. Mickey had been on the staff of *International Times*, and later became its editor. He was the founder of the British White Panther Party, the singer and lyricist with the Social Deviants, whose 'Let's Loot The Supermarket' was a punk anthem years before its time. He was a science-fiction author, counter-cultural activist and a specialist in conspiracy theories. Mickey first took me to the *NME* offices in May 1974 to meet the editor Nick Logan and features editor Neil Spencer, but I didn't actually write anything for them until I returned from Cuba in September 1975. To succeed as a freelancer you needed a speciality.

Mickey Farren had gone to work there only on condition that he didn't have to write about music – he wanted to write think-pieces – though he did discover an interest in the rebellious end of country music and wrote about that. By this time many of the underground press writers had joined the music press, but they were constrained by the fact that *NME*, *Melody Maker (MM)* and *Sounds*, the big three, were all commercial papers owned, in the case of *NME* and *MM*, by the giant publishing conglomerate IPC. Caroline Coon, who started Release, was writing for *MM*, and on the *NME* staff in addition to Mickey Farren were Nick Kent, writer for *Frendz*, Penny

Smith, photographer on *Frendz*, and Charles Shaar Murray, one of the original *Oz* schoolkids. I began attending their weekly editorial conferences and picking up the odd writing job: interviews, concert reviews or record reviews that no staffer wanted. Their offices were on Long Acre, conveniently located for roadies – always a good source of rock news – to drop in and gossip in exchange for a few drinks or a smoke. Even a few stars made an appearance to promote new albums, concert tours or to raise their profile.

The 11 a.m. editorial meetings usually opened with Tony Tyler rubbing his hands and asking, 'Who're we gonna number this week?' It was usually Brian Ferry, someone for whom Tyler nursed a particular hatred. The paper was seen as being a bit edgy and critical, though it was firmly in the hands of the advertising department. Very occasionally someone like Island Records – Ferry's label – would withdraw advertising for a couple of issues if they objected to an article or review of one of their artists, usually because of pressure from the artist, but they always came back because it was a target market.

Any suggestions for articles about corruption, payola, chart fixing or everyday music business activities involving drugs and groupies were totally out of bounds. The paper was there to make money for IPC by selling ads and selling copies. It made a fortune and no one wanted to rock the boat. If a bit of swearing was needed to give it street credibility, that was OK, but that was virtually all that was allowed. There were strict rules to be adhered to: 'fuck', 'bugger' and 'asshole' could be used in moderation but 'cunt' or any other slang word for genitalia, male or female, was strictly forbidden. Whereas on the underground papers people had written freely and openly about drugs, for *NME* at that time the subject was completely forbidden. Rock stars did not take drugs, end of story. I was very amused to sit in on an editorial meeting between Nick Logan, Neil Spencer and Charles Shaar Murray. Murray had interviewed Keith Richards, who, naturally, had passed Charles a joint. Charles mentioned this in his piece but no way was that going to be allowed in the paper. In the end they reached a compromise where it was presented in his piece as a dream sequence; he fantasised that Keith had passed him a joint. Such was the 'cool' *NME*.

I had not worked for the big commercial music press before. In the sixties I had interviewed McCartney, Lennon, Harrison, Jagger, Pete Townshend and others for *International Times*, but that had been on an informal basis, just by asking them, rather than going through publicists or their record companies: I would go to their home or, more often, they would drop by my place in the afternoon for tea and a chat. Now I saw the straight side of rock journalism: the press conferences, the phoney excitement generated by the press office for a new act or a new record, the free T-shirts, albums and business lunches, the free trips, free alcohol and, often as not, the free drugs. As a freelancer, I quickly learned that a morning press conference was in fact a free breakfast, and would find myself at the Café Royal, hearing how much Dolly Parton loved England, while stuffing myself with smoked salmon and champagne, or listening to Elkie Brooks' new single at Les Ambassadeurs. The press officers didn't mind freelance liggers because they needed a big crowd to please their bosses and the artist's management.

Many of the press events were like factory assembly lines with a room full of journalists – Fleet Street as well as music press – being ushered in to see the star at fifteen-minute intervals. I remember one such at the Hyde Park Hotel, already running late, to talk with Harry Nilsson about his new album, *Knnillssonn*. Harry had recently finished making *Pussy Cats*, produced by John Lennon in his so-called Long Weekend period in Los Angeles. It quickly turned out that we had many friends in common – I first met him at Apple in the late sixties – and to the intense irritation of the other journos in line – someone from *MM* had already been waiting more than an hour – Harry cancelled all the remaining interviews, produced a full bottle of Rémy Martin and locked the door. He admitted that the high speed that some of the tracks on *Pussy Cats* were taken at was the result of too much coke and had seemed funnier at the time than on later hearings, by which time it was too late. We finished up in Tramp on Jermyn Street at 3 a.m.; I was rather the worse for wear but Harry looked as if he could go on all night.

Obviously the staff got all the best jobs so I decided to pursue my interest in electronic and avant-garde music: so-called 'Kraut rock', ambient, progressive and so on. I also had a few contacts and so I was able to write about Captain Beefheart, having spent time with him in Los Angeles in the late sixties. The German electronic trio Tangerine Dream (TD) interested me because every concert was different; they improvised the whole time like avant-garde jazz groups instead of playing regular numbers, and yet they presented themselves as a rock band. Everything they did on stage with their three large custom-built synthesisers – which were enormous in those days – was spontaneous improvisation, letting one idea lead to another, responding to each other's creations and developing them into long, beautiful melodic passages. The closest in contemporary jazz would have been the recently issued *Köln Concert* by Keith Jarrett. Audiences were sometimes confused. The group did nothing much on stage except manipulate great banks of switches and flashing lights, a bit like an old-fashioned telephone exchange; it was impossible to tell who was making which sound and there was no jumping about or stage act, though later Edgar Froese took to playing guitar as part of the set.

When I interviewed TD's Chris Franke for *NME* he said, 'It is composed in the moment; it happens live. That is my definition of the thing we are doing.' I thought they were an interesting development in popular music and interviewed them several times for *NME*, reviewed concerts at the Albert Hall, and also concerts in Washington and New York, which led me to writing the programme notes for their British and American tours. It was refreshing to see that the ideas about electronic music impacting rock 'n' roll that I had first discussed with Paul McCartney and John Lennon back in the mid-sixties had come to fruition.

It was through Tangerine Dream that I was properly introduced to the more hedonistic side of the music business. In order to review TD's American concerts, Richard Branson took Alan Lewis, the editor of *Melody Maker*, and me to the States on Concorde to see them. We flew into Washington, then to New York the next day, and the day after that returned to London. I had been in New York only the week before on a press trip and was barely over jet lag, but Concorde was different; there didn't appear to be any jet lag or else I wasn't in the country long enough to notice it.

In the Concorde departure lounge at Heathrow there was the usual curious combination of high tech and wood-panelled tradition that the British are actually quite good at. It was like a no-expense spared wedding reception: there were tables of food, including plates of cold meats and fruit, and even cigarettes in little jars. Waiters brought round champagne – 'A little champagne, sir? Very settling for the stomach' – which I managed to spill over Richard's trouser leg. The plane was parked right outside, and when the flight was called we all tottered aboard, to be met with a thousand apologies that the champagne on board was a different brand. When the plane took off we were literally pressed against the backs of our seats and the deep throaty roar made it the Harley Davidson of jets.

I liked the fact that the windows were small, and when you touched them, instead of being icy cold as they are on a regular jumbo, they were warm because of the friction. Also, when you looked up through the window, instead of the deep blue of normal flights, the sky was really quite black because we were twice as high as usual. Then of course there was the fun of arriving before you left, London time. Compared with the austerity of living on Allen's farm, or my days as an impoverished art student, this was unbelievable luxury. Rock journalism enabled me to see up close how the rich live, but it did not, of course, provide the income for me to be anything other than a tourist in this other world. It was an added plus; something that I had not encountered when I was writing rock journalism in the sixties for the underground press.

In the spring of 1975 I had been introduced to a French rock critic called Hervé Muller by my friend Larry Debay. Larry lived on Maida Avenue in St John's Wood, next to the canal. He was French, with long red hennaed hair and a long bright green beard, jodhpurs and knee-length riding boots. I often saw him walking his two large and very impressive Borzois, nodding convivial greetings to his puzzled neighbours. He had a record shop on Portobello Road specialising in garage and proto-punk records by the likes of Iggy Pop, Zappa and so on; he also did a nice line in bootlegs, though those were usually available only from his home. In the best tradition of a salesman he casually displayed hundreds of rarities in a row of tatty cardboard boxes, which only made them more desirable.

Hervé wrote for *Rock et Folk* and had lived for a time in London. He was skinny in the best rock 'n' roll tradition, and wore the standard jeans and leather jacket of the rock critic. His hair was long and very dark. He cared passionately about his hair, and introduced me to his hairdresser, who ran an outfit called Rock Hair from a small apartment (pronounced, of course, 'rock air'). It was one of the best haircuts I've ever had, but just as we were leaving, Hervé could not resist having a few final adjustments made to his own hair, which had been cut only the day before. Hervé's girlfriend, Jenny Beer, was a tall, thin Englishwoman with impeccable French taste in clothing, who ran the international section of CBS Records in Paris. They lived in a tiny flat on the rue Crozatier in the Bastille area of Paris, a flat I came to know very well.

Hervé had befriended Jim Morrison when he moved to Paris in 1971 and took the last known photographs of him; looking puffy and drunk at a table on the terrace of the Alexander Hotel on avenue George V. Morrison gave Hervé a copy of his spoken-word album of poems, *An American Prayer*, and asked whether it would be possible for him to translate it into French, but Morrison died before anything could be done.

According to Hervé, on the night of 3 July 1971, Morrison had been at the late-night music business club the Rock 'n' Roll Circus on the rue de Seine, a regular hang-out of his, and in his drunken state had taken a line of heroin thinking it was cocaine. He did not speak French, which may have added to the confusion; also, French street heroin was considerably stronger than anything he may have taken in the USA. He passed out in the toilets, and to the considerable relief of the frantic management, who feared that they would lose their licence, the two drug dealers who had given him the heroin bundled him out the back way through the kitchens of the Club Alcazar on the rue Mazarine, and from there in a cab or car back to his flat on rue Beautreillis in the Marais.

It was here that his girlfriend, Pamela Courson, attempted to revive him by putting him in a cold bath. Pamela was herself taking heroin but should have known that this often-used method of revival is nothing but junkie folklore and does not work. Morrison was dead by the time the paramedics arrived. There are many differing accounts of Morrison's death, some quite fanciful, but this seems a very likely one as Hervé heard the story from the club's manager, Sam Bernett, a good friend of his, who witnessed the door to the toilet being broken down and saw Morrison's body slumped inside.

Hervé often found himself in London to interview a group or attend a concert and would usually stay at my place. One time, after he left for Paris on a morning flight, I wandered into the back room where he had slept. There was a workbench running the full length of the wall and sitting in the middle of it, arms wrapped around her knees, was a naked girl waiting for me to get up. She was from the record company and had spent the night with Hervé but I had forgotten that she was there. She stayed a week or more, going to work each day, and in the evening we would go to a gig and she would come back to my place. These were young women out to have fun; that was why they worked in record companies. The pay was not great, but the expenses were huge, and it was their job to entertain the press and keep the bands happy by providing expensive meals and quantities of alcohol. Having sex with journalists and musicians was not a part of the job; the record companies neither encouraged nor discouraged it, but it often happened when

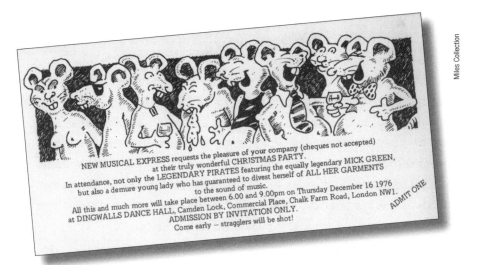

Miles Collection

NEW MUSICAL EXPRESS requests the pleasure of your company (cheques not accepted)
at their truly wonderful CHRISTMAS PARTY.
In attendance, not only the LEGENDARY PIRATES featuring the equally legendary MICK GREEN,
but also a demure young lady who has guaranteed to divest herself of ALL HER GARMENTS
to the sound of music.
All this and much more will take place between 6.00 and 9.00pm on Thursday December 16 1976
at DINGWALLS DANCE HALL, Camden Lock, Commercial Place, Chalk Farm Road, London NW1.
ADMISSION BY INVITATION ONLY.
Come early – stragglers will be shot!

ADMIT ONE

The designer of *International Times*, Edward Barker, one of many ex-underground newspaper people to work for the music press, did the *NME* Christmas party invitation for 1976

publicists, bands and journalists found themselves at a loose end on the road with the hotel bar just closing. These were the innocent, pre-AIDS days when sixties ideas of free love still held. It was not seen as exploitative, or sexist. Sex had always been a major part of the music business, and this was its attraction for many people, male and female.

The people who started Dingwalls Dance Hall in Camden Town – Tony Macintosh, Tchaik Chassey, John Armit et al – decided that they wanted something a little more exclusive: a members-only bar with little or no live music, cocktails and a higher standard of food. In the spring of 1976 they opened the Zanzibar Club in Great Queen Street, Covent Garden, across from the giant, ugly Freemasons' head-quarters that dominates the street. The architect Julyan Wickham based his design for Zanzibar on a photograph of a thirties Italian fascist bar. It was a long thin room, so he ran the bar down most of the left-hand side, terminating at the back in a small, mirrored bandstand and a mirrored door leading to the bathrooms. There were raised banquettes on the right-hand side, served by waitresses. The bar itself was shaped like a series of waves so that people could sit around a projecting curve and face each other more directly than at a conventional bar. At regular intervals, small square mirrors were set flush into the bar's surface.

Julyan said this was for women to check their make-up but this was the mid-seventies and cocaine was everywhere. Periodically a group of customers would close ranks, as if huddled over a fresh kill, and put the mirrors to use. Food came from the Anti-Opera restaurant next door, high quality, high price. My friend Pearce Marchbank was asked to design the signage for Zanzibar, which he based on that of a twenties French café, so we spent many pleasant luncheons and evenings trying out the bar before it officially opened.

He was then married to Sue Miles, my first wife, and at that time he and I were putting together a book called *The Rock Almanac* for Paddington Press. We continued to work together on projects and he gave me a desk in his art studio on Newman Street in the basement of the Music Sales building, which was very convenient because I had access to a photocopy machine and was on the spot whenever they needed an introduction to a book of sheet music or a song selection made for a greatest hits songbook.

Ann had no interest in the rock 'n' roll world and concentrated her attention on Tibetan Buddhism and a political group she founded called the Committee for Puerto Rican Independence. I was also involved in the CPRI and wrote press releases, designed flyers and even spoke at conferences on a couple of occasions, but my heart wasn't in it the way that hers was as, ultimately, it seemed like a lost cause: there was no way that the USA was going to give Puerto Rico its independence. The best they could hope for was to get the same environmental and social protection offered to mainland American citizens. Ann was also involved with a group of Buddhists who squatted in a house in North London and did it up for their Tibetan teacher. A great deal of her spare time was taken up by working on the building, and when they eventually moved in she began spending more and more time there. In the end she moved in with them and, though we were still very good friends, Ann and I were no longer a couple.

Meanwhile, my flat in Hanson Street became very much a rock 'n' roll pad as I concentrated on paying the rent by writing about popular music. In addition to Zanzibar, I became a regular at the Marquee and quickly familiarised myself with the best routes across the floor to avoid the unpleasant squishing sensation beneath one's feet from the beer-soaked carpets that had not been properly cleaned in a decade. It was possible to review the band from the bar at the Marquee, which is where most of the journos could be found. One *MM* writer even managed to review a set by a band who didn't show up: the cause of some embarrassment and much ribbing. The main area in front of the stage was to be avoided if there was an audience of any size because it was unbearably hot and hard to escape from.

I would also hang out at the Ship, the roadies' pub on Wardour Street a few doors up from the Marquee, which was a good place for gossip, and at Frank Coe's La Chasse, located between the two at 100 Wardour Street, a small private upstairs drinking club. I paid £5 to join, but no one ever had their membership checked; all that mattered was whether you were buying drinks. It was an old-time rock 'n' roll joint. In the sixties Jon Anderson had been the barman there and had sometimes slept on the couch until he and other La Chasse regulars got together in May 1968 to form Yes. A decade later it was much favoured by the likes of Keith Moon, who sometimes acted as barman, surreptitiously putting triple vodkas into people's pints of beer and roaring with laughter as they rapidly became almost as drunk as he was, and all of it delivered in his fake upper-class accent: 'Another little drinky-poo?' He liked to play spoken-word tapes by poets such as Dylan Thomas when behind the bar and would chant along with *Under Milk Wood*.

Moon was a lot of fun to be with but it was easy to get into scrapes with him. In May 1977 I was in the Albany Hotel in Glasgow with a bunch of fellow journalists. We had been to see the Eagles play the Apollo and were staying in the same hotel as the band. After they had drunk the bar clean of tequila the Eagles made their way to their rooms and, as it was about 4 a.m., the rest of us were contemplating doing the same. Just then there was a sudden commotion and in burst Keith Moon, closely followed by Viv Stanshall, and behind them a Glasgow police inspector. Moon had in his hand a large white megaphone clearly labelled as belonging to the Glasgow police. Moon insisted on addressing all his remarks to the policeman through the megaphone, which brought all of us to tears of laughter, wondering how he was going to get out of this one.

Enraged by our laughter, the police inspector, who had several other uniformed men with him, turned on us and demanded to know many things. Unfortunately I couldn't understand a word he was saying – I was drunk and he had a powerful Glaswegian accent – and I had to keep asking him to repeat himself. This irritated him even more and he grabbed me, and two of my colleagues, with the obvious intention of taking us down to the station. At this point a Scottish journalist who was with us, who could understand the man's thick accent, piped up, intending to explain that we were but passive observers. Delighted at having made contact, the police inspector immediately arrested the Scottish journalist and before we could protest, he whisked him out of the door, which was then barred by two of his men.

'Such impudence!' screamed Moon. 'Intolerable behaviour! We must launch a formal protest forthwith.' Having prevented us from intervening, the two uniformed police had now left. We followed Moon outside. He and Stanshall had what appeared to be a Second World War German staff car parked at the kerb, and with Stanshall at the wheel, and Moon standing up in the open back, still clutching the stolen megaphone, which the police had presumably forgotten about, they lurched off through the empty 4 a.m. streets in search of the police station. I never did find out what happened. It was now so late that there seemed little point in even going to our rooms so we all took a cab to the airport for breakfast and caught the first shuttle back to town.

It was the seventies, not the sixties, which should be known as the era of sex and drugs and rock 'n' roll, and working as a rock journalist dropped me right in the middle of it. Drugs were everywhere: you could turn up at a record company at 10 a.m., ready to take a coach or limo to an out-of-town gig or attend a press conference, and there would be the band's manager or minder, flipping out a test tube full of coke attached to a silver chain about his neck and flourishing a small silver coke spoon – often rather nice Victorian salt spoons – licking his lips and rolling his eyes. It was like a miniature version of the early eighties moment when the man in the moon came down over the dance floor at Studio 54 and snorted a glittering line of star-spangled coke and the music was cranked up a few decibels louder and on the huge dance floor the young men with their shirts off all leapt up and down and screamed. Well, the rock journalists didn't scream at these early morning jaunts: many of them needed their medicine just to summon the energy to clamber on board. One friend of mine flew to Detroit to review a band. A limo was waiting to take him in from the airport but no representative from the record company was there. That was fairly normal. At the hotel he checked in and went to his room. He opened the door and there in a huge king-size bed were two naked black girls with a big bowl of cocaine between them on the sheets. Not that this affected his review of the band, of course.

The contrasts from one day to the next were sometimes almost surreal. A day might begin with a press conference with Abba in the expensive surroundings of the Café Royal, followed by lunch at Langan's and an evening watching Gentle Giant mix their latest album at Advision before going on to catch the second set by Linda Lewis at Ronnie Scott's. The next evening it might be Ian Dury at the Nashville pub, drinking beer from battered plastic pint glasses, hanging out with the West London locals.

I got to know Wilko Johnson, the guitarist from Dr Feelgood, who shared my interest in William Burroughs. One evening he was visiting with his girlfriend Maria, a dancer at the Raymond Revue

Bar, and I put Bill Burroughs' 'Ali's Smile' tape on the Revox. The TV was on with no sound. Wilko and Maria were flopped out on the carpet. 'Rome has fallen…' said William on the tape. The TV news cut to St Peter's Square, Rome. 'I like the job, wouldn't you?' intoned Burroughs. On the TV the new Pope spoke to the assembled crowds through a microphone, spreading his arms and gesturing to the crowd. We all cracked up laughing.

When I visited New York I was always welcome to stay at Allen Ginsberg's flat, but there was often a problem about where to sleep as so many people fetched up there and the beds were usually full, often with multiple occupancy. In March 1973 he had moved from the apartment on East 10th Street, where I had been tied up and robbed, to a much larger place in a slightly more salubrious neigh-bourhood, at 437 East 12th Street between First Avenue and Avenue A. Apartment 23 consisted of six rooms and had been created by roughly joining together two small three-room slum apartments. There were extraneous doors and, rather incongruously, a sink in the living room next to the front window. There was no entrance system and people had to yell up, above the din of Avenue A, to get in; then someone would throw the key down in a sock. People usually telephoned from the corner, as it was impossible to be heard unless someone was in the office or front room. I had my own key, as did many of Allen's regular visitors. Allen and Peter Orlovsky had two of the front rooms and another became Allen's office. Denise had a tiny room off the kitchen, which also led to the office, where Allen's new secretary, Bob Rosenthal, and a team of volunteer researchers kept track of the Ginsberg cottage industry: filing articles, clipping news-papers, compiling a bibliography, running his various campaigns and his poetry foundation. The room was filled with four-drawer file cabinets, each different, all battered, sometimes two piled on top of each other. Several drawers were labelled 'F.B.N.C.' (Faded Brown Newspaper Clippings). Everything was oriented towards poetry and political activism. It was only in the eighties that Allen's shrink suggested that he make a comfortable space in his flat and try to entertain friends instead of working all the time.

With all the rooms in use, Allen had no room for guests, so when it became free, he rented the apartment next door. This was in even worse shape than his main apartment but they tidied it up, and when Peter Orlovsky's brother Julius came out of the mental hospital, this is where he had his bedroom. The other rooms also had beds in them and it served as an annexe to Allen's flat. I was staying there one night when there was a terrible crash, what sounded like rocks falling in an avalanche. I put on the light, but it didn't seem to be working. Then I realised that there was a dim glow from the ceiling, but the room was full of thick dust or smoke, obscuring the light. I thought the building must be collapsing and ran through to Julius's bedroom. The dust in there was even thicker and I felt my way around the room and opened the window, all the time calling to Julius. As the dust billowed out of the window, I saw Julie, still in bed. All around him was rubble, with several large pieces on his pillow, but he seemed unhurt and just lay there, mute, his fingers holding the top of his cover, staring upwards. The ceiling of his room had fallen in and could have killed him, but he lay there unscathed. By this time Allen had arrived, alerted by the noise, and began cursing the landlord, who had done no repairs to the building in years. In the morning we saw what a lucky escape Julie had: almost the entire ceiling had fallen and one huge slab of plaster and laths had missed his pillow by inches.

Rather than risk my luck or even my life at Allen's, I usually found it more convenient to stay with my friend Victor Bockris at his apartment on Perry Street in the West Village. It was almost on the corner with Hudson, a short walk from the White Horse Tavern, in an old brownstone that once had a high stoop but had been crudely converted into apartments. The brickwork on one wall of the apartment was exposed and there was a working fireplace. In the summer you could sit out on the fire escape and look at the large tree in the backyard. I was first introduced to Victor by Allen Ginsberg at a reading Allen was giving at Barnard College. He gestured for me to come over and said, 'You two Brits should meet. You'll like each other.' He was right; we quickly became friends, sharing a love for the Beat Generation writers, rock 'n' roll and Andy Warhol.

Victor had the confidence of an English public school boy – he had gone to Rugby – but his accent was now half American as his family moved to the States when he was a teenager. British people always assumed he was American whereas Americans could hear his British accent. When he and his fellow poet Andrew Wylie were driving across the country, they came up with the idea of starting a small poetry press, intending to do for their generation what City Lights Books had done for the Beats. Andrew rented a small shopfront on Jane Street in Greenwich Village and opened a bookshop for the press. They brought out ten books in a uniform edition, including two each by themselves, two by Aram Saroyan, one by Gerard Malanga and Patti Smith's first book, *Seventh Heaven*. Victor was a great believer in collaboration, and he and Andrew began a writing partnership called Bockris Wylie, publishing as if they were a single entity. They were writing every day, giving poetry readings almost every week, publishing books and arranging poetry tours. They were having a good time, they were flying.

Victor bought his suits from the boys' department of Brooks Brothers – he is small of stature and they are much cheaper there. Andrew bought bigger ones. Sometimes Victor wore a top hat; he had studied drama and was a consummate showman. His poetry readings were lively affairs, filled with grand gestures and action; not for him to mutter through an open book.

Much as Victor loved the poetry of the St Mark's crowd, he found that they were much more interesting as people than their poems. It was after interviewing Peter Schjeldahl, now the art critic for the *New Yorker*, that he realised that the poetry of human speech was more interesting than written poetry. It changed his life. Bockris Wylie switched from poetry to interviewing, publishing the transcripts in obscure little literary magazines.

In 1973, Victor and Andrew changed gear: they made a list of

Victor Bockris and William Burroughs in Los Angeles

one hundred people they wanted to interview and began selling the interviews to *People* magazine, *Oui*, *Penthouse* and *Viva*. They interviewed Salvador Dali, Halston, François Truffaut, John Huston, Andy Warhol and John Lennon, They were tenacious and just kept telephoning people until they agreed. As Victor put it, they were the Gilbert and George of the interviewing world. They did a series of interviews with Muhammad Ali, which they published as *Ali: Fighter, Poet, Prophet.* They were perhaps too good at interviewing because their subjects sometimes had second thoughts about having intimate details of their lives revealed in print.

In one week they interviewed Mick Jagger, William Burroughs and Lou Reed. Then Jagger's lawyers wrote to *Playboy* asking them not to run the interview, William Burroughs had his lawyer write to them, and though the Lou Reed interview was great, they couldn't find a publisher for it. Bockris Wylie broke up, amicably, in 1975, with Andrew eventually becoming a literary agent, and Victor extending his interviews into full-blown biographies. He created a book about William Burroughs by setting up a series of dinner parties at William's place on the Bowery and tape-recording the results: dinners with Burroughs and Andy Warhol, Lou Reed, Mick Jagger, Joe Strummer, Blondie, Christopher Isherwood or Susan Sontag, published as *Report from the Bunker.* His love life was turbulent, perhaps best summed up by two of his better-known pieces, 'Negative Girls' and 'Why I Hate My Girlfriend'.

Back then Victor was an intuitive Situationist: he created situations, both in his life and work. It was easy to tell whether Victor was bored: he would fiddle, turn his napkin into a mask or put it on his head. Once in Mickey Ruskin's Chinese Chance restaurant, he leapt up from a large table of people where the conversation was going nowhere and threw himself at the huge wall mirror, not once but repeatedly, until Mickey came and remonstrated with him. On another occasion at the Mudd Club, his evening was not going well so he climbed out of the window and hung on to the ledge just by his fingertips.

During the punk period, Victor was working with Andy Warhol on *Interview* magazine, writing the book about Burroughs and conducting a series of interviews with Debbie Harry and Chris Stein for a book about Blondie that the three of them would co-author. Victor had embraced the negative punk ethic and the living room was dominated by a large trestle table illuminated by an anglepoise lamp that was always, uncomfortably, shining in your eyes as in a police interrogation. When I complained, Victor explained that it was intentional. I dropped by one day to find Rope Burns, the punk country and western artist, seated at the table in his cowboy boots with Victor and Legs McNeil from *Punk* magazine, seated on either side, earnestly questioning him. He looked distinctly uncomfortable. Victor wrote himself notes on his hands, his clothing, on the walls and on the kitchen counter. Periodically, if he had the money, he would have a cleaning agency come and scrub the apartment down. Then he would entertain guests to dinner with flowers on the table and the floor clean of cigarette ends, but after a few weeks the writing on the wall would begin again and the apartment become a shambles.

15 1976
punk

After a period of stagnation, there was a new subject for rock journalists to gossip about: punk. It spread like Chinese whispers, provoked by Kate Simon's photographs of Malcolm McLaren attacking a hippy in the front row of the Sex Pistols' gig at the Nashville on 23 April 1976; a piece of gratuitous violence sparked by Vivienne Westwood, who had suddenly begun slapping the face of the girl next to her, a complete stranger. When the girl's boyfriend took exception, McLaren joined in, closely followed by Johnny Rotten. Vivienne had been 'bored'. Then came the International Punk Rock Festival held at the 100 Club on Oxford Street on 20 and 21 September. The second night featured the Sex Pistols, the Clash, Subway Sect and Siouxie and the Banshees, the last two acts having never before played live and, in the case of Siouxie, having never played before at all, having formed that night. Their drummer was Sid Vicious, who threw a beer glass at the audience, which shattered against an iron pillar, cutting several members of the audience and blinding a girl in one eye. Sid was arrested, and when Caroline Coon, the founder of Release, now a writer on *Melody Maker*, went to investigate the charges against him the police arrested her too, though she was later given an absolute discharge. Though hardly any journalists had been there, the Punk Festival and the violence surrounding punk became the subject of considerable debate; most of it negative. It was clear and new, high-energy rock 'n' roll was developing. I had seen it for myself on 16 May 1976 when Patti Smith played the Roundhouse.

I went along to see her, going first to the Portobello Hotel, the current 'in' hotel for rock bands. When I arrived she was in the basement bar-restaurant, eating an early dinner, having just flown in from Amsterdam, where she had played the Paradiso the previous night. She had the same nervous energy I'd noticed when I first met her in 1969, making little stabbing gestures in the air as she talked. In between mouthfuls she periodically shouted, in her clipped South Jersey accent, 'Gee, you girls sure know how to make a great steak!' or 'Gee, you girls sure know how to make a great salad!' As we talked she flipped through the daily papers, looking for any mentions of herself. She froze halfway through turning a page. 'Keith Relf dead?'

We had been joined by this time by Lenny Kaye, her guitarist, previously best known for compiling the famous *Nuggets* anthology of garage bands. Keith was added to the growing list of rock's casualties. I remembered how fond of the Yardbirds Patti had been in the sixties and how surprised she was when I explained that, important and well loved though they were, in the mind of the British public they were not up there with the Beatles and Stones. She didn't believe me; she seemed to get most of her information from *16* magazine and *Tiger Beat*. Nonetheless, she was a walking rock 'n' roll encyclopedia.

Patti: 'Same initials as Keith Richards' (her other great love).

Lenny: 'Same first name as Keith Richards.'

Patti: 'Brian Jones was asthmatic too. Maybe it's that blond hair...'

They decided to dedicate a song to him at the concert that evening.

We talked about the old days at the Hotel Chelsea: 'I always said I'd move back into the Chelsea when I had some bread but I never did. I guess I want to protect the memories of those great days.' She told Lenny: 'Miles knew me when I was just a nobody.' It was rather strange to see her in her new life, famous, with fans and her photograph on the cover of *Rolling Stone*, hailed as the saviour of rock 'n' roll, with a huge black limo to take her and the band to the gig.

It took me a while to get into her new persona as a rock 'n' roller; to me she was a poet. I mentioned that I had seen Robert Mapplethorpe a few weeks before in New York. I had been walking along West Street in the West Village and passed the Ramrod, a gay bar on the corner of Christopher Street. There were three figures standing outside, leaning against the wall, catching some early spring sunshine. All three were dressed in rubber bondage gear, including tight-fitting masks. As I passed, one of them pulled the stopper out of his mouth – Pop! – and said 'Hi, Miles!' It was Robert. Laughing.

There were some fan letters waiting for Patti in the dressing room at the Roundhouse. 'This is a good one for you to read aloud, Lenny,' she said. 'It's in rhyme. It says, "Marry me. I want to fuck you," and it's from someone who says he lives in a council house.' I explained that was a project. Patti was delighted. Though they had been playing together for some time, I had not seen the band before. It didn't surprise me that they were immediately recognisable as from New York City. I wrote in *NME*:

> Lenny Kaye adopts the classic stance, legs wide apart and then that familiar New York music begins. And they are *very* New York. Patti doesn't mess around. Just grabs the audience and takes them up there. She has tremendous stage presence, not showbizz, not glitter, just a personal magnetism, which keeps all eyes, beamed straight at her. 'Redondo Beach is a place where women love each other (kiss, kiss)' she announces. A pair of little lesbians in front of me hug each other with glee and then yell, 'Yeah, tell it to them Patti.' But Patti is not a woman rock and roller as such. There's plenty of sex drive in her act but it's not specifically male or female by any usual archetypes, it's just a stack of burning energy bursting through. Not even so much sex as love because for all the sullen street punk imagery she is really warm and friendly.

She said: 'When there are 1,000 people in the audience and
500 of them are guys and 500 are girls, why just talk to half
of them? Why should I, being a girl, just sing to boys? I want
everybody to love me. I want to communicate with everybody. I
don't really think of myself sexually or other people sexually, I
just think of sex period.'

Though much discussed, hardly any punk music had made it
on to record yet, partly because A&R men could not see a way to
capture the energy and excitement of a live punk performance on
tape. The musicians could barely play, and all their inadequacies
would become immediately apparent. The Ramones' first album
was produced like a commercial pop record by Craig Leon and
Tommy Ramone and worked well, and Patti Smith's *Horses* came
from the hands of fellow musician John Cale, the most musical
member of the Velvet Underground. Australian punks the Saints
had released their high-energy 'I'm Stranded' on their own Fatal
label with a black-on-black label, and the Damned, the first British
punk band to release a record, had 'New Rose' on Stiff, the first time
many people had heard just how fast punk bands played. I was very
interested in the whole movement because the music seemed to be
coming from an inchoate alternative community and the counter-
culture had always been my territory. Bernie Rhodes, the manager
of Subway Sect, Snatch Sounds and the Clash, invited me to see
his bands perform at the Institute of Contemporary Arts (ICA) at a
gig billed as 'A Night of Pure Energy' on 23 October 1976. *NME* had
not yet mentioned the Clash, though from what I'd heard, they were
more politically committed than the Sex Pistols and their lyrics were
more interesting, so I went along. I found Subway Sect virtually
impossible to listen to and I was talking with Bernie Rhodes when
Snatch Sounds were on and returned only for the Clash.

As soon as the Clash took the stage, the punks erupted in a frenzy
of activity. Pogo dancing was supposedly invented by Sid Vicious,
slam-dancing at the 100 Club, and had not yet completely taken over

as the only correct punk mode of rhythmic expression; there was also prizefight sparring, the rocking-horse ride, several examples of *West Side Story*-style knife-fight choreography and even some old hippy high-steppin' and boogying-on-down, though a hard core in the centre pogoed furiously, slamming into each other and twisting and turning with the music, rather like seals leaping up to be fed in a crowded aquarium.

I had seen the Patti Smith Group play the previous night, but they had been too distant, too New York cool and arrogant to really connect with the audience, and I had not liked them as much as at their gig five months before, which had been less studied. I preferred Patti as a poet. Now Patti was in the Clash audience to check out the competition and clearly felt that her own dance moves were being overshadowed by the crowd, so she climbed on stage alongside the band to dance where everyone could see her.

The Clash was everything that *Sniffin' Glue* magazine had promised. Fast, high energy, with intelligent lyrics, though it was hard to actually decipher them: songs such as 'I'm So Bored With The USA', 'Career Opportunities' and 'White Riot'. It was this last title which made my editor at *NME*, Neil Spencer, wonder whether the paper should be publicising them because to him it sounded racist. I was worried too as there were a number of swastika armbands and patches on display and the audience was brimming with aggression.

At this time the Clash line-up consisted of Joe Strummer, lead singer, Mick Jones on guitar, Paul Simonon on bass and Terry Chimes (known as Tory Crimes) on drums. Terry left soon after, unable to deal with the violence of the fans. A wine bottle had shattered on his high-hat, showering him with shards of glass. The other members of a group can dodge if they see a missile, but the drummer is seated, an obvious target. He was replaced by Topper Headon.

Joe Strummer was born in Ankara, a public schoolboy whose father was in the diplomatic corps, but he hid his undeniable middle-class origins with a slurred working-class London accent even less

Allen Ginsberg, Joe Strummer and Mick Jones backstage at Bonds, New York City, 1981

authentic than that of Mick Jagger. He spent months learning how not to speak proper and even advising his middle-class friends how to do likewise. Like most punks, the Clash were not quite as street as their audience, or as young for that matter; Strummer was only nine years younger than me, born in 1952, a hippy child of the sixties, like it or not. He had previously been known to his hippy friends as Woody and before joining the Clash he sang in an energetic pub-rock band called the 101ers. His hippy background showed through when he cast the *I-Ching* to decide whether or not to join the band.

Much of the excitement of punk came from the audiences; both from their amphetamine-fuelled enthusiasm and their creative apparel: the punks dressed to startle. The girls wore men's shirts with rips in them safety-pinned together with the names of bands crudely written on them in felt-tip pen or ballpoint and torn fishnet stockings. They wore old jumpers from Oxfam that had been torn so that they were unravelling; black bin-liners were very popular, as were see-through plastic macs, the ubiquitous safety pins, through both fabric and flesh, and later occasional full nudity. More important than the clothes was the face paint and make-up, which was wonderfully creative, with geometric shapes painted across cheeks, noughts and crosses, with lashings of black eyeliner. Hair was spiked and multicoloured. Some of the kids wore swastikas, hoping to shock, but they were more likely to cause exasperation.

The men concentrated on spiky hair and safety pins through cheeks, earlobes and nose, though mostly just on their clothes. A friend of mine took a punk home to her bed and was astonished to find that he had a safety pin through his foreskin. She insisted that he took it out. How they got in from the suburbs dressed like that without encountering major hassles was hard to imagine, but they did. Most of the clothes were home-made, and all the more creative for it, but some came from Sex, Vivienne Westwood and Malcolm McLaren's expensive clothes boutique on the King's Road.

I found it hard to imagine a viable musical or social revolution coming from a Chelsea dress shop, and was always suspicious of the Sex Pistols for the same reason; they had, after all, been put together by Malcolm McLaren as a group just like the Monkees, and from what I could gather, he saw himself as an old-time Jewish manager, just like Don Kirshner, who invented the Monkees. 'My little Artful Dodgers', McLaren called them. McLaren's hero was Larry Parnes, the fifties and early sixties manager known as Mr 'Parnes, shillings and pence'.

Onstage at the ICA the Clash launched into a furious set. Strummer took his name from his playing technique, which, at double-time speed, was more like strumming a banjo than playing conventional rhythm guitar. Then Joe peered down at the audience in front of the stage and muttered, 'I don't believe what's happening down here at the front...'

An out-of-it young couple had been nibbling and fondling each other amid broken beer bottles when she suddenly lunged forward and appeared to bite off his earlobe. As the blood spurted she reached out to paw it with a hand tastefully clad in a rubber glove, and after smashing a Guinness bottle on the front of the stage she was about to add to the gore by slashing her wrists when the security men finally reached her, pushing through the crowd, who, apparently in a trance, watched but did not attempt to get involved. 'Anyone's into violence, go home and collect stamps!' Strummer yelled at them. 'Collecting stamps is much tougher.' It turned out that not all the earlobe was lost and its owner, Shane MacGowan, later went on to front the multimillion-selling band the Pogues and his girlfriend Mad Jane became Jane Modette of the Modettes. MacGowan later told *Zigzag* magazine: 'I was up the front at this Clash gig in the ICA, and me and this girl were having a laugh, which involved biting each other's arms 'til they were completely covered in blood and then smashing up a couple of bottles and cutting each other up a bit. Anyway, in the end she went a bit over the top and bottled me in the side of the head. Gallons of blood came out and someone took a photograph. I never got it bitten off – although we had bitten each other to bits – it was just a heavy cut.'

I brought up the issue of violence when I interviewed the band for *NME* two weeks later at Rehearsal Rehearsals, their studio space next to the Roundhouse in Camden Town. Mick Jones was vehement: 'We ain't advocating it. We're trying to understand it… It ain't hip. *We definitely think it ain't hip.* We think it's disgusting to be violent.' When I mentioned the earlobe incident he turned to Joe: 'On that gig, it put me an' you off, didn't it? I mean, when I came offstage I didn't feel particularly good.'

I got the sense that Joe didn't agree, but he cleverly redirected the conversation: 'But it's energy, right? And we wanna channel it in the right directions.' Paul Simonon had the words 'Creative Violence' stencilled on his painted boiler suit. Since I wanted to know about violence Joe explained further: 'Suppose I smash your face in and slit your nostrils with this, right?'

Joe had been opening and closing his flick-knife in a vaguely threatening way throughout the interview. Now he held it close to my face. '...Well, if you don't learn anything from it, then it's not worth it, right? But suppose some guy comes up to me and tries to put one over on me, right? And I smash his face up and he learns something from it. Well, that's in a sense creative violence.

'And this sort of paintwork is creative violence too, right?' he said, pointing to Paul's white stencils and clashing colours. It seemed to me that Joe had a fascination with violence that was at odds with his generally left-wing sympathies. I felt the same ambivalence in their lyrics and their political slogans, and I thought their audience would like a clear, unambiguous statement of their position. Joe spelled it out for me: 'I think people ought to know that we're anti-fascist, we're anti-violence, we're anti-Racist and we're pro-creative. We're against ignorance.'

Mick Jones: 'We urge people to learn fast.'

I arrived at Rehearsal Rehearsals not feeling my best, having been up all night, and I had not had time to even go home and brush my teeth before my late morning appointment with the Clash to hear some tapes. Seeing the poor shape I was in, Joe Strummer naturally insisted that what I needed was some fresh air and insisted, quite forcefully in his bossy public-school way, that I must play five-a-side football with them as they needed a fifth person to make up the numbers. They always kicked a ball about before rehearsals.

I protested that I had not engaged in any kind of sport since I left school in 1959, and then only under duress, but it was no good and I soon found myself in goal on a piece of waste ground, later turned into a small park, next to the railway arches at the corner of Camden Street and Kentish Town Road. Our opponents were five skinny blokey punk males dressed in black who had been rehearsing at the studio, a mixed team of members of Subway Sect and the Moors Murderers. I later learned that Steve Strange and Chrissie Hynde were in the latter band but they were not there that day. Bernie Rhodes also managed Subway Sect. I saw them rehearse earlier and was particularly struck by one song that reduced punk rock to an absolute minimal statement: it consisted of shouting 'Oh fuck it!' over and over, very quickly, for about a minute, to a buzzsaw guitar backing. Maybe it was because Subway Sect knew it was me who described them as 'terrible' in the *NME* that they seemed inordinately determined to score goals and embarrass me in the eyes of the Clash, but I only let in four, and managed to deflect many, many more. 'You did your best,' Strummer grunted when the game was finally determined to be over.

Of all the British punk bands, I thought the Clash were the most interesting. They were good entertainment and energised their audience but were also genuinely concerned for them in a way that is rare in rock 'n' roll. In conversation they recognised the boredom of living in the high-rise council blocks – Mick Jones still lived at home on the eighteenth floor of one, overlooking the Westway – and though they were all from a rather more middle-class background than they admitted to, they knew the dole queues, and the mind-destroying jobs offered to poorly educated unemployed school leavers. They talked about there being no clubs that stayed open late, of how Britain had no rock 'n' roll radio stations, of how there was nothing for young people to do.

Paul Simonon said he used to get drunk every night and go around kicking people and smashing up phone boxes, but now he had the band as a means of expression and he hoped the audience would start their own bands, or find some creative outlet for their energy. I found this astonishing, as I knew Paul had studied at the private Byam Shaw art school in Chelsea. 'I used to draw blocks of flats and car dumps.'

There was a certain amount of myth-making going on, even at this early stage in their career before a record contract or serious press attention. I believed Joe when he told me, 'We're dealing with subjects we really believe matter. We're hoping to educate any kid who comes to listen to us, right, just to keep 'em from joining the National Front when things get really tough in a couple of years. I mean, we just really don't want the National Front stepping in and saying, "Things are bad. It's the blacks!" We want to prevent that somehow, you know?... We want to sing about what we think is relevant and important.'

Mick Jones: 'We want to bring things to the attention of other people to help them learn faster. That's the important thing... to try and understand what's going down.'

I saw them a lot, at the Electric Ballroom in Camden, the Roxy in Covent Garden, in recording studios and rehearsal rooms. They never seemed to have any money. I was struck by the fact that after they played three sell-out nights at the Rainbow Theatre, I saw Bernie Rhodes pull away in a car with personalised number plates reading CLA5H, while Mick Jones was waiting for a bus outside. He came back to my place and we talked until 7 a.m. I tried, unsuccessfully, to convert him to Zappa; but he regarded the track 'Hey Punk' as insulting, even though it was recorded in the hippy era. Though the punks affected to despise the hippies, they were actually intrigued by that whole period; it was only decades later, however, that they were able to admit it publicly. As someone said, they were really hippies with short hair.

In 1978, problems with Bernie Rhodes grew worse and the Clash approached Ellie Smith, the chief press officer at their record label, CBS, and myself, with a view to us managing them. The idea was to form a six-way company with equal shares, much as the Pink Floyd had done with their original managers Pete Jenner and Andrew King. But first Ellie and I had to see the books; it appeared very likely that the Clash really needed a management team with substantial capital behind them rather than two well-meaning believers. The books showed that even though CBS had advanced them more than a hundred thousand pounds, the band was broke and the individual members had seen very little of it. It sounded as if managing the band would consist very much of a series of lawsuits against Bernie and very little on the creative side. Added to this was that Joe retained a fondness for Bernie. At one meeting, Ellie and I were expressing astonishment at some of the financial dealings while Joe lolled on the settee in the corner, smoking a huge joint, which cracked and popped because he had not bothered to sort the seeds out, and said, 'Aw, Bernie's all riiight, really!' It seemed unlikely that we would ever get the full, enthusiastic support of the band, so Ellie and I pulled out. For the idea to have worked it would have required a new spirit, a new beginning in the band that just wasn't there.

But money problems obviously continued to plague them and later that year, the day after a press reception for a new album, I found Joe and drummer Topper Headon selling clothes at a cold open-air stall in Dingwalls Market in Camden Town. 'We're broke, man, so you just have to do what you can.' Strummer shrugged. 'Bernie kicked us out of our rehearsal studio and changed the locks.' I was with Rosemary Bailey, who was to become the great love of my life, and when she wandered away and began looking at other stalls, Joe said to me, 'Is that your girlfriend? She's very pretty.' With his guard down, he suddenly struck me as very young, vulnerable, sensitive like a schoolkid, but the pressure never seemed to let up and he was forced to assume the aggressive muscular stance he used onstage with 'Hate & War' stencilled on his boiler suit as a reaction to the hippies' 'Love and Peace'. He thought his slogan was a more accurate description of what was happening around him.

The biggest problem in the band was that Joe believed many of the half-digested ideas presented to him by Bernie, whereas the other three were more interested in becoming a successful rock 'n' roll band. Joe certainly went along with the posing and pouting – none of the other punk bands came anywhere near the Clash in terms of adopting classic rock 'n' roll stances as soon as a photographer removed their lens cap, and the music rags were happy to print the pictures of the Clash looking moody in front of burnt-out buildings, in front of bare brick walls, the Clash in camouflage fatigues in Northern Ireland, the Clash posing in much the same way that all of the pop groups of the sixties posed, in fact. Never a smile; they were masters of the cool profile and the moody attitude, particularly Paul

Miles Collection

ROXY CLUB
41-43 NEAL ST.W.C2   TEL: 836 8811
(OPEN 830-1)

THURSDAY 31ST MARCH
CANCELLED

FRIDAY 1ST APRIL   £1-25
EATER
SIOUXSIE AND BANSHEES
WIRE

SATURDAY 2ND APRIL   £1-50
BUZZCOCKS
JOHNY MOPED BAND
X RAY SPEXS

The Roxy was the best punk club in London but only lasted four months

Simonon, who became a real pin-up in punk circles.

It paid off eventually, of course, and they went on to become one of the most successful bands of the era, a seventies equivalent of the Rolling Stones, until Joe took Bernie's advice and sacked Mick Jones. With the only musically talented member of the band gone, the Clash degenerated into a parody of its old self and folded.

For many people, punk lasted only about four months, neatly encompassed by the lifespan of Andy Czezowski's Roxy Club, which opened in December 1976 and effectively closed in April 1977, though it continued under new management for a bit longer after that. The Roxy was at 41 Neal Street in Covent Garden. It was in a dark basement, quite large, with a low ceiling supported by round iron columns. Because the ceiling was so low, the stage was also low, which made seeing the bands difficult. I could finally see the point of pogoing; it was the only way to see what was going on onstage.

You would sometimes catch a glimpse of a musician leaping up to smash the polystyrene tiles, sometimes intentionally, other times inadvertently, as they swung the microphone stand or leapt in the air, striking the ceiling with the machine head of their guitar. Pogoing punks could also reach the tiles and the ceiling was in pretty bad shape. The floor was scattered with shards of plastic from broken beer glasses, which crunched underfoot, as well as saliva from the punks' obnoxious habit of spitting at bands, blood from their nihilistic habit of cutting themselves, vomit from their tendency to drink too much, and spilt beer from the difficulties experienced in trying to negotiate past a pogoing mob with a full glass of beer in hand. The walls were painted matt black and covered in graffiti and there were many large mirrors, which the punks enjoyed, liking few things better than to pose and look at themselves.

Andy Czezowski let people do pretty much anything they wanted and so, as usual, the ladies' room was the centre of the action. Girls teased their hair into bizarre shapes while people chopped up lines of coke next to the sink. There were smears of blood on the mirror and one time I saw the bass player from a band getting a blow-job in a stall with the door left open. The DJ was Don Letts, a rasta punk; one of the few. As very few punk records had yet been released he played mostly reggae and ska with the bass turned up really loud. His brother and some other rastas sold pre-rolled spliffs; the punks were too incompetent to roll their own.

The sound system was awful, but it didn't really matter because most of the bands could not play very well. Of all the bands I saw there the Damned were the most professional, always doing a long sound check even though there were only three working microphones in the place. There was a Valentine's Day gig, when they shared the bill with the Adverts, that was particularly good. The lead singer, Dave Vanian, had developed a striking Count Dracula look, complete with swirling cape, long jet-black hair greased back

and heavy black eyeshadow above and below his eyes. Drummer
Rat Scabies was like a younger Keith Moon, with a disconcerting
habit of rolling his eyes skyward as he played to make them look
completely white. Captain Sensible wore a nurse's outfit.

I particularly liked the Damned because they injected humour
into punk, something sadly lacking with bands like the Clash. I
was sitting with Captain Sensible in a pub garden in Cambridge
one afternoon, having driven up with them to report on a gig that
evening, and just as we were coming to some agreement about the
merits of the various line-ups of the Soft Machine, the pub's owner
came storming up and threw us out, just because the Captain was
wearing a dress – a rather fine tutu in fact. I produced a tape recorder
and asked the publican his reasons but this appeared to outrage him
even more. I suppose being insulted on a regular basis by punting
aristocrats was bad enough without having a cross-dresser in his
beer garden. The Captain was unfazed by it, and said it happened
all the time. Theirs was the humour of the Dadaists and Surrealists,
designed to shock and make people think twice. They didn't expect
everyone to get it and were not surprised when they didn't.

I also liked the Adverts, even though they had been playing
live for only four weeks, because TV Smith's lyrics were a few
cuts above most guttural punk utterances, often critical of the herd
instinct among punks. Of course, both he and Gaye Advert went to
art school, as did many punks. Their look was studied, with Gaye
the obvious centre of attention: her jet-black hair, pale face, heavy
eye make-up and blank stare became an iconic punk image. She
habitually wore a black T-shirt, tight jeans and a black leather jacket;
onstage she sometimes wore nothing beneath it, just did up the top
button so her midriff was exposed. This was very effective because
there was little or no sex onstage in the punk movement and the
audience was largely composed of teenage males. She played a large
Rickenbacker bass which she cared about but was often too out of it
to tune it properly.

It turned out that I was responsible for them getting a manager.

A few years before, I had met Michael Dempsey, not the bass player from the Cure but another of Emma Tennant's Irish ex-husbands, though, unlike the aristocratic Anglo-Irish Cockburns, Michael was from a 'black Irish' family who he claimed spent their time crawling up mountains on their knees to visit holy shrines; though I always suspected Michael of exaggeration. He had wild curly hair and a round cherubic face, puffy from alcohol. He was ever ebullient, enthusiastic, excited. The most mundane was deemed fabulous.

As a publisher at Hutchinson he struck lucky by signing up Frederick Forsyth's *The Day of the Jackal* before joining Granada Publishing, where he was the youngest senior editor in the business. He brought much new American talent to the company, including Hunter S. Thompson and Ed Sanders' *The Family*. In 1973 he gave Mick Farren his publishing break by bringing out *The Texts of Festival* and that same year was instrumental in getting J. G. Ballard's *Crash* into print. But Dempsey's lifestyle and that of the 'suits' in charge of the money didn't gel and he is famous for throwing one of the most expensive Frankfurt Book Fair parties ever known, a gesture involving drinks and prostitutes being charged to expenses and a chair being thrown out of a fifth-floor hotel window in the middle of the night, which cost him his job, but only after a decent settlement was made which enabled him to set up on his own.

He lived at 4 West London Studios, Fulham Road, next to Chelsea football stadium, in a modern block of flats with a huge wall-size south-facing picture window in the living room. The room was flooded with light, even on a cloudy day. He first suggested that we do a book on Dylan back in May 1974, but we didn't actually bring anything out until 1978, and then it was little more than an enlarged souvenir booklet.

Another potential idea was a Tammy Wynette combination cookbook, memoir and compendium of household tips, which never got off the ground. Dempsey just wanted to visit the custom-made trailer home she used on tour.

Evenings with Dempsey usually finished at the Zanzibar or some other Soho or Covent Garden club. When punk came along in 1976, he was very interested and came with me to the Roxy Club. He knew punk must be good because the tabloids attacked it so much. The first time he visited he saw the Damned and, like most people, he was impressed by their energy and theatricality. The next time we went was the 1977 Valentine's Day concert with the Damned and the Adverts. Afterwards, Michael and I headed over to the Zanzibar, on nearby Great Queen Street, taking TV Smith and Gaye Advert with us. After a few drinks I casually said to Michael, 'You should manage them, they need a manager.' I thought no more of it until a few days later when Michael called up and asked, 'What sort of van should I get?' I was astonished, Michael knew nothing about punk or rock and roll management. I said I assumed that a Ford Transit, as every other band had, was in order.

In one of the few interviews he gave about the band, Dempsey described the gig: 'It could only have been their second or third gig ever, but I thought they were dynamic, especially Tim's lyrics. I've always been nuts about talent, and Tim had talent. I saw that straight away. The thing with the Adverts, they were always being lumped in with the rest of the No Future brigade, but they were taking a far more realistic view of things. Tim might have believed in the ideals of the punk thing, but he also understood its limitations, which is something that very few people did, especially at that time. While everyone else was celebrating how "different" they were, how outrageous, Tim was saying "so what?", asking them what they were trying to prove. While they were challenging the establishment, he was challenging the challengers.'

The band's first record was on Stiff. Jake Riviera had seen them at the Roxy and whipped out one of his one-off contracts saying, 'Sign this and I'll make you broke.' They did and he did. But Riviera was good for one thing; he really knew about publicity. He followed up the Damned's first single with the Adverts' 'One Chord Wonders', launched with full-page ads for the singles and live gigs in the music press which read: 'The Damned can now play three chords, the Adverts can play one. Hear all four at...' They gained from the association with Stiff, and were getting known, but when Dempsey appeared on the scene they owed money on their equipment and were still more or less destitute.

Michael clearly enjoyed his new role. I went with him and the band to several out-of-town gigs. After one, on the way back from Manchester, we pulled into a late-night truck stop for something to eat. As soon as the van stopped, Gaye pulled off her black leather jacket and leapt out of the van, topless. She ran towards the parked lorries. I've never seen Dempsey move so fast; in a flash he was out of the van and in hot pursuit, laughing all the way. He calmly guided her back to the Transit while several envious truck drivers looked on, wondering what was going on in there. Michael was devoted to them and when one journalist wrote a bad review of Gaye's playing, Dempsey gave him a beating.

Dempsey embraced the lifestyle, publishing books on the Roxy Club and an anthology taken from *Sniffin' Glue*. Members of the band stayed at his flat, which was rapidly trashed, with windows broken, graffiti spray-painted on his pristine walls and blood splattered all over them.

But Michael loved it. He got the Adverts a proper recording contract, and they recorded a third single, which I produced at a cheap-rate recording studio in Brighton. My previous experience consisted of various spoken-word albums with Charles Bukowski, Lawrence Ferlinghetti and so on, and one musical outing, Allen Ginsberg singing William Blake's *Songs of Innocence and Experience*, which featured Archie Shepp and Elvin Jones. The Adverts single was called 'Safety In Numbers' and it was not as catchy or clever as 'Gary Gilmore's Eyes' but it still made number 28 in the charts. Michael then got a proper producer and they made an album, *Crossing the Red Sea with the Adverts*.

On 6 December 1981 Michael died a classic alcoholic's death, trying to change a light bulb at the head of the stairs on a stepladder while drunk.

As punk was getting under way, the comics, which was how the music business quite rightly referred to *NME*, *MM* and *Sounds*, each chose a position to take. Though Caroline Coon recognised the value of punk at once, her bosses at *MM* were very slow off the mark and rather missed the boat by not encouraging her. She did, however, write most of the best early articles on the phenomenon. Once *Sounds* saw that punk was flavour of the month, they pushed it to the hilt, and succeeded to a certain extent. Their coverage was so extensive that they became the 'official' punk paper. *NME* was initially wary. Neil Spencer reviewed the Sex Pistols but was initially sceptical about the other groups. There was no one on the staff who knew about punk except Nick Kent, who had actually been in an earlier line-up of the Sex Pistols and knew all the bands, but his musical taste was wide ranging and it was obvious that he could not be expected to focus on punk; particularly if the Rolling Stones were touring.

When Tony Tyler decided to leave *NME*, Nick Logan, the editor, had him conduct the interviews to find his replacement. He chose an inexperienced young man from Essex, a prototype example of the new laddism, called Tony Parsons. He had large features and a slightly puzzled look on his face. A week or so later, Nick Logan also hired Julie Burchill, a sixteen-year-old from Bristol whom he thought would know all about punk, feeling that the two of them together would just about replace one competent journalist as they were both new to writing; Julie, for instance, refused to write anything longer than 800 words, the length of the longest school essay she had ever written. Parsons, however, when taken to the pub, told us that he had just published a novel with New English Library called *The Kids* and also a guide to the Greek islands, proving that, like many punks, he was quite clearly several years older than he claimed to be (he was born in 1953).

Around this time, *NME* moved to King's Reach Tower, a thirty-one-floor eyesore by Richard Seifert, on Stamford Street overlooking Blackfriars Bridge. Reed International were in such a hurry to get their scattered magazines into the building that the lifts were not properly functioning when *NME* moved and several times staff had to climb to the twenty-seventh floor, taking more than half an hour, to arrive exhausted, sweating and cursing. The staff were furious at having to move, and after one liquid lunch at the local pub Mick Farren attempted to throw a typewriter through the office window but it was built to withstand high wind pressure and did not even crack. Unlike the typewriter.

NME was on the same floor as *Mickey Mouse Monthly*, *Horse and Hound* and a scurrilous weekly rag called *Reveille*. It was not difficult to tell which paper people worked for when you found yourself in the lift with them and they were all headed for your floor.

I was not on the staff, but I wrote regularly for the paper and was listed in the contributors' box. That meant I was invited to the weekly editorial meeting, essential for freelancers because that was where the jobs were handed out. It was important to have a few ideas to suggest; preferably ones that no one on the staff would want and pre-empt.

One of the most insightful and intelligent writers there was Nick Kent, but by the time I joined, he was hopelessly addicted to heroin, which meant that, by his own later admission, he was not writing to the best of his ability. However, he was still not one to be taken in by press office hyperbole and his pieces were always spot on in terms of recognising talent, and identifying bullshit.

One day I was in the office and, as no one else was around, I answered the internal phone. It was security, asking whether Nick Kent worked there. They wouldn't let him in because he didn't have his pass and they insisted that someone come down to get him. I went down and found an affronted Nick Kent, running his fingers through his hair, head thrown back in high dudgeon. 'I don't understand it, man. They didn't think I looked like a journalist!' Nick was wearing a copper band around his neck which had left a green ring, a girl's blouse, too small for him, which exposed his bare midriff, and a pair of black leather trousers, the seams of which had split so that his balls could clearly be seen. 'He's a *rock 'n' roll* journalist,' I explained to the jobsworths at the door. Nick certainly lived the rock 'n' roll life 24/7.

Julie Burchill was living at the YWCA on Great Russell Street and had only visited London a few times before with her parents. She spoke in a high-pitched Betty Boop voice with a pronounced West Country accent: 'Eyem from Briss-Toll.' Several people on the staff felt sorry for her: she knew no one and was clearly out of her depth. Several of the women on the staff felt that Nick Logan should not have hired her; at sixteen she was too young. She said that the only reason she joined *NME* was to meet Patti Smith, her idol, so when Patti came to town for a concert, I took Julie along to meet her.

There was a press reception at the Intercontinental Hotel but Patti appeared to be on amphetamine or something and behaved badly, walking about on the tables, kicking people's food and drinks on the floor, shouting and laughing loudly. She had been angered by the poor reception afforded her new album, *Radio Ethiopia*, by the notoriously fickle and opinionated British rock press. When one journo asked her why her tickets weren't selling, she screamed, 'Fuck you! You're a drag. Get out of here,' and tried to throw food at him. This was of course exactly what the pressmen wanted. 'Which Beatles newsreel are you acting now?' shouted one.

This was when Patti climbed on the table. 'I'm the Field Marshal of Rock 'n' Roll!' she told them. 'I'm fucking declaring war! My guitar is my machine gun!' And she stalked from the room. It was a pity that she had not yet learned how to play her guitar, which up until that point she used as a symbol, not an instrument. Julie was horrified and burst into tears; real tears, her shoulders shaking. It must have been a tipping point for all the fears and stress of being in London, from working with a staff of mostly stoned, cynical, macho journos. I took her next door to the Hard Rock Café and bought her a large brandy, which seemed to calm her down, then put her in a cab. It was the shattering of a fantasy, one of the reasons she came to London in the first place.

In the course of adjusting to her new life in London Julie spent one night with Tony Parsons. After this she developed something of a crush on Mick Farren and arrived at his flat one morning, suggesting that he might like to introduce her into the mysteries of S&M. A few days later at the office, Parsons saw some bruises on her arms and took a proprietary stand, leaping on Mick, throwing punches. Mick naturally refused to fight and simply protected himself as best he could while a number of us leapt on the flailing bundle of testosterone and dragged him off. Tony ran from the office, slamming the door. Julie sat on her desk, kicking her legs. She was still too young to vote.

Tony Parsons never knew that I once saved him from a very uncomfortable experience. Because Nick Logan insisted that all punk-related stories went through Parsons and Burchill, the record companies and the members of bands began to court them assiduously. As the *NME*, for some reason, was regarded as the most important of the weekly music papers, they soon found themselves in a very powerful position, able to virtually make or break new or emerging bands. As I was spending a lot of time in New York, I naturally filed stories on many of the new American punk and New Wave bands such as the Ramones, Dead Boys and Blondie. I did interviews with bands like Talking Heads and even got a cover story with an interview with Willy de Ville from Mink de Ville. I can only imagine that Parsons and Burchill thought they should have done the Mink de Ville interview themselves because they took against them, and when Mink de Ville were set to play London to promote their new album, they sent a note to the EMI Records press office which read: 'Dear Tom and Lynne. Willy De Ville's career stops *here*. Love, Julie + Tony.'

The press office, rather foolishly, showed it to the band. Now Willy de Ville was not the usual downtown New York musician: he grew up in the working-class Belltown district of Stamford,

DEAR TOM + LYNNE

WILLY DE VILLE'S
CAREER STOPS
HERE

261
6683

LOVE,
JULIE + TONY

The note

before quitting high school to move to the Lower East Side, where he lived among the Puerto Rican and Italian street gangs, on streets filled with junkies, crackheads, muggers and murderers. He was in a variety of bands, in Greenwich Village, then San Francisco and Oakland, before returning to New York. He and Toots, whom he married when she was seventeen, lived on East 7th Street and then on East 6th Street in the slums of Alphabet City in the Lower East Side, the centre of the heroin and cocaine trade, dealt from boarded-up, burned-out tenement buildings. Dealers and enforcers were their friends and neighbours. They naturally took the note at face value.

One of their roadies, rumoured to have been responsible for more than one murder in the past, proposed simply rubbing them out. Attractive as this sounded, it did seem a bit drastic: these were just two pale middle-class English journalists whose egos had run away with them. Then again, Mink de Ville had come up out of the slums and were not about to let a couple of journos damage their career. The band settled on a plan. They told me that just before the concert, roadies would bundle Parsons into the boot of a car and drive him out to Hackney Marshes, which someone had assured them was just like the New Jersey marshes, where he would be left, stripped of money, and possibly his trousers, and unable to review

Miles Collection

Doreen D'Agostino,
Willy de Ville and the
author backstage
somewhere in New
York City, 1977

the concert. I took the note to Nick Logan, who I assume had a quiet word with them. I told the band that Parsons and Burchill would not be reviewing the concert and Parsons was saved from the roughing up that would inevitably have occurred had Mink de Ville's loyal roadies got their hands on him. Several of my fellow journalists were sorry to hear that the planned action was called off. I still have the note.

Though he was no longer strung out on heroin when I knew him, Willy still used a bewildering quantity of drugs. One night, at 3.30 a.m. in Dallas, Texas, after a concert and a meal, I sat in his hotel room and watched as he and his girlfriend organized their stash:

Willy, licking his finger and dipping it into one of three opened wraps of white powder: 'This is the speed.'

Girlfriend: 'No, that's the charlie.'

Willy, dipping his finger into the next wrap: 'This is the charlie. That one's the smack.'

Girlfriend, licking her finger and dipping it into the third wrap: 'No, this one's the smack.'

Willy, trying the third wrap himself. 'This is the speed, the first one's the smack.'

And so it went until they were both so befuddled that it didn't really matter which was which. I returned to my room, making sure to close their door behind me as they sat muttering to each other, sucking their fingers.

On 13 July 1977, I was at a Boz Scaggs concert at Alice Tulley Hall in Lincoln Center, New York, with my friend, photographer Joe Stevens, when halfway through the set, at 9.27, the lights went out. Emergency back-up safety lights kicked in and the stage was immediately crawling with roadies with flashlights, who assumed that they were responsible. Then the head of the road crew, in torn T-shirt, long hair and beard, marched to centre stage, and, shining the flashlight on his face, yelled to the audience: 'The whole city's out!' Half a beat later everyone cheered, 'Yeeaaaah!' as if it was a big rock 'n' roll moment. We sat for a bit, fidgeting, expecting this to be only a temporary power cut, but then people began to drift away and Joe and I decided to go; it was quite a long walk back to Greenwich Village and we assumed the subway was not running and that buses and cabs would be impossible to get.

Once we got outside, the smell of smoke was already in the air. There was chaos at the nearest subway stop, where emergency workers were rescuing the more than four thousand people trapped on subway trains and leading them down the tracks to the nearest stations. Traffic lights were out and cops were directing traffic at some intersections; others, however, had been taken over by crazy people, waving their arms, blowing whistles and causing minor accidents. Most drivers were wary and travelling very slowly. The low swirling clouds from the electric storm that caused the blackout sometimes parted and you could see stars. It was amazing; not since the previous blackout of November 1965 had the stars been properly visible in Manhattan.

'Everybody has a smile on their face,' commented Joe. 'It takes something really big to make a New Yorker smile.' At Times Square the sidewalks were filled with people jumping in the air and waving as Channel Five News turned their spotlights and cameras on them for a live report. People jostled forward, desperate to be interviewed. Light suddenly flickered on and a massive cheer went up, cars hooted and there was a feeling like that of the victory celebrations at the end of the war, but almost immediately the power failed again. Then came a collective groan, mixed with a few scattered cheers. People were in a good mood. By the time we reached Joe's apartment on Thompson Street, his instincts as a photographer were fully aroused and we decided to look for riots and looting.

We took his car and headed for the South Bronx. It was a hot night and people had rigged up enormous speakers to their car stereos that blasted out into the night as people danced in the streets. We saw some broken shop windows but most of the looting was over in Brooklyn and we missed it. As we bumped through the crowds we were very conscious of being the only white people in sight. 'I'd hate to break an axle here,' commented Joe as we bottomed out on yet another pothole, almost invisible because the hydrants were on and they were all full of water.

Radio reports were confusing, but it seemed as if most of the action was in Bedford-Stuyvesant, so we sensibly decided to return to the Village. Over in Brooklyn, two blocks of Broadway, which separates Bushwick from Bedford-Stuyvesant, were ablaze, 134 stores looted and forty-five set on fire. Twenty-five fires were still burning the next morning. We missed the biggest mass arrest in New York's history when 3,776 looters were arrested; and many more got away. So many were held, the police had to detain them in basements, storerooms and guarded corridors. All told, 1,600 stores were ransacked and over a thousand fires were started. A congressional study estimated the cost of damages as more than $300 million.

The looting and rioting were confined mostly to the poor neighbourhoods, but even Brooks Brothers on Madison Avenue was struck by looters. In the more wealthy neighbourhoods the blackout provided the excuse for a street party. We went down to the Village and ran into Bleeker Street Bob – Bob Plotnik – outside his rare record store. I first met him through Frank Zappa in 1967 when he invited me back to see his record collection. I had been astonished: records were filed in fireproof metal cabinets by catalogue number. They were not there to play, he had other copies for that purpose; these were complete runs of some of the rarest record labels of all time, all in mint condition. 'See this? This is the Cobra label,' he would say, indicating a file drawer full of singles, carefully housed in protective sleeves, and pull out a 45 I'd never heard of.

He was one of those record collectors who discussed records by catalogue number rather than by name; the characters in *High Fidelity* had hardly started compared to Bob. He always queried me for details about British groups, being particularly concerned that there were not enough Jewish musicians in England. 'Now Peter Asher,' he said. 'He *has* to be Jewish.' I had to disabuse him on this, pointing out that Asher was an old English name for a spear-carrier because spear handles were made of ash. He was pleased, however, to hear that Marc Bolan's real name was Mark Feld.

Bob had quickly realised that the blackout was going to last all night and, ever one with an eye for the main chance, he called up the owner of the candle shop next to his record store and made him an offer for his complete stock. Bob sat up all night outside his store, selling candles at outrageous prices, and made a $2,000 profit.

In the Village there was a party atmosphere on the streets with everyone out, talking to each other. People sat out on their stoops, their portable radios tuned to New Jersey stations as the New York ones were all out. Outside the deli next to the Blarney Stone Bar on 23rd Street someone sat tending a huge portable radio and a small crowd sat around listening. It was 1 a.m.: 'Four or five officers entered a darkened building in East Harlem through the shattered windows and confronted up to a hundred and twenty-five looters in the dark.' A pair of cops strolled up, listened for a while then walked on. A couple of girls from the Hotel Chelsea wearing tiny hot pants came up and demanded that they change to a music station. 'I want music!' one screamed, and stormed off when people told her they needed to hear the news. In the deli they were charging round figures – $3 for a six-pack, 50 cents for a beer – and not making change; their till was electric and they couldn't open it. The line inside for beer was candlelit and very hot. Some people brought out pitchers of sangria and paper cups for passers-by, others had huge plates of sandwiches. People danced to rock 'n' roll stations and passed around wine and joints.

In the dark city, the blind came into their own and there were numerous reports of blind people charging to help people find their front doors in the big pitch-black apartment blocks. I made two attempts to find my own tenth-floor apartment at the Hotel Chelsea. It was hard enough to find the correct floor, as the building was completely dark except for the lobby, where people had lit candles and were sitting around strumming guitars and drinking wine. I got lost on my first try; found the stairs again and went back down to the lobby. After hanging out for an hour or so I had another go, this time with the aid of a pack of book matches. I found my apartment and looked out over the darkened city. I was facing south and, framed between two black towers in the financial section, like cardboard silhouettes, the Statue of Liberty stood out, lit up in bright white light. She stands in New York Harbour but gets her power from the State of New Jersey.

The next day it was 88 degrees. Sound trucks roamed the streets urging people not to loot and to take pride in their communities. At the Chelsea, the El Quijote bar was not letting any more people

in. It looked cool inside through the blue glass doors but I doubt
it was. The Angry Squire bar down the street was packed out and
sweltering hot. By the time the power was restored at 10.30 in the
evening the novelty had worn thin and New Yorkers had returned
to their usual ratty selves.

16 1978

on the bowery

In New York, the upstairs bar at Max's Kansas City was a place to hear new bands and I often went there before heading down to CBGBs. One night in October 1978, a smacked-out Sid Vicious was there, out on $50,000 bail after the murder of his twenty-year-old girlfriend Nancy Spungen. It was a horrible sight: fawning punks, all trying to buy him drinks or hand him drugs, surrounded Sid. He staggered about, puffy-faced, completely out of it, one eye almost closed, focusing his attention only enough to use his new pulling line on the most attractive of the punk girls hanging on his arm: 'You know, I 'aven't been with a woman since Nancy died.'

In some ways Sid fitted right in. The New York punk scene was populated by a much more aggressive, unfeeling, purposely nasty breed of punk. Whereas the London punks could hardly be said to be nice to each other, there was, nonetheless, a sense of community; they were mostly working-class and they often resembled nothing more than a schoolyard full of children playing. Theirs was a world filled with jokes, put-ons, practical jokes and sticking a finger up to teacher. In New York the punk scene was, for the most part, an incoherent scream of rage from a lot of middle-class kids trying desperately to find an identity. They posed harder, took heavier drugs, were ruder, more aloof and, ultimately, more lonely. They had the petulance of a spoiled child.

One time, at the bar at CBGBs, which was lit entirely with neon advertisements for beer, a punk girl in leather jacket and chains pushed in next to me and knocked over my beer. When I pointed this out to her she simply bellowed, 'Fuck you!' I couldn't help noticing that the hair above her right ear was slicked down by what looked suspiciously like semen; perhaps the cause of her angst was an amorous encounter that had not gone entirely to plan. The ladies' room at CBGBs was like a psychiatrist's waiting room, filled with girls getting their own back on Daddy. Considering how out of it most of the men were, it's amazing that any of them could get it up at all, but there was a fair amount of action and the walls of the cubicles were graffitied with intimate details, sometimes including measurements, of various musicians' proclivities and endowments.

Despite its initial similarity to the Roxy, or other dingy London clubs, CBGBs was a much more professionally run establishment where you could reserve tables in the elevated seating area and there was waitress service. The first time I saw Talking Heads was from just such a table right next to the stage: David Byrne looking self-conscious and nervous against the incongruous backdrop of double-life-size photographs of Victorian bathing beauties, stuttering his way through 'Psycho Killer'. The place had a somewhat studied scruffiness, enhanced by the fact that Hilly Krystal's dog Jonathan was allowed to shit wherever it wanted around the club, giving CBs a unique ambience: a mixture of sweat, BO, stale beer and dog turds. Over the years the place got completely covered with graffiti and advertising stickers from unknown bands; the mirror in the bathroom, the urinals, the steps and risers and every inch of the stage and the huge speakers either side of it had a thick layer of stickers and spray paint, so that in the end it was just a characterless tip.

Unlike the London punks, who struck a rebellious chord with an entire generation of British youth, the American punks were still firm supporters of the American way of life; in fact, many of them were ardent followers of newly elected Ronald Reagan. They believed wholeheartedly in American imperial might and, if anything, they were proud of their lack of moral judgement (something that could also be said of the Warhol crowd). For a time in the late seventies I wore a ring, made of metal from an American plane shot down over Vietnam, mention of which often provoked quite unreasonable levels of hostility, often combined with irrational suggestions that the British National Health system was a hotbed of communist activity and suggestions that I, myself, might be some kind of pinko, if not a pinko faggot. It was better to steer the subject back to something they knew about: sex, beer and rock 'n' roll.

In the summer, big crowds would sometimes gather on the street outside CBGBs on the wide Bowery sidewalk, with people sitting on parked cars and the action enlivened by arrivals and departures in yellow cabs and the occasional stretch limo. A lot of them were very young teenage girls from the suburbs who were not normally allowed into premises where alcohol was served but somehow CBGBs allowed it. Some of them became falling-over drunk, but as CBGBs was next door to a Bowery flophouse the streets were already littered with drunks and they fitted right in. The cops certainly didn't even bother to slow down as they cruised past.

As is often the case, the musicians and their close circle were more worldly and better informed than their fans. They took care to appear part of the scene even if in private they had a more defined lifestyle by being part of the musical community of roadies, recording engineers, studio staff and session musicians. One of my favourite bands was the Ramones, largely for their tremendous sense of humour. They had created their entire act as a living cartoon strip. Their lyrics were minimalist and funny, their look – black leather jackets, blue jeans and T-shirts – became an instant rock 'n' roll brand, and their name – all of them called Ramone – was inspired.

It came from Dee Dee Ramone, who used to call himself that even before the band was formed because he was a big Paul McCartney fan and Paul had used Paul Ramon as a stage name when the Silver Beetles backed Johnny Gentle on his 1960 Scottish tour. I once had a long talk with Dee Dee about their name. I told him that Paul once told me that the name Paul Ramon was a take-off on the name of society hairdresser Raymond Cohen, known as Mr Teasy Weasy, who demonstrated ladies' hairstyles on television in the fifties. Paul liked him because he was an impossibly suave-looking fellow with slicked-back black hair and a pencil moustache. Dee Dee was delighted because he had previously worked as a beautician's assistant in a beauty salon. And so a hairdresser from Birmingham was indirectly responsible for the name of one of the world's greatest punk bands. It was very appropriate: the Ramones were lower-middle-class kids from Forest Hills, they loved Herman and the Hermits, the soundtrack from *Hair*, songs like 'Yummy Yummy Yummy I've Got Love In My Tummy', late-night television movies, mindless American and UK pop, nothing intellectual, nothing cool, nothing avant-garde. Nonetheless they were great and I always enjoyed seeing them play.

Of all my evenings with Burroughs in New York, two were particularly memorable. One evening Bill and I had dinner together at Phoebe's on the Bowery and he insisted on introducing me to the refined taste of a green chartreuse, which he spotted on the shelves above the bar. This was a drink from his youth in the twenties: Jay Gatsby serves it to his friends in *The Great Gatsby*. We allowed a number of glasses of this viscous sweet green liquid to ooze down our throats while Bill extolled the virtues of living on the Bowery, which he proudly proclaimed as much cheaper than his place in London. This was not surprising as in London he had lived just a few blocks from St James's Palace, one of the most expensive areas in Europe, if not the world. Eventually we decided to call it a day, paid and left.

I walked Bill the few blocks down the Bowery towards the Bunker, the windowless concrete gym and locker room of an abandoned YMCA at 222 Bowery where he lived, intending to go on from there to CBGBs down the block. I invited him to join me but he had been once and said he did not intend going again (in fact, he went only twice in his whole life, despite reports to the contrary). En route to the Bunker we encountered a group of bums clustered around a burning garbage can. Flames leapt into the air, head height, throwing sparks and fragments of burning paper into the night sky. Their faces were strangely illuminated by the fire, as if in a seventeenth-century Dutch painting.

Bill had been remembering New York in the forties, reminiscing about the Third Avenue Elevated Railroad, which once ran down the centre of the Bowery, and was clearly feeling nostalgic. The bums were passing round a bottle, which they offered to us. Bill enthusiastically joined in, taking a swig and wiping his lips with the sleeve of his jacket in an exaggerated gesture. Whatever it was it tasted dreadful, and I surreptitiously wiped the neck of the bottle before taking my turn. I couldn't understand a word they said, but I gathered that they knew Bill was a resident of the Bowery and that they were friendly. Very friendly. They had a stock of bottles and we stayed for several more rounds before I insisted that we make our way to the Bunker. Bill was elated and talked and laughed loudly, slurring his words, as we staggered to his door. When I spoke with him the next day he had no memory of the incident. I blamed the green chartreuse.

The other evening that sticks in my mind was in 1979 when I took Rosemary with me to New York for the first time, and Victor had arranged a dinner for us at the Bunker. Rosemary, Victor and I arrived at exactly 6 p.m., carrying a pint of vodka and extra tonic waters. After going through the usual rigmarole of the four locked doors – Bill had to lock each one of them behind him – we reached the Bunker itself. The poet John Giorno, who lived upstairs, soon joined us. The conversation was typically Burroughsian, beginning with a discussion about a white gorilla pictured in the latest *National Geographic* that Bill had seen. Bill ruminated about what a perfect CIA front *National Geographic* would be; always having to go on

Mick Jagger, William Burroughs and Andy Warhol at one of Victor Bockris's dinners at the Bunker

trips to foreign countries, making maps and surveys. The conversation then turned to a particularly gruesome rape that was getting massive coverage in the *Daily News* and the *New York Post*. 'At exactly what point were the girl's arms cut off, would you say?' Bill asked. 'How far across the desert did she crawl like that?' She had managed to survive by hiding in a drainage pipe and was able to confront her attacker in court. When she saw him, she threw up.

At this point the phone rang and Victor answered it. It was Allen Ginsberg calling from the corner of the block to say he was outside. Victor went down to let him in and Bill began to discuss his armoury. He produced a mace gun, used to ward off muggers by temporarily blinding them and dyeing them a bright orange colour. Rosemary, who had been seated to Bill's left in the traditional manner, now attempted to assert herself in this bizarre milieu, having been effectively left out of most of the conversation, and ventured to suggest that she doubted whether it would really work. Bill spun round. 'You challenge the efficacy of my weapon?' he growled, and proceeded to demonstrate.

'Careful, Bill, this is a closed space!' warned John, but it was too late. The room filled with clouds of noxious fumes. At this moment Allen Ginsberg entered, bringing with him Raymond Foye, a young friend just arrived from San Francisco. Instead of the sophisticated New York literary soiree that Allen had envisaged, they were greeted by a room filled with coughing, spluttering people, frantically trying to escape the gas, which burned the throat and eyes. Holding wet cloths in front of our faces, we all retreated to Bill's spare room, next door, and fanned the door to the apartment, trying to clear the gas, as Bill cackled to himself. 'Bill, what have you done? What have you done?' demanded Allen, but Bill couldn't talk. He sat on the spare bed, his shoulders shaking with mirth as tears rolled down all our cheeks. 'Bill, you don't seem to be taking this at all seriously,' chided Allen. It took more than an hour before we could eat: Bill flitted around the room waving his handkerchief to clear the fumes, still chuckling to himself, and remained in exceptionally good humour all evening.

afterword

After writing for the *NME* for three years I was keen to move on: rock journalism, for the most part, was seen as a job for the very young. Any depth of understanding or historical perspective on it was generally not appreciated by editors, making it the only art form where a knowledge of the subject was frowned upon.

The obvious direction seemed to be to write books. I had written the introductions to a couple of William Burroughs' French-language editions – *Exterminateur!* in 1974 and *Le Métro Blanc* in 1976 – and through my friend Pearce Marchbank I began compiling song selections for books of sheet music, writing discographies and generally doing music-related editorial work for Music Sales, a sheet music company where Pearce had his in-house art studio. I also wrote press biographies for record companies and worked on and off with Emma Tennant on *Bananas*. Some form of writing seemed to be the way forward.

In 1978 Pearce came up with the idea of doing *The Illustrated Rock Almanac*, showing who was born or died on each day and listing major rock 'n' roll events on the day they occurred. I wrote the text and Pearce did the design. It was published that year by Paddington Press, who went out of business not long afterwards. The book took much longer than we expected it to do, but it showed that Pearce and I could work together.

That same year, 1978, Pearce and I attended the Picnic at

Blackbushe, a one-day festival, held at Blackbushe Aerodrome near Camberley, Surrey. That year it featured Graham Parker and the Rumour, Joan Armatrading, Eric Clapton and Bob Dylan. On 15 July, Pearce and I drove there in his Citroën DS. Before leaving we studied a large-scale Ordnance Survey map of the area and found a tiny country lane that came out just by the backstage entrance. From here we plotted a route along country lanes and were able to drive there avoiding all the traffic jams. I had backstage passes so we made straight for the CBS hospitality area, which was housed in a Routemaster double-decker (Dylan was on CBS). Hervé and Jenny were there along with Mick Jones and Joe Strummer from the Clash.

The aerodrome was a bleak place to hold a festival but there was a good atmosphere and people were anxious to hear Dylan, who did a fine set and included a lot of recent stuff as well as his classics. As soon as he'd completed his encore, 200,000 people attempted to drive home. Apparently it took many people six hours to get back to London. Fortunately our country lane was still completely empty as we sailed along towards the capital.

Then, pulled up on the grass verge just ahead, looking like a beached whale, we saw a stretch limo. Standing next to it, looking incredibly pissed off, reluctantly hitchhiking, was Bianca Jagger. Naturally Pearce pulled over and offered her a lift. She muttered something nasty to the cowed-looking driver and jumped in. We sped along, the new Talking Heads album on full volume, chemical stimulants to hand. Pearce took her right to her door on Cheyne Walk and was rewarded with a nice long kiss.

That summer, Pearce Marchbank and I took over as editors of *Time Out*: I edited the words, he controlled the layout and graphics, just as we had done with the *Rock Almanac*. Pearce and Tony Elliott, the owner, were friends from way back. Pearce had been involved with the magazine in the early days and had designed their distinctive logo. We were hoping to transform *Time Out* into a London equivalent of Clay Felker's *New York* magazine only with more listings, but we were up against a formidable office culture, resistant to change. In many ways *Time Out* was like a dozen small arts magazines stapled together, with each section editor fighting desperately to retain or enlarge their number of column inches. Everyone was paid the same wage – a relic of the magazine's sixties origins – but the workload was by no means shared equally: the film section clamoured to get articles in every week whereas the music section was content to run two or three a year.

The music section was also the cause of a certain opprobrium because it received every new album, the vast majority of which were taken straight down to Berwick Street and Hanway Place to sell, an additional income that many of the staff felt should also be shared equally. It was the news section, however, which presented the most obdurate, unified front against change and which was also the cause of most of the magazine's difficulties; a problem most succinctly summed up, curiously enough, by Mick Jagger.

One evening Mick and his old friend Mark Palmer joined Rosemary and me at our table at Zanzibar. Jagger's young girlfriend wanted to dance. Mick thrust a large note into her hand, 'Here's some pocket money,' and said he'd pick her up from Blitz later. Blitz was a few doors away. 'I'm just down from your gaff,' he said, meaning the Savoy Hotel, which was at the end of Southampton Street where *Time Out*'s offices were then located. We talked about the magazine and I told him we were interviewing focus groups to try to find out what people wanted from the magazine and what they disliked about it. 'The biggest problem,' he said, 'is the news section in the front. It's like having to cross a picket line to get to the rest of the magazine.'

He was absolutely correct. Our researches confirmed this; in fact, sales would have gone up had the news section been dropped altogether, but that would have resulted in endless strike action and was not an option. The news staff were good people, and politically I probably agreed with them, but they were marred by the years of infighting on the British left, which often put an unfortunate slant on their stories, too many of which were internecine attacks on obscure political groupings. The other staff members were intimidated by them. One time I was talking with Sarah Kent, the art critic, as we walked towards my office. Without thinking I turned into the news compound, taking her with me. Afterwards she said that in all the years she had worked there she had never been into the newsroom; I had noticed the startled looks as I entered but I thought it was just me.

It turned out that transforming *Time Out* was an impossible task and in the end Pearce resigned, and, as our editorship was a joint one, I had to follow suit, though I stayed on a month or two more until a new editor had been appointed. I did not run as a candidate; I was relieved to be out of it.

There were many roads not taken: at the beginning of the decade, Peter Asher had proposed various jobs in record production, which was an area that interested me a lot and I had many friends in the industry, but it would probably have meant living in Los Angeles. I received job offers from two different New York bookshops to take charge of their rare book departments, but that would also have meant leaving London, though I did a couple of catalogues for New York book dealers; several new music magazines started up during the decade and asked whether I would care to be on the staff, but though I usually wrote for them, I chose to remain freelance. *Time Out* might have worked out had not Pearce Marchbank found it too stressful and quit, but how I would have weathered their protracted strike I don't know. I am glad that Ellie Smith and I did not attempt to manage the Clash; I would certainly have become an alcoholic. But at the end of the decade, there seemed to be only one area open to me: freelance book editing and the possibility of becoming a writer myself, which is what I did.

In the early eighties, after a spell as a freelance editor, I moved to New York with Rosemary, where I wrote the first of a series of biographies about the people who had played such a big part in my life: beginning with Allen Ginsberg and continuing on through William Burroughs, Frank Zappa, Paul McCartney and Charles Bukowski. I first sent off my $1 to City Lights Books in San Francisco in 1960 for a copy of *Howl*, and that same year managed to buy an under-the-counter copy of *The Naked Lunch* in Archer Street, Soho. In 1986 I edited the original text facsimile edition of *Howl* with Ginsberg himself and in 2003 co-edited the Revised Text Edition of *Naked Lunch* that is now used as the standard text worldwide. In a sense I had come full circle.

index